PRENTICE HALL

SCIENCE EXPLORER

Animals

PRENTICE HALL
Needham, Massachusetts
Upper Saddle River, New Jersey

Animals

Program Resources

Student Edition
Annotated Teacher's Edition
Teaching Resources Book with Color Transparencies
Animals Materials Kits

Program Components

Integrated Science Laboratory Manual
Integrated Science Laboratory Manual, Teacher's Edition
Inquiry Skills Activity Book
Student-Centered Science Activity Books
Program Planning Guide
Guided Reading English Audiotapes
Guided Reading Spanish Audiotapes and Summaries
Product Testing Activities by Consumer Reports™
Event-Based Science Series (NSF funded)
Prentice Hall Interdisciplinary Explorations
Cobblestone, Odyssey, Calliope, and *Faces* Magazines

Media/Technology

Science Explorer Interactive Student Tutorial CD-ROMs
Odyssey of Discovery CD-ROMs
Resource Pro® (Teaching Resources on CD-ROM)
Assessment Resources CD-ROM with Dial-A-Test®
Internet site at www.science-explorer.phschool.com
Life, Earth, and Physical Science Videodiscs
Life, Earth, and Physical Science Videotapes

Science Explorer Student Editions

Staff Credits

The people who made up the *Science Explorer* team—representing editorial, editorial services, design services, field marketing, market research, marketing services, on-line services/multimedia development, product marketing, production services, and publishing processes—are listed below. Bold type denotes core team members.

Kristen E. Ball, **Barbara A. Bertell,** Peter W. Brooks, **Christopher R. Brown, Greg Cantone,** Jonathan Cheney, **Patrick Finbarr Connolly,** Loree Franz, Donald P. Gagnon, Jr., **Paul J. Gagnon, Joel Gendler,** Elizabeth Good, Kerri Hoar, **Linda D. Johnson,** Katherine M. Kotik, Russ Lappa, Marilyn Leitao, David Lippman, **Eve Melnechuk, Natania Mlawer,** Paul W. Murphy, **Cindy A. Noftle,** Julia F. Osborne, Caroline M. Power, Suzanne J. Schineller, **Susan W. Tafler,** Kira Thaler-Marbit, Robin L. Santel, Ronald Schachter, **Mark Tricca,** Diane Walsh, Pearl B. Weinstein, Beth Norman Winickoff

Acknowledgment for pages 180–181: Excerpt from *Dragons and Dynasties: An Introduction to Chinese Mythology,* by Yuan Ke, selected and translated by Kim Echlin and Nie Zhixong, published by Penguin Books, 1993. First published in the People's Republic of China by Foreign Languages Press, Beijing, 1991. Copyright © Foreign Languages Press, 1991, 1992, 1993. Reprinted by permission of Penguin UK.

Cover: A polar bear cub rests comfortably on its mother.

ISBN 0-13-434477-4

8 9 10   05 04 03 02 01

Program Authors

Michael J. Padilla, Ph.D.
Professor
Department of Science Education
University of Georgia
Athens, Georgia

Michael Padilla is a leader in middle school science education. He has served as an editor and elected officer for the National Science Teachers Association. He has been principal investigator of several National Science Foundation and Eisenhower grants and served as a writer of the National Science Education Standards.

As lead author of *Science Explorer,* Mike has inspired the team in developing a program that meets the needs of middle grades students, promotes science inquiry, and is aligned with the National Science Education Standards.

Ioannis Miaoulis, Ph.D.
Dean of Engineering
College of Engineering
Tufts University
Medford, Massachusetts

Martha Cyr, Ph.D.
Director, Engineering
    Educational Outreach
College of Engineering
Tufts University
Medford, Massachusetts

Science Explorer was created in collaboration with the College of Engineering at Tufts University. Tufts has an extensive engineering outreach program that uses engineering design and construction to excite and motivate students and teachers in science and technology education.

Faculty from Tufts University participated in the development of *Science Explorer* chapter projects, reviewed the student books for content accuracy, and helped coordinate field testing.

Book Author

Jan Jenner, Ph.D.
Science Writer
Talladega, Alabama

Contributing Writers

Fred Holtzclaw
Science Instructor
Oak Ridge High School
Oak Ridge, Tennessee

Theresa K. Holtzclaw
Former Science Instructor
Clinton, Tennessee

Evan P. Silberstein
Science Instructor
Spring Valley High School
Spring Valley, New York

Reading Consultant

Bonnie B. Armbruster, Ph.D.
Department of Curriculum
    and Instruction
University of Illinois
Champaign, Illinois

Interdisciplinary Consultant

Heidi Hayes Jacobs, Ed.D.
Teacher's College
Columbia University
New York, New York

Safety Consultants

W. H. Breazeale, Ph.D.
Department of Chemistry
College of Charleston
Charleston, South Carolina

Ruth Hathaway, Ph.D.
Hathaway Consulting
Cape Girardeau, Missouri

Tufts University Program Reviewers

Content Reviewers

Teacher Reviewers

Stephanie Anderson
Sierra Vista Junior
    High School
Canyon Country, California

John W. Anson
Mesa Intermediate School
Palmdale, California

Pamela Arline
Lake Taylor Middle School
Norfolk, Virginia

Lynn Beason
College Station Jr. High School
College Station, Texas

Richard Bothmer
Hollis School District
Hollis, New Hampshire

Jeffrey C. Callister
Newburgh Free Academy
Newburgh, New York

Judy D'Albert
Harvard Day School
Corona Del Mar, California

Betty Scott Dean
Guilford County Schools
McLeansville, North Carolina

Sarah C. Duff
Baltimore City Public Schools
Baltimore, Maryland

Melody Law Ewey
Holmes Junior High School
Davis, California

Sherry L. Fisher
Lake Zurich Middle
    School North
Lake Zurich, Illinois

Melissa Gibbons
Fort Worth ISD
Fort Worth, Texas

Debra J. Goodding
Kraemer Middle School
Placentia, California

Jack Grande
Weber Middle School
Port Washington, New York

Steve Hills
Riverside Middle School
Grand Rapids, Michigan

Carol Ann Lionello
Kraemer Middle School
Placentia, California

Jaime A. Morales
Henry T. Gage Middle School
Huntington Park, California

Patsy Partin
Cameron Middle School
Nashville, Tennessee

Deedra H. Robinson
Newport News Public Schools
Newport News, Virginia

Bonnie Scott
Clack Middle School
Abilene, Texas

Charles M. Sears
Belzer Middle School
Indianapolis, Indiana

Barbara M. Strange
Ferndale Middle School
High Point, North Carolina

Jackie Louise Ulfig
Ford Middle School
Allen, Texas

Kathy Usina
Belzer Middle School
Indianapolis, Indiana

Heidi M. von Oetinger
L'Anse Creuse Public School
Harrison Township, Michigan

Pam Watson
Hill Country Middle School
Austin, Texas

Activity Field Testers

Nicki Bibbo
Russell Street School
Littleton, Massachusetts

Connie Boone
Fletcher Middle School
Jacksonville Beach, Florida

Rose-Marie Botting
Broward County
    School District
Fort Lauderdale, Florida

Colleen Campos
Laredo Middle School
Aurora, Colorado

Elizabeth Chait
W. L. Chenery Middle School
Belmont, Massachusetts

Holly Estes
Hale Middle School
Stow, Massachusetts

Laura Hapgood
Plymouth Community
    Intermediate School
Plymouth, Massachusetts

Sandra M. Harris
Winman Junior High School
Warwick, Rhode Island

Jason Ho
Walter Reed Middle School
Los Angeles, California

Joanne Jackson
Winman Junior High School
Warwick, Rhode Island

Mary F. Lavin
Plymouth Community
    Intermediate School
Plymouth, Massachusetts

James MacNeil, Ph.D.
Concord Public Schools
Concord, Massachusetts

Lauren Magruder
St. Michael's Country
    Day School
Newport, Rhode Island

Jeanne Maurand
Glen Urquhart School
Beverly Farms, Massachusetts

Warren Phillips
Plymouth Community
    Intermediate School
Plymouth, Massachusetts

Carol Pirtle
Hale Middle School
Stow, Massachusetts

Kathleen M. Poe
Kirby-Smith Middle School
Jacksonville, Florida

Cynthia B. Pope
Ruffner Middle School
Norfolk, Virginia

Anne Scammell
Geneva Middle School
Geneva, New York

Karen Riley Sievers
Callanan Middle School
Des Moines, Iowa

David M. Smith
Howard A. Eyer Middle School
Macungie, Pennsylvania

Derek Strohschneider
Plymouth Community
    Intermediate School
Plymouth, Massachusetts

Sallie Teames
Rosemont Middle School
Fort Worth, Texas

Gene Vitale
Parkland Middle School
McHenry, Illinois

Zenovia Young
Meyer Levin Junior
    High School (IS 285)
Brooklyn, New York

Contents

Animals

Activities

DISCOVER
Exploration and inquiry before reading

Sharpen your Skills
Practice of specific science inquiry skills

TRY THIS
Reinforcement of key concepts

Interdisciplinary Activities

EXPLORING

Visual exploration of concepts

AN AMAZON DISCOVERY

Dr. Russell A. Mittermeier is President of Conservation International and a leader in the effort to understand and preserve biodiversity around the world. Since 1977, he has served as chairman of the Primate Specialist group of the World Conservation Union Species Survival Commission. He has described several previously unknown species of monkeys.

If you think scientists spend their days in clean, white laboratories and their nights hunched over computers and notebooks, you haven't met Dr. Russell Mittermeier. An adventurer and well-known authority on primates (monkeys, apes, and similar animals), Dr. Mittermeier tells captivating tales of his treks.

He recalls a major expedition he made into the Amazon rainforest in 1973. Dr. Mittermeier was traveling on the powerful Amazon River, carrying his photographic equipment, binoculars, notebooks, and other gear in a motorized canoe. In the choppy waves, his boat took on water and sank beneath him into the river. To reach shore safely, he had to swim past hungry crocodile-like black caimans. He made it, but lost all his gear except a plastic cup he carried for his toothbrush! Fortunately, the event didn't discourage him. Mittermeier accepts such setbacks when studying animals in the wild.

The dwarf marmoset is the second smallest monkey ever discovered. Its scientific name is *Callithrix humilis.* It measures about 10 centimeters and weighs around 158 grams.

An Early Interest in Wildlife

Dr. Mittermeier traces his interest in animals and adventure to his childhood in New York. "When I was young, my mother read books to me about Africa and South America. She dragged me every week to the Museum of Natural History and to the Bronx Zoo. So from a very early age, I grew up interested in wildlife. In first grade, when teachers asked what we wanted to be when we grew up, my answer was a jungle explorer. In today's language that would probably be a field biologist."

Though Dr. Mittermeier's driving interest is in science, he admits that the spirit of adventure still moves him. "At the age of thirteen, I discovered Edgar Rice Burroughs' Tarzan books. I've been very, very much a Tarzan fan ever since."

In 1997 Dr. Mittermeier set out on an extraordinary expedition to Brazil's Amazon jungle to search for the world's second smallest monkey. The adventure really began in 1996, when Dr. Mittermeier visited his long-time colleague Marc Van Roosmalen in the Brazilian city of Manaus. A local man had brought an orphaned baby monkey to Van Roosmalen's primate clinic. The man said he'd found the monkey about 500 kilometers away.

Van Roosmalen "showed me this tiny, little, baby monkey. It was about the size of my fist. We looked at each other and realized it was a new species, and a really distinctive one," Dr. Mittermeier relates. Finding a new kind of monkey is a rare scientific accomplishment.

The tiny monkey looked similar to the pygmy marmoset, the world's smallest monkey, which also lives in

The triangle of land between the Madeira River and the Aripuanã River is a small part of the huge Amazon rain forest. It was in this isolated area that scientists found the tiny monkeys.

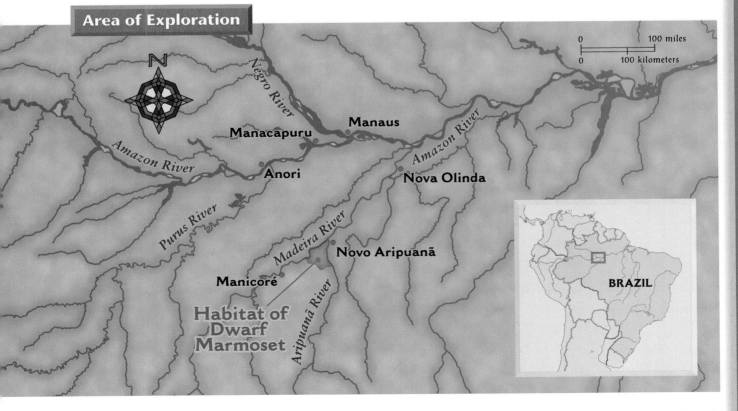

Area of Exploration

Negro River

Amazon River

Manaus

Manacapuru

Amazon River

Anori

Nova Olinda

Purus River

Madeira River

Novo Aripuanã

Manicoré

Aripuanã River

Habitat of Dwarf Marmoset

BRAZIL

0   100 miles
0   100 kilometers

Like other monkeys in the Amazon rain forest, this little monkey feeds on the sap of rain forest trees.

the Brazilian rain forest. But this dwarf marmoset was slightly larger and its color and markings were different. It had white fur around its face, a black crown, and a black tail with no rings. Its ears had less hair and its mane was shorter than that of the smallest known monkey. Until the scientists could give the new monkey a scientific name, they called it "Little Fellow."

But one captive monkey, no matter how unusual, is not enough to establish a new species. The scientists needed to find more of these monkeys living in the rain forest. Dr. Mittermeier knew that finding them would be no easy task.

> **One captive monkey. . . is not enough to establish a new species.**

"This is like finding a needle in a haystack, going out in the middle of the largest rain forest on Earth and trying to find a tiny monkey species that has never before been seen by scientists."

The Amazon rain forest is the haystack that Dr. Mittermeier referred to. It covers almost 7 million square kilometers, including much of northern Brazil and parts of eight other South American countries. It's a challenging place to explore. Dense vegetation, tropical diseases, poisonous snakes, and flesh-boring worms are just a few of the hazards of the rain forest. Dr. Mittermeier knew that sending an expedition to find this monkey would be danger-ous as well as expensive.

◄ The orphaned dwarf marmoset at 2 months (left) and at 7 months (right) at the primate clinic.

To obtain money, Dr. Mittermeier returned to the United States. He is president of an international organization that works to protect the rich variety of plants and animals living on Earth. He splits his time between that Washington-based conservation group and the rain forests of the world. Back in the United States, Dr. Mittermeier was able to obtain money for Van Roosmalen's expeditions.

After several unsuccessful attempts, Van Roosmalen finally located monkeys like "Little Fellow." They were in an area isolated from the rest of the rain forest by two rivers. This dwarf marmoset was given the scientific name *Callithrix humilis*. Finally, in 1997 Dr. Mittermeier joined the group of scientists in the Brazilian rain forest who were photographing and observing these monkeys in the wild. They found that the behavior and eating habits of the monkeys were similar to those of other Amazon monkeys. They feed on the sap of rain forest trees.

"Nonhuman primates" says Dr. Mittermeier, "are our closest living relatives, and you would think they would be very well known. In fact, since 1990 we've managed to find seven new ones just in the country of Brazil. That doesn't count the new ones we've found in Madagascar and a few other places."

It's not that surprising when someone finds a new tropical forest canopy beetle or a soil microorganism in the floor of the rain forest. But the discovery of a new primate species indicates that there may still be many creatures in the world that people don't even know exist.

In Your Journal

In a paragraph, write what interests you about Russell Mittermeier as a scientist. What do you think motivates him? What surprises you about how he works? What skills does a scientist like Mittermeier need?

Sponges, Cnidarians, and Worms

The graceful tentacles of this yellow cup coral help it to lure and catch food.

WHAT'S AHEAD

PROJECT 1

Alive and Well

When you hear the word *animal*, what picture comes to mind? You probably do not think of anything like this fingerlike yellow coral waving in the ocean current. But just like horses or sparrows, corals are animals, too.

Do animals such as corals really have anything in common with horses and sparrows? Keep this question in mind as you begin your study of animals. Instead of just reading about animals, though, you and your classmates will create a zoo in your classroom. Your zoo will feature crickets, earthworms, and other animals not usually found in zoos. In your role as zookeeper, you will select one animal to care for and study.

Your Goal To keep an animal safe and healthy for three weeks while you study its characteristics, needs, and behaviors.

To complete the project successfully, you must
◆ provide a healthy and safe environment for your animal
◆ keep the animal alive and well for the entire time of the project, and observe the animal's behavior
◆ prepare a report or illustrated booklet to show what you have learned about your animal
◆ follow the safety guidelines in Appendix A

Get Started After you have chosen an animal you want to care for, work with a partner to brainstorm questions you have about its survival needs. Then plan a way to find answers to your questions.

Check Your Progress You'll be working on this project as you study this chapter. To keep your project on track, look for Check Your Progress boxes at the following points.

Section 1 Review, page 22: Research your animal's needs and prepare its home.
Section 3 Review, page 33: Record your daily observations.
Section 4 Review, page 41: Analyze what you've learned and prepare your presentation.

Wrap Up At the end of the chapter (page 45), you will introduce your animal to your classmates and share your knowledge.

SECTION 4 Worms

Discover What Can You Learn About a Flatworm by Looking at It?
Sharpen Your Skills Observing
Skills Lab Earthworm Responses

SECTION 1 What Is an Animal?

DISCOVER

·····ACTIVITY·····

Is It an Animal?

1. Carefully examine each of the organisms that your teacher gives you.

2. Decide which ones are animals. Think about the reasons for your decision. Wash your hands after handling each of the organisms.

Think It Over
Forming Operational Definitions What characteristics did you use to decide whether each organism was an animal?

GUIDE FOR READING

◆ What characteristics do all animals have in common?
◆ How are animals classified into groups?

Reading Tip Before you begin to read, write your own definition of *animal*. Add to it or change it as you read.

In the waters off the north coast of Australia, a young box jellyfish floats along, looking more like a tiny transparent flower than an animal. After a time the young *jellyfish* will change form. As an adult, it will resemble a square bubble of clear jelly trailing bunches of long, wavy, armlike structures called tentacles.

To capture food, a box jellyfish's tentacles fire deadly venom at unlucky animals that happen to touch them. Humans are no exception. A swimmer who brushes the tentacles of a box jellyfish can die in only four minutes. In spite of their harmless appearance, adult box jellyfish have one of the strongest venoms on Earth.

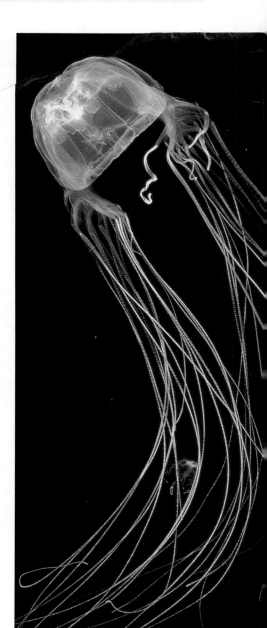

Figure 1 Don't be fooled by the delicate-looking tentacles of the Australian box jellyfish. Animals that brush against them can be killed by their venom—and become the jellyfish's next meal.

Characteristics of Animals

The box jellyfish may not look like most of the animals that you are familiar with, but it is indeed an animal. Biologists, scientists who study living organisms, have described over 1 million different animal species, and there are certainly many more. A **species** is a group of organisms that can mate with each other and produce offspring, who in turn can mate and reproduce.

All species of animals, including the beautiful but deadly box jellyfish, are similar in some important ways. **Animals are many-celled organisms that must obtain their food by eating other organisms.** In addition, most animals reproduce sexually and can move from place to place. Biologists look for these characteristics in deciding whether an organism is an animal.

How Animal Cells Are Organized All animals are multicellular; that is, their bodies are composed of many cells, the tiny working units that make up all living things. The cells of most animals are grouped together to form different kinds of tissue. A tissue is a group of similar cells that perform a specific job. For example, muscle tissue allows animals to move, while nerve tissue carries messages from one part of the body to another. Tissues may combine to form an organ, which is a group of different tissues that work together to perform a specific job that is more complex than the functions of each tissue by itself. Organs are made up of different types of tissue—your thigh bone, for example, is an organ that contains bone tissue, nerve tissue, and blood. In most animals, different organs combine to form an organ system, such as your skeletal system, shown in Figure 2.

How Animals Obtain Food Every animal is a **heterotroph** (HET ur oh trohf)—it cannot make food for itself, and must obtain food by eating other organisms. Contrast this with a green plant, which is an **autotroph** (AW toh trohf), an organism that makes its own food. Most animals take food into a cavity inside their bodies. Inside this cavity, the food is digested, or broken down into substances that the animal's body can absorb and use.

How Animals Reproduce Animals typically reproduce sexually. **Sexual reproduction** is the process by which a new organism forms from the joining of two sex cells—a tiny male sperm cell combines with a much larger female egg cell. The joining of egg and

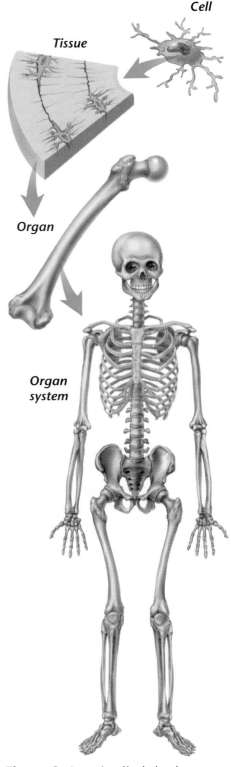

Figure 2 An animal's skeletal system has different levels of organization. Bone cells make up tissues, and tissues make up organs such as the thigh bone. *Classifying Is the skull best classified as an organ or as a tissue?*

Get Moving

Design an animal with a new and different way of moving. Your design should help your animal obtain food or get out of danger.

ACTIVITY

1. Make and label a drawing that shows how the animal would move.

2. Using clay, pipe cleaners, aluminum cans, construction paper, and whatever other materials are available, create a three-dimensional model of your animal.

3. Compare your animal to those of other classmates. What are some similarities? What are some differences?

Making Models What features of your design help your animal obtain food or escape danger?

sperm is called **fertilization.** Sperm and egg cells carry information about the characteristics of the parent that produced them—characteristics such as size and color. When sperm and egg unite, the resulting new individual has a combination of characteristics from both parents. It is something like each parent, but not exactly like either one.

Some animals can reproduce asexually as well as sexually. **Asexual reproduction** is the process by which a single organism produces a new organism identical to itself. Asexual reproduction does not involve a joining of sex cells from two individuals. Instead, the parent organism may divide to form two or more new organisms, or it may produce offspring from buds that grow on its body. A tiny animal called a hydra, for example, reproduces asexually by forming buds that eventually break off to form new hydras.

How Animals Move Animal movement can be fascinating to watch. Much of the movement is related to obtaining food, reproducing, and escaping danger. Barnacles, for example, wave feathery arms through the water to collect tiny food particles. Some geese must fly thousands of miles each spring to the place where they mate and lay eggs. And you've probably seen a cat claw its way up a tree trunk to get away from a snarling dog.

Some animals don't move from place to place. Adult oysters, sponges, and corals all stick firmly to underwater rocks and other solid surfaces. But most animals move freely at some point in their lives. For example, for its first few weeks of life, an oyster is a tiny swimmer—so tiny that you need a microscope to see it. Then the young oyster swims to a solid surface and attaches itself. It glues itself in place and undergoes changes in its form, eventually becoming an adult oyster within a shell.

☑ *Checkpoint Contrast the ways in which heterotrophs and autotrophs obtain food.*

Figure 3 Animals such as this Arabian stallion move with grace and power.

How Animals Meet Their Needs

If someone asked you to make a list of the things that you need to stay alive, you would probably write down *water*, *food*, and *oxygen*. Like all living things, animals need water because the chemical reactions that keep them alive, such as the breakdown of food, take place in water. Food provides animals with raw materials for growth and with energy for their bodies' activities, such as moving and breathing. To release that energy, the body's cells need oxygen. Some animals get oxygen from air; others absorb it from water.

Water, food, and oxygen must come from an animal's environment, or surroundings. An animal needs to be able to respond to its environment—for example, to find food and to run away from danger. Animals' bodies and behaviors are adapted for tasks such as these. An **adaptation** is a characteristic that helps an organism survive in its environment or reproduce.

Adaptations for Getting Food

Unlike plants that make their own food using sunlight, animals must obtain their food. Some animals eat plants, other animals eat animals, and still others eat both plants and animals.

Herbivores Animals that eat only plants are called **herbivores**. Grasshoppers, termites, and garden snails are some common smaller herbivores. Larger herbivores include cows, horses, and pandas. Herbivores have adaptations such as teeth with broad, flat surfaces that are good for grinding tough plants.

Carnivores Animals that eat only other animals are **carnivores**. Many carnivores are **predators** that hunt and kill other animals. Predators have adaptations that help them capture the animals

Figure 4 Animals have different adaptations for obtaining food. **A.** A carpet snake is a carnivore that feeds on lizards and other animals. **B.** A macaw is an herbivore that feeds on fruits and seeds. *Observing What feeding adaptations do you see in the photos?*

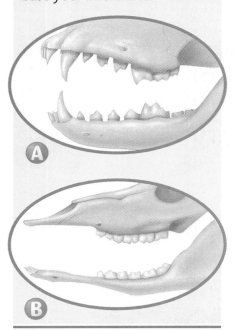

they feed upon, their **prey**. Wolves, for example, run down their prey. A wolf's adaptations include sharp claws, speed, and excellent hearing and eyesight. The teeth of most carnivores are sharp and pointed—they are adapted for cutting and stabbing.

Unlike wolves, sit-and-wait predators hide quietly and attack suddenly. Most of them blend in with their surroundings. Think of a frog sitting quietly by a pond. An insect flying by doesn't see the frog. Suddenly the frog flicks out its sticky tongue and catches the unsuspecting insect.

Omnivores Some animals eat both plants and animals; such an animal is an **omnivore**. A grizzly bear eats berries and roots, as well as insects, fish, and other small animals. Humans are also omnivores, as you know if you like hamburgers with tomato.

☑ *Checkpoint* *Describe some feeding adaptations of carnivores.*

Adaptations for Escaping Predators

In addition to feeding adaptations, animals have adaptations that help them avoid being eaten by predators. Some animals, such as box turtles and hedgehogs, have hard shells or spiny skins. Opossums and pill bugs "play dead" when they are attacked, so their predators lose interest. Stingers, claws, bitter-tasting flesh, or smelly sprays protect other animals. If you see a skunk, you stay far away from it. So do most predators.

Classification of Animals

Biologists classify animals in the animal kingdom into about 35 major groups, each of which is called a **phylum** (plural *phyla*). As you read this book, you will learn the characteristics of some of these phyla. Notice that in Figure 6, the phyla are arranged like the branches on a tree.

Figure 5 Hedgehogs, like this African pygmy hedgehog, roll up into spiny balls to protect themselves from possible predators.

Figure 6 This branching tree shows how the major animal phyla are related to one another, and the approximate order in which they evolved. *Interpreting Diagrams To which group are flatworms more closely related—roundworms or mollusks?*

The branching tree shows how biologists think the different phyla are related. For example, from their positions on the tree, you can see that segmented worms are more closely related to arthropods than to sponges.

The tree also shows the order in which biologists think animal life has evolved, or changed over time. This evolution process has resulted in all the different phyla that exist today. Biologists do not know the exact way in which evolution took place—they can only make inferences on the basis of the best evidence available. Notice that biologists think all animals arose from unicellular, or single-celled, ancestors, as shown at the base of the tree.

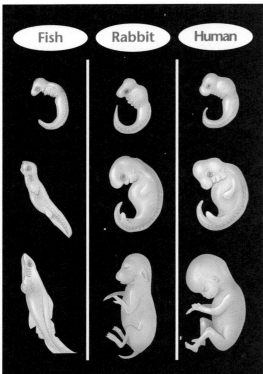

Fish   Rabbit   Human

Figure 7 Biologists often study embryo development when classifying animals. *Comparing and Contrasting* *Compare the embryos of three vertebrates—a fish, a rabbit, and a human. Which two animals show greater similarity in their development?*

Animals are classified, or put into groups, according to how they are related to other animals. **When biologists classify an animal, they look at the structure of its body and the way it develops as an embryo at the very beginning of its life. Biologists also examine the animal's DNA, which is a chemical in cells that controls an organism's inherited characteristics.** The more similar two animals are in those characteristics, the more closely they are probably related.

For example, look at the developing embryos shown in Figure 7. You can see that a rabbit embryo is more similar to a human embryo than it is to a fish embryo. This similarity provides one piece of evidence indicating that rabbits are more closely related to humans than they are to fishes. The structure of the animals' hearts provides another piece of evidence. The hearts of rabbits and humans are similar—but are quite different from the hearts of fishes.

One important structural characteristic used to classify animals is the presence or absence of a backbone, which is a series of bones that run down the center of the back. An animal that does not have a backbone is called an **invertebrate**. Jellyfishes, worms, snails, crabs, spiders, and insects are all invertebrates. Most animal species—about 95 percent—are invertebrates. In contrast, a **vertebrate** is an animal that has a backbone. Fishes, amphibians, reptiles, birds, and mammals are all vertebrates.

Aside from having—or not having—a backbone, animals also differ in the overall shape of their bodies. Although a few animals have lopsided bodies, most do not, as you will learn in the next section.

Section 1 Review

1. Describe two characteristics that all animals share.
2. List the major characteristics that are used to classify animals into groups.
3. List three needs that all animals must meet in order to survive.
4. **Thinking Critically** **Comparing and Contrasting** Contrast the ways in which wolves and frogs obtain their food, and identify one food-getting adaptation of each animal.

Check Your Progress   CHAPTER PROJECT 1

By now, you should have chosen your animal and learned from library research how to meet its needs. Discuss with your teacher your plans for obtaining, housing, and caring for your animal. After preparing your animal's home and obtaining some food for it, put the animal in its new home. (*Hint:* Be sure to consider how your animal will survive holidays and weekends.)

SECTION 2 Symmetry

DISCOVER ⋯⋯⋯⋯⋯⋯⋯⋯⋯⋯⋯⋯⋯⋯⋯⋯⋯ACTIVITY⋯

How Many Ways Can You Fold It?

1. Trace the triangle onto a sheet of paper and cut it out. Then draw a circle by tracing the rim of a glass or other round object. Cut out the circle.

2. Fold the triangle so that one half matches the other. Do the same with the circle.

3. See how many different ways you can fold each figure so that the two halves are identical.

Think It Over

Classifying Can you think of animals whose body shape could be folded in the same number of ways as the triangle? As the circle?

With its wings closed, a bright and colorful butterfly perches lightly on a flower, drinking nectar. Its delicate but strong wings are motionless as it drinks. Then, suddenly, those fragile-looking wings begin to move, and they lift the butterfly, seemingly effortlessly, into the air.

As you can see from the photo of the large copper butterfly in Figure 8, a butterfly's body has two halves, and each half looks almost like a reflection of the other. This balanced arrangement, called symmetry, is characteristic of many animals. A butterfly's symmetry contributes to its pleasing appearance. More importantly, the balanced wings help the butterfly to fly more easily.

GUIDE FOR READING

◆ What types of symmetry do complex animals exhibit?

Reading Tip Before you read, preview the illustrations in Figures 8 and 9. Predict how body shape is important to an animal.

Figure 8 If you could draw a line through this butterfly's body, it would divide the animal into two mirror-image halves. *Applying Concepts What is this balanced arrangement called?*

The Mathematics of Symmetry

In Figure 8, you can see that a line drawn down the middle of the butterfly produces two halves that are the same—they are mirror images. This dividing line is called a line of symmetry. An object has line symmetry, or **bilateral symmetry,** if there is a line that divides it into halves that are mirror images. A large copper butterfly has bilateral symmetry, as do an oak leaf, a spoon, and a pair of eyeglasses.

Contrast the butterfly's symmetry to that of a sea anemone. A sea anemone is circular if you look at it from the top, as in Figure 9. Any line drawn through its center will divide the sea anemone into two symmetrical halves. Like the sea anemone, many circular objects exhibit **radial symmetry**—they have many lines of symmetry that all go through a central point. Pie plates and bicycle wheels have radial symmetry.

☑ *Checkpoint* *How is radial symmetry different from bilateral symmetry?*

Symmetry in Animals

There are a few animals, such as most sponges, that exhibit no symmetry. These asymmetrical animals generally have very simple body plans. Sponges, for example, have no hearts, brains, kidneys, or nerve cells. **The bodies of complex animals all have either radial or bilateral symmetry.**

Animals with Radial Symmetry The external body parts of animals with radial symmetry are equally spaced around a central point, like spokes on a bicycle wheel. Because of the circular arrangement of their parts, radially symmetrical animals, such as jellyfishes, sea anemones, and sea urchins, do not have distinct front or back ends.

Animals with radial symmetry have several characteristics in common. All of them live in water. Most of them do not move very fast—they either stay in one spot, are moved along by water currents, or creep along the bottom. Few radially symmetrical animals are able to go out in search of prey. Instead, their watery environment carries food to them.

For a water animal that does not actively chase prey, the absence of a front end creates no disadvantage. Animals with radial symmetry learn about their environment primarily through senses of touch and taste, which function on the surfaces of their bodies. Because the animals are able to sense their environment in all directions, they can be ready to grab food coming from any direction.

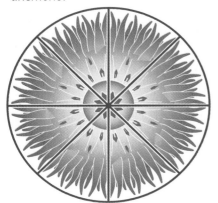

Figure 9 Sea anemones have radial symmetry. A radially symmetrical object has many lines of symmetry that all go through a central point. *Observing How would you describe the shape of the sea anemone?*

Animals with Bilateral Symmetry Most animals you are familiar with have bilateral symmetry. For example, a fish has only one line of symmetry that divides it into mirror images. Each half of a fish has one eye, one nostril, half of a mouth, and one of each of the fish's pairs of fins. Your body also has bilateral symmetry.

In general, bilaterally symmetrical animals are larger and more complex than those with radial symmetry. Animals with bilateral symmetry have a front end that goes first as the animal moves along. These animals move more quickly and efficiently than most animals with radial symmetry. This is partly because bilateral symmetry allows for a streamlined, balanced body. In addition, most bilaterally symmetrical animals have sense organs in their front ends that pick up information about what is in front of them. Swift movement and sense organs help bilaterally symmetrical animals get food and avoid enemies.

Figure 10 Radially symmetrical animals, like the sea urchin at left, have no distinct front or back ends. In contrast, bilaterally symmetrical animals, like the tiger above, have a front end with sense organs that pick up information. Because of its balanced body plan, a tiger can also move quickly.

Section 2 Review

1. What two types of symmetry do complex animals exhibit? Describe each type.
2. How can bilateral symmetry be an advantage to a predator?
3. Draw a view of a bilaterally symmetrical animal to show its symmetry. Draw the line of symmetry.
4. **Thinking Critically** Applying Concepts Which capital letters of the alphabet have bilateral symmetry? Radial symmetry?

Science at Home

With a family member, observe as many different animals as possible in your yard or at a park. Look in lots of different places, such as in the grass, under rocks, and in the air. Explain to your family member the advantage to an animal of having a distinct front end. What is this type of body arrangement called?

A TALE TOLD BY TRACKS

Suppose that, on a chilly winter day, you hike through a park. You suspect that many animals live there, but you don't actually see any of them. Instead, you see signs that the animals have left behind, such as mysterious tracks in the snow. These tracks are evidence you can use to draw inferences about the animals, such as what size they are and what they were doing. Inferences are interpretations of observations that help you to explain what may have happened in a given situation.

Problem

What can you learn about animals by studying their tracks?

Skill Focus

observing, inferring

Procedure

1. Copy the data table into your notebook.
2. The illustration at the top of the next page shows the tracks, or footprints, left in the snow by animals living in a park. The illustration has been divided into three sections. Focus in on the tracks in Section 1.
3. Make two or more observations about the tracks and record them in your data table.
4. For each observation you listed, write one or more inferences that could be drawn from that observation.

	DATA TABLE	
Section	Observations	Inferences
Section 1		
Section 2		
Section 3		

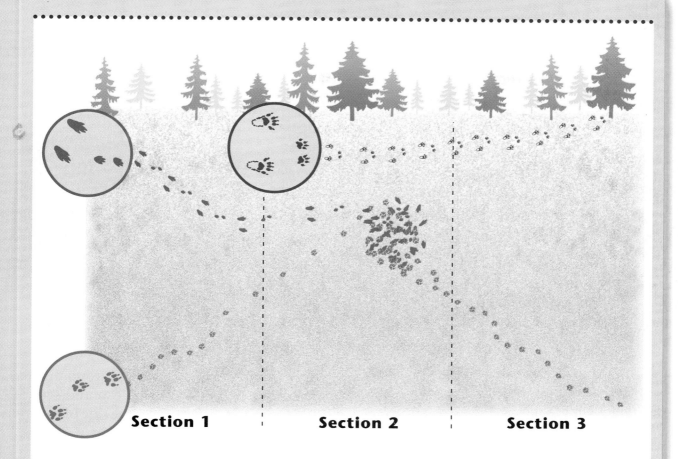

Section 1   Section 2   Section 3

5. Now look at the tracks in Section 2. Write two or more observations in the data table. For each observation, write one or more inferences.

6. Study the tracks in Section 3. Write two or more observations in the data table. Write at least one inference for each observation.

Analyze and Conclude

1. How many types of animals made the tracks shown in the illustration? Explain.
2. What inferences, if any, can you make about the relative sizes of the animals based on their tracks? Explain.
3. What can you infer about the speed of the animals' movements? Are they walking? Running? How can you tell?

4. In a paragraph, explain what you think happened to the animals and the order in which the events happened.
5. What inference do you feel most confident about and why? Which inference do you feel least confident about and why?
6. **Apply** How might making inferences be important in the work of a real detective? Explain.

More to Explore

Take a walk around your community looking for indirect evidence of animal life such as tracks, feathers, empty nests, and holes in the ground or in dead trees. For each discovery, record its location, at least two observations, and one or more inferences to explain each observation.

SECTION

3 Sponges and Cnidarians

DISCOVER ·· ACTIVITY

How Do Natural and Synthetic Sponges Compare?

1. Examine a natural sponge, and then use a hand lens or a microscope to take a closer look at its surface. Look carefully at the holes in the sponge. Draw what you see through the lens.

2. ✂ Cut out a small piece of sponge and examine it with a hand lens. Draw what you see.

3. Repeat Steps 1 and 2 with a synthetic kitchen sponge.

Think It Over

Observing What are three ways a natural and synthetic sponge are similar? What are three ways they are different?

GUIDE FOR READING

◆ How is the body of a sponge organized?

◆ What are the main characteristics of cnidarians?

Reading Tip Before you read, preview *Exploring a Sponge* on page 29. Then write a brief description of a sponge.

Eagerly but carefully, you and the others in your group put on scuba gear, preparing to dive into the ocean and see firsthand what lies beneath the surface. Over the side of the boat you go; the salty ocean water feels cool on your skin. As you slowly descend, you notice that you are surrounded by animals. You see many kinds of fishes, of course, but as you get to the ocean bottom, you notice other animals, too, some as strange as creatures from a science fiction movie. Some of these strange creatures may be sponges.

Sponges live all over the world—mostly in oceans, but also in freshwater rivers and lakes. Sponges are attached to hard surfaces underwater, and they are well adapted to their watery life. Moving currents carry food and oxygen to them, and these same currents take away their waste products. Water plays a role in their reproduction and helps their young find new places to live.

Sponges

Sponges don't look or act like most animals you know. In fact, they are so different that for a long time, people thought that sponges were plants. Like plants, adult sponges stay in one place. But unlike most plants, sponges take food into their bodies, which qualifies them for membership in the animal kingdom. These strange animals have been on Earth for about 540 million years.

◀ **Pink sponges on a Caribbean coral reef**

The bodies of most sponges have irregular shapes, with no symmetry. While some of their cells do specialized jobs, sponges lack the tissues and organs that most other animals have.

The Structure of a Sponge You might use a brightly colored, synthetic sponge to mop up a spill. That sponge is filled with holes, and so are the animals called sponges. **The body of a sponge is something like a bag that is pierced all over with openings called pores.** In fact, the name of the phylum to which sponges belong—phylum Porifera—means "having pores." Notice the many pores in the sponge in *Exploring a Sponge*.

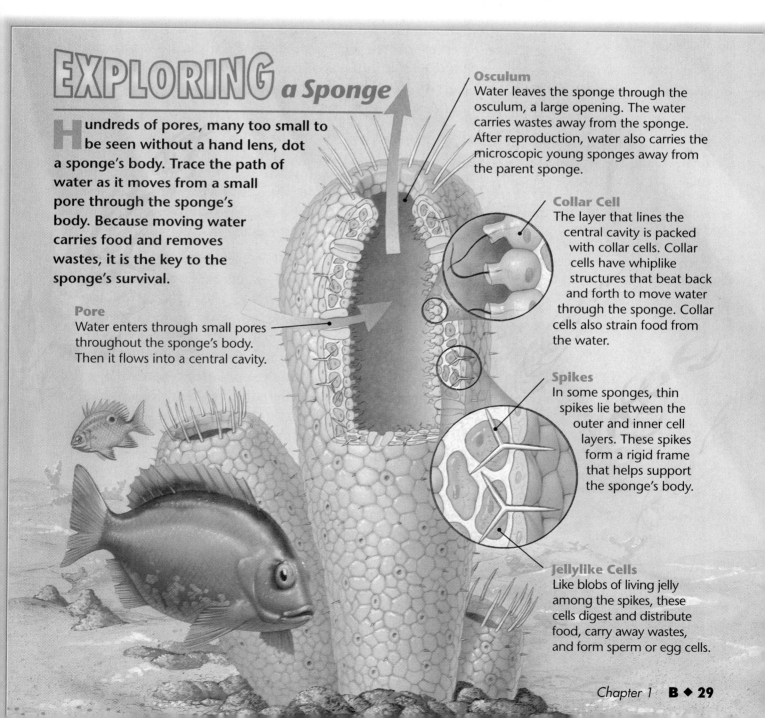

EXPLORING a Sponge

Hundreds of pores, many too small to be seen without a hand lens, dot a sponge's body. Trace the path of water as it moves from a small pore through the sponge's body. Because moving water carries food and removes wastes, it is the key to the sponge's survival.

Pore
Water enters through small pores throughout the sponge's body. Then it flows into a central cavity.

Osculum
Water leaves the sponge through the osculum, a large opening. The water carries wastes away from the sponge. After reproduction, water also carries the microscopic young sponges away from the parent sponge.

Collar Cell
The layer that lines the central cavity is packed with collar cells. Collar cells have whiplike structures that beat back and forth to move water through the sponge. Collar cells also strain food from the water.

Spikes
In some sponges, thin spikes lie between the outer and inner cell layers. These spikes form a rigid frame that helps support the sponge's body.

Jellylike Cells
Like blobs of living jelly among the spikes, these cells digest and distribute food, carry away wastes, and form sperm or egg cells.

In the paragraph that describes how sponges defend themselves, notice how the author says that a sponge dinner would be "like a sandwich made of thorns, sand, and cement, with a little awful-tasting goo mixed in." The author's description is a simile, which is a comparison using the word *like* or *as*. Writers use similes to paint lively word pictures and create vivid impressions.

In Your Journal

You can use similes in your own writing. For instance, you might say that a racehorse launches itself from the starting line like a rocket. Choose three different animals and write a simile describing each one. For each simile, identify the characteristic that you are trying to convey.

Getting Food and Oxygen from Water Sponges feed by straining food particles from water. As water enters a sponge, it carries tiny organisms such as bacteria and protists. Collar cells on the inside of the central cavity trap these food particles and digest them. Sponges are very efficient at removing food particles from water. A sponge the size of a teacup is able to remove food from 5,000 liters of water per day. That's enough water to fill a truckload of two-liter soft-drink bottles!

INTEGRATING CHEMISTRY A sponge gets its oxygen from water too. The water contains oxygen, which moves from the water into the sponge's cells in a process known as diffusion. In diffusion, molecules of a substance move from an area in which they are highly concentrated to an area in which they are less concentrated. Oxygen is more highly concentrated in the water than it is in the sponge's cells. So the oxygen moves from the water into the sponge. Diffusion also carries waste products from the sponge's cells into the water.

Spikes The soft bodies of most sponges are supported by a network of spikes. Those spikes can be as sharp as needles, as anyone who has touched a live sponge knows. In addition, many sponges are tougher than wood, and some produce irritating substances. Even so, some fish eat sponges. A sponge dinner is probably like a sandwich made of thorns, sand, and cement, with a little awful-tasting goo mixed in.

Sponge Reproduction Sponges reproduce both asexually and sexually. Budding is one form of asexual reproduction in sponges. In budding, small new sponges grow from the sides of an adult sponge. Eventually these tiny sponges detach and begin life on their own. Sponges reproduce sexually too. Sponges do not have separate sexes—a single sponge forms eggs at one time of the year and sperm at a different time. At any one time of the year, some sponges are producing eggs and others are producing sperm. When a sponge produces sperm, the water currents that move through the sponge carry sperm from the sponge into the open water. The sperm may then enter the pores of another sponge and fertilize egg cells in that sponge.

After fertilization, a larva develops. A **larva** (plural *larvae*) is the immature form of an animal that looks very different from the adult. A sponge larva is a hollow ball of cells that swims through the water. Eventually the larva attaches to a surface and develops into a nonmoving adult sponge.

Checkpoint As water flows through a sponge's body, what functions does it enable the sponge to perform?

Cnidarians

Some other organisms you might notice on an underwater dive are jellyfishes, sea anemones, and corals. At first glance, those animals look like they could be creatures from another planet. Most jellyfishes look like transparent bubbles that trail curtains of streamerlike tentacles. Sea anemones look like odd, underwater flowers. Some corals have branches that make them look like trees. Jellyfishes, sea anemones, and corals are **cnidarians** (nih DAIR ee uhnz), animals that have stinging cells and take their food into a hollow central cavity. **Members of the phylum Cnidaria are carnivores that use their stinging cells to capture their prey and defend themselves.** The stinging cells are located on the long, wavy tentacles.

Unlike sponges, cnidarians have specialized tissues. For example, because of muscle-like tissues, many cnidarians can move in interesting ways. Jellyfishes swim through the water, and hydras turn slow somersaults. Anemones stretch out, shrink down, and bend slowly from side to side. These movements are directed by nerve cells that are spread out like a spider web, or net. This nerve net helps the cnidarian respond quickly to danger or the presence of food.

Cnidarian Body Plans Cnidarians have two different body plans, both with radial symmetry. As you read about these two body plans, refer to Figure 12. A **polyp** (PAHL ip), such as a hydra, sea anemone, or coral, is shaped something like a vase, with the mouth opening at the top. Most polyps do not move around; they are adapted for a life attached to an underwater surface. In contrast, the bowl-shaped

Figure 11 All cnidarians live in watery environments. **A.** Hydras live in freshwater ponds and lakes, where they reproduce by budding. **B.** The Portuguese man-of-war is actually a colony of cnidarians living together. **C.** Sea anemones are large cnidarians that often live in groups in the ocean. *Comparing and Contrasting* What characteristics do these three cnidarians share?

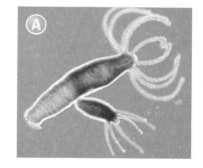

medusa (muh DOO suh), such as a jellyfish, is adapted for a free-swimming life. Medusas, unlike polyps, have mouths that open downward. Some cnidarians go through both a polyp stage and a medusa stage during their lives. Others are polyps or medusas for their whole lives.

How Cnidarians Feed A cnidarian captures its prey by using its stinging cells to inject venom, a poisonous substance that paralyzes fish and other prey. Then the cnidarian's tentacles pull the prey animal to its mouth. From there the food passes into a body cavity where it is digested. Because cnidarians have a digestive system with only one opening, undigested food is expelled through the mouth.

Cnidarian Reproduction Cnidarians reproduce both asexually and sexually. For polyps, such as the hydra in Figure 11, budding is the most common form of asexual reproduction. Amazingly, in some polyps the entire animal splits into pieces. Each piece then forms a new polyp. Both kinds of asexual reproduction allow the numbers of cnidarians to increase rapidly in a short time.

Sexual reproduction in cnidarians occurs in a variety of ways. Some species of cnidarians have both sexes within one individual. In others, the sexes are in separate individuals, as in humans.

Checkpoint **How does a cnidarian obtain and digest food?**

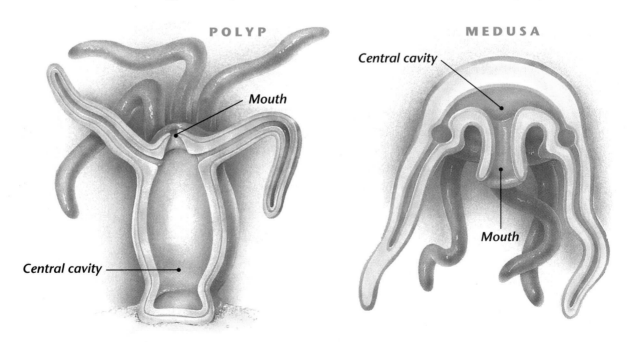

Figure 12 Cnidarians have two basic body forms, the vase-shaped polyp and the bowl-shaped medusa. *Comparing and Contrasting* *Contrast the location of the mouth in the polyp and the medusa.*

Life on a Coral Reef

In some warm, shallow ocean waters, just below the surface, you can find one of the most diverse ocean environments—a coral reef. Coral reefs seem to be made of stone. But in fact, coral reefs are built by cnidarians. At the beginning of its life, a free-swimming coral larva attaches to a solid surface. A broken shell, a sunken ship, or the skeleton of a once-living coral animal will do just fine.

The coral polyp reproduces asexually, and then its offspring reproduce asexually, too. The coral polyp then produces a hard, stony skeleton around its soft polyp body. Over time, that polyp may give rise to thousands of polyps, each with a hard skeleton. When the coral polyps die, their skeletons remain behind. Over thousands of years, as live corals add their skeletons to those that have died, rocklike masses called reefs grow up from the sea floor. Coral reefs can become enormous. The Great Barrier Reef off the coast of Australia is about 2,000 kilometers long.

Coral reefs, like the one in Figure 13, are home to more species of fishes and invertebrates than any other environment on Earth. Hundreds of sponge species live among the corals, constantly filtering water through their bodies. Worms burrow into the coral reef. Giant clams lie with their huge shells slightly open. Shrimp and crabs edge out of hiding places below the corals. At night, bright blue damsel fish settle into pockets in the coral. At dawn and dusk, sea turtles, sea snakes, and sharks all visit the reef, hunting for prey. These living things interact in complex ways, creating an environment that is rich and beautiful.

Figure 13 Coral reefs provide homes and hunting grounds for a vast variety of sea animals. The bottom photo is a close-up of a group of individual coral polyps.

Section 3 Review

1. Describe the structure of a sponge's body.
2. Explain how cnidarians capture prey and defend themselves. In your explanation, refer to specific body structures.
3. Draw a diagram to show how water travels through a sponge. Show the path with an arrow.
4. **Thinking Critically** **Classifying** Why is a sponge classified as an animal?

Check Your Progress

CHAPTER PROJECT 1

You should be observing your animal every day and writing your observations in your journal. Record how the animal looks, feeds, and behaves. Note any changes in the animal. Talk to your teacher before making any changes to your animal's home, feeding schedule, or other living conditions.

Coral Reefs in Danger

Coral reefs off the coasts of many nations are endangered, damaged, or threatened with destruction. Reefs house and protect many species of sea animals, including sponges, shrimp, sea turtles, and fishes. In addition, reefs protect coastlines from floods caused by ocean storms.

Although coral reefs are hard as rocks, the coral animals themselves are quite delicate. Recreational divers can damage the fragile reefs. Is it possible to protect the reefs while still allowing divers to explore them?

The Issues

What's the Harm in Diving? About 3.5 million recreational divers live in the United States. With so many divers it is hard to guarantee that no harm will occur to the coral reefs. In fact, divers can cause significant damage by standing on or even touching these fragile reefs. Carelessly dropping a boat anchor can crush part of a reef. Although most divers are careful, not all are, and accidents can always happen.

Harm to the reefs is even more likely to occur when divers collect coral for their own enjoyment or to sell for profit. You can see brightly colored coral from the sea in jewelry and in decorations.

Should Reefs Be Further Protected? The United States government has passed laws making it illegal, under most circumstances, to remove coral from the sea. Because a few divers break these laws, some people want to ban diving altogether. However, many divers say it's unfair to ban diving just because of a few lawbreakers.

Many divers consider coral reefs the most exciting and beautiful places in the ocean to explore. As recreational divers, photographers, scientists, and others visit and learn more about these delicate coral reefs, they increase their own and other's awareness of them. Public awareness may be the best way to ensure that these rich environments are protected.

More Than a Diving Issue Coral reefs in the Western Atlantic—such as those in Bermuda, the Bahamas, the Caribbean Islands, and Florida—are major tourist attractions that bring money and jobs to people in local communities. If diving were banned, local businesses would suffer significantly. Also, although divers can harm coral reefs, other human activities, such as ocean pollution, oil spills, and fishing nets, can also cause harm. In addition, natural events, such as tropical storms, changes in sea level, and changes in sea temperature, can also damage the fragile reefs.

You Decide

1. Identify the Problem

In your own words, explain the controversy surrounding diving near coral reefs.

2. Analyze the Options

List the arguments on each side of the issue. Note the pros and cons. How well would each position protect the reefs? Who might be harmed or inconvenienced?

3. Find a Solution

Write a newspaper editorial stating your position on whether diving should be allowed near coral reefs. State your position and reasons clearly.

SECTION 4 Worms

What Can You Learn About a Flatworm by Looking at It?

1. Your teacher will give you a planarian, a kind of flatworm. Pick the worm up with the tip of a small paintbrush. Place it carefully in a small, transparent container. Use a dropper to cover the planarian with spring water.

2. Observe the planarian with a hand lens for a few minutes. Look for a head and tail region. Look for two spots in the head region. Draw a picture of the planarian.

3. Observe and describe how the planarian moves.

4. Gently touch the planarian with a toothpick and observe how it behaves. Then return the planarian to your teacher, and wash your hands.

Think It Over

Observing What are some ways in which a planarian is different from a sponge?

Y ou might think that all worms are small, slimy, and wriggly. But many worms do not fit that description. Some worms are almost three meters long and are as thick as your arm. Others look like glowing, furry blobs. Worms can flutter and glide or climb around with paddle-like bristles. Still others are very small and live in white tubes cemented to rocks.

What Worms Have in Common

It's hard to say exactly what worms are, because there are many kinds of worms, all with their own characteristics. **Biologists classify worms into several phyla—the three major ones are flatworms, roundworms, and segmented worms.** Flatworms belong to the phylum Platyhelminthes (plat ee HEL minth eez);

GUIDE FOR READING

◆ What are the three main groups of worms?

◆ What are the characteristics of each group of worms?

Reading Tip As you read, list the characteristics of flatworms, roundworms, and segmented worms.

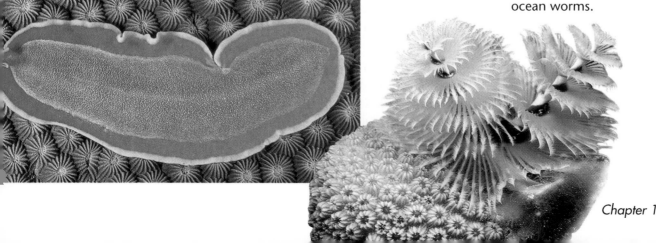

Figure 14 The ocean flatworm, left, and the segmented Christmas tree worm, right, show some of the wide variety of ocean worms.

Figure 15 As you can tell from this spectacular spaghetti worm, not all worms are gray and tube shaped.

roundworms belong to the phylum Nematoda; segmented worms belong to the phylum Annelida.

All worms have some characteristics in common. All worms are invertebrates, and they all have long, narrow bodies without legs. In addition, all worms have tissues, organs, and organ systems. Also, all worms have bilateral symmetry. Unlike sponges or cnidarians, worms have head and tail ends.

Worms are the simplest organisms with a brain, which is a knot of nerve tissue located in the head end. Because a worm's brain and some of its sense organs are located in its head end, the worm can detect objects, food, mates, and predators quickly, and it can respond quickly, too. Sense organs, such as organs sensitive to light and touch, pick up information from the environment. The brain interprets that information and directs the animal's response. For example, if an earthworm on the surface of the ground senses a footstep, the worm will quickly return to its underground burrow.

Both sexual and asexual reproduction are found in the worm phyla. In many species of worms, there are separate male and female animals, as in humans. In other species each individual has both male and female sex organs. A worm with both sexes does not usually fertilize its own eggs. Instead, two worms mate and exchange sperm. Many worms reproduce asexually by methods such as breaking into pieces. In fact, if you cut some kinds of worms into several pieces, a whole new worm will grow from each piece. Earthworms cannot do this, but if you cut off the tail end of an earthworm, the front end will probably grow a new tail. This ability to regrow body parts is called **regeneration.**

☑ *Checkpoint* **What type of symmetry do worms exhibit?**

Flatworms

As you'd expect from their name, flatworms are flat. The bodies of flatworms, such as planarians, flukes, and tapeworms, are soft as jelly. Although tapeworms can grow to be 10 to 12 meters long, other flatworms are almost too small to be seen.

Most flatworms are parasites that obtain their food from their hosts. Instead of living on its own, a **parasite** is an organism that lives inside or on another organism. The parasite takes its food from the organism in or on which it lives, called the **host**. Parasites may rob their hosts of food and make them weak. They may injure the host's tissues or organs. Sometimes a parasite will kill its host, but usually the host survives.

Tapeworms Tapeworms are one kind of parasitic flatworm. A tapeworm's body is adapted to absorbing food from the host's digestive system. Some kinds of tapeworms can live in human hosts. Many tapeworms live in more than one host during their lifetime. Notice that in *Exploring the Life Cycle of a Dog Tapeworm*, the tapeworm has two different hosts—a rabbit and a dog.

EXPLORING *the Life Cycle of a Dog Tapeworm*

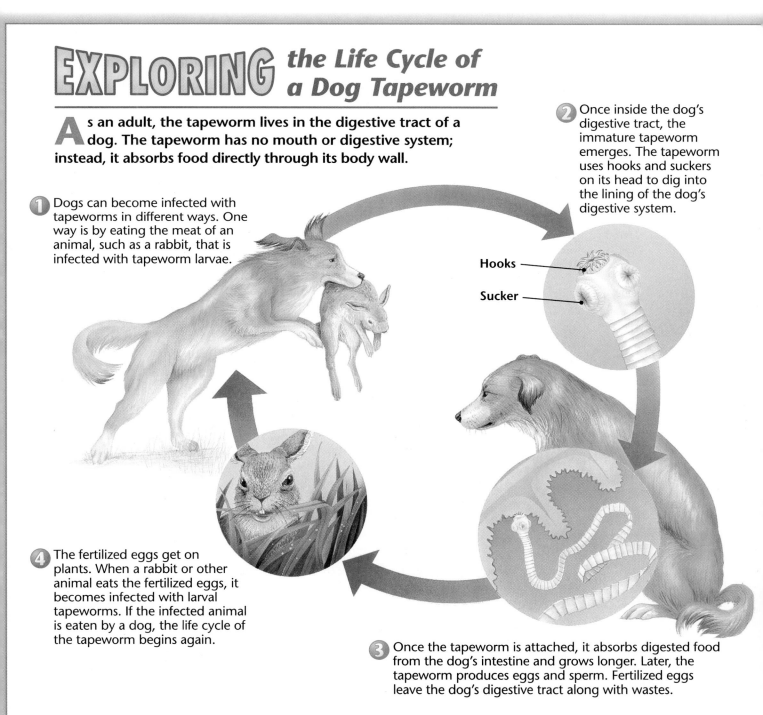

As an adult, the tapeworm lives in the digestive tract of a dog. The tapeworm has no mouth or digestive system; instead, it absorbs food directly through its body wall.

1 Dogs can become infected with tapeworms in different ways. One way is by eating the meat of an animal, such as a rabbit, that is infected with tapeworm larvae.

2 Once inside the dog's digestive tract, the immature tapeworm emerges. The tapeworm uses hooks and suckers on its head to dig into the lining of the dog's digestive system.

Hooks

Sucker

4 The fertilized eggs get on plants. When a rabbit or other animal eats the fertilized eggs, it becomes infected with larval tapeworms. If the infected animal is eaten by a dog, the life cycle of the tapeworm begins again.

3 Once the tapeworm is attached, it absorbs digested food from the dog's intestine and grows longer. Later, the tapeworm produces eggs and sperm. Fertilized eggs leave the dog's digestive tract along with wastes.

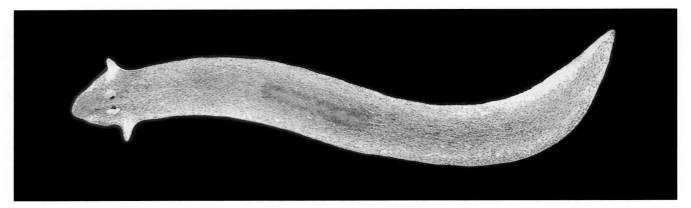

Figure 16 Planarians are flatworms that live in ponds, streams, and oceans. The eyespots on the planarian's head can distinguish between light and dark. *Inferring How is having a distinct head end an advantage to a planarian?*

Planarians Some flatworms are nonparasitic, or free-living. Unlike parasites, free-living organisms do not live in or on other organisms. Small free-living flatworms glide over the rocks in ponds, slide over damp soil, or swim slowly through the oceans like ruffled, brightly patterned leaves.

Planarians, such as the one in Figure 16, are scavengers—they feed on dead or decaying material. But they are also predators and will attack any animal smaller than they are.

If you look at a planarian's head, you can see two big dots that look like eyes. These dots are called eyespots, and they function something like eyes, although they cannot see a specific image like human eyes can. A planarian's head also has cells that pick up odors. Planarians rely mainly on smell to locate food. When a planarian smells food, it moves toward the food and glides onto it.

A planarian feeds like a vacuum cleaner. The planarian inserts a feeding tube into its food. Digestive juices flow out into the food, where they begin to break down the food while it is still outside the worm's body. Then the planarian sucks up the partly-digested bits of food. Digestion is then completed within a cavity inside the planarian. Food is distributed to body cells by diffusion. Like cnidarians, planarians have one opening in their digestive system. Undigested wastes exit through the feeding tube.

Roundworms

The next time you walk along a beach, consider that about a million roundworms live in each square meter of damp sand. Roundworms can live in nearly any moist environment—including forest soils, Antarctic sands, and even pools of super-hot water. Most are tiny and hard to see, but roundworms may be the most abundant animals on Earth.

Unlike flatworms, roundworms have cylindrical bodies. As you can see in Figure 17, they look like tiny strands of cooked spaghetti that are pointed at each end. If you look at roundworms under a microscope, you'd see their bodies thrashing from side to side.

Figure 17 The transparent bodies of these roundworms have been stained for better viewing under a microscope.

While many roundworms are carnivores or herbivores, others are parasites. Have you given worm medicine to a pet dog or cat? The medicine was probably meant to kill roundworm parasites, such as hookworms.

Unlike cnidarians or flatworms, roundworms have a digestive system that is like a tube, open at both ends. Food enters at the animal's mouth and wastes exit through an opening, called the **anus,** at the far end of the tube. Food travels in one direction through the roundworm's digestive system, as it does in most complex animals.

A one-way digestive system has certain advantages. It is something like an assembly line, with a different part of the digestive process happening at each place along the line. Digestion happens in orderly stages. First food is broken down by digestive juices. Then the digested food is absorbed into the animal's body. Finally wastes are eliminated. The advantage of this type of digestive process is that it enables the animal's body to use foods efficiently, by enabling it to absorb a large amount of the needed substances in foods.

☑ *Checkpoint* *You are using a microscope to look at a tiny worm. What would you look for to tell whether it is a roundworm?*

Segmented Worms

If you have ever dug in a garden in the spring, you have probably seen earthworms wriggling through the moist soil. Those familiar soil inhabitants are segmented worms. So are the exotic sea-floor worms that you see in Figure 18. Parasitic blood-sucking leeches are also segmented worms. Since their bodies are long and narrow, some segmented worms look a bit like flatworms and roundworms. But segmented worms may be more closely related to crabs and snails.

Figure 18 These segmented sea-floor worms belong to the same phylum as earthworms.

Sharpen your Skills

Observing ACTIVITY

Observe earthworms in a container filled with soil. Make your observations on several different days—if possible, at different times in the day. Note the worms' general sizes, colors, and appearances. Also observe their behavior—for example, how the worms move and how they tunnel through the soil. How is an earthworm's behavior adapted to surviving in its environment?

Figure 19 An earthworm's body is divided into over 100 segments. Some organs are repeated in most of those segments; others exist in only a few. *Interpreting Diagrams How does blood move through an earthworm's body?*

Segmented worms occupy nearly all environments, and most live in burrows or tubes. The burrow helps the worm hide both from possible predators and from possible prey. Many segmented worms are sit-and-wait predators that leap out of their burrows to attack animals that come too close.

Segmentation When you look at an earthworm, you notice that its body seems to consist of a series of rings separated by grooves, something like a vacuum-cleaner hose. **Earthworms and other segmented worms have bodies made up of many linked sections called segments.** An earthworm usually has more than 100 segments. On the outside, the segments look nearly identical. On the inside, some organs are repeated in most segments. For example, each segment has tubes that remove wastes . Other organs, however, such as the worm's reproductive organs, are found only in some segments. Nerve cords and a digestive tube run along the length of the worm's body. Like roundworms, earthworms have a one-way digestive system with two openings.

A Closed Circulatory System Segmented worms have a closed circulatory system. In a closed circulatory system, like your own, blood moves only within a connected network of tubes called blood vessels. In contrast, some animals, such as insects, have an open circulatory system in which blood leaves the blood vessels and sloshes around inside the body. A closed circulatory system can move blood around an animal's body much more quickly than an open circulatory system can. Blood quickly carries oxygen and food to cells. Because of this, an animal with a closed circulatory system can be larger and more active than one with an open circulatory system.

In segments 9 through 13, an earthworm has five paired pumping organs that act like hearts. They pump blood through large blood vessels that run the length of the worm's body. Find the earthworm's hearts and blood vessels in Figure 19.

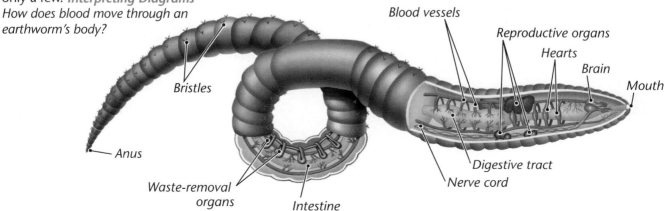

Blood vessels · Reproductive organs · Hearts · Brain · Mouth · Bristles · Anus · Waste-removal organs · Intestine · Nerve cord · Digestive tract

How Earthworms Live Earthworms tunnel for a living. They are scavengers that eat decayed plant and animal remains in the soil. On damp nights earthworms come up out of their burrows. They crawl on the surface of the ground, seeking leaves and soft fruits to drag underground and eat.

Night is a safe time for an earthworm to crawl on the surface, because many worm predators are asleep then. At night the air is damp, and this dampness helps keep the worm's skin moist. If a worm dries out, it will die, because it obtains oxygen through moisture on its skin.

Well-developed muscles let an earthworm move through its burrow. Stiff bristles stick out from each of the worm's segments. To crawl forward, an earthworm sticks its bristles in the ground and pulls itself along, much as a mountain climber uses an ice ax. Mountain climbers drive ice axes into a slippery slope and then pull themselves up.

Earthworms and Soil Earthworms are among the most **INTEGRATING EARTH SCIENCE** helpful inhabitants of garden and farm soil. They benefit people by improving the soil in which plants grow. Earthworm droppings make the soil more fertile. Earthworm tunnels loosen the soil and allow air, water, and plant roots to move through it. You have probably seen an earthworm tunnel entrance without realizing what it was—they are extremely common in lawns. To find one, look for a small, round hole in the ground with little lumps of soil next to it.

Section 4 Review

1. List the three major phyla of worms and give an example of each.
2. How does a dog tapeworm obtain its food?
3. Contrast a roundworm's digestive system to that of a planarian.
4. Describe the structure of an earthworm's body.
5. **Thinking Critically Relating Cause and Effect** How does keeping a dog on a leash reduce its risk for getting a tapeworm?

Check Your Progress

CHAPTER PROJECT 1

Begin to analyze what you have learned about your animal from your observations. Did you see a daily pattern to the animal's behavior? Think about what each kind of behavior accomplishes—whether it helps the animal obtain food or escape from danger, for example. Choose how you are going to present what you have learned—a written report, a talk, captioned illustrations, or some other method. Prepare charts or other visual aids.

Earthworm Responses

In this lab, you will practice the skill of making hypotheses to learn more about earthworms.

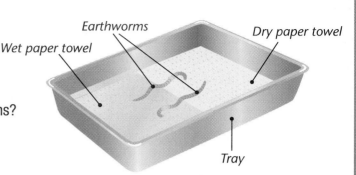

Earthworms

Wet paper towel

Dry paper towel

Tray

Problem

Do earthworms prefer dry or moist conditions? Do they prefer light or dark conditions?

Materials

plastic dropper	water	cardboard
clock or watch	paper towels	flashlight
2 earthworms	storage container	tray

Procedure

1. Which environment do you think earthworms prefer—dry or moist? Record your hypothesis in your notebook.
2. Use the dropper to sprinkle water on the worms. Keep the worms moist at all times.
3. Fold a dry paper towel and place it on the bottom of one side of your tray. Fold a moistened paper towel and place it on the other side.
4. Moisten your hands. Then place the earthworms in the center of the tray. Make sure that half of each earthworm's body rests on the moist paper towel and half rests on the dry towel. Handle the worms gently.
5. Cover the tray with the piece of cardboard. After five minutes, remove the cardboard and observe whether the worms are on the moist or dry surface. Record your observations.
6. Repeat Steps 4 and 5.
7. Return the earthworms to their storage container. Moisten the earthworms with water.
8. Which do you think earthworms prefer—strong light or darkness? Record your hypothesis in your notebook.

9. Cover the whole surface of the tray with a moistened paper towel.
10. Place the earthworms in the center of the tray. Cover half of the tray with cardboard. Shine a flashlight onto the other half.
11. After five minutes, note the locations of the worms. Record your observations.
12. Repeat Steps 10 and 11.
13. Moisten the earthworms and put them in the location designated by your teacher. Wash your hands after handling the worms.

Analyze and Conclude

1. Which environment did the worms prefer—moist or dry? Bright or dark? Did the worms' behavior support your hypotheses?
2. Use what you know about earthworms to explain how their responses to moisture and light help them survive.
3. **Think About It** What knowledge or experiences helped you make your hypotheses at the start of the experiments?

Design an Experiment

Do earthworms prefer a smooth or rough surface? Write your hypothesis. Then design an experiment to answer the question. Check with your teacher before carrying out your experiment.

SECTION 1 — What Is an Animal?

Key Ideas

◆ Animals are multicellular organisms that obtain food by eating other organisms. Animals can move. Most reproduce sexually.

◆ Animals need water, food, and oxygen to survive. Some animals are carnivores, or meat eaters. Others are herbivores, or plant eaters. Omnivores eat both plants and animals.

◆ When biologists classify an animal, they look at the structure of its body, its DNA, and the way its embryo develops. Some animals are vertebrates; most animal species are invertebrates.

Key Terms

species	heterotroph
autotroph	sexual reproduction
fertilization	asexual reproduction
adaptation	herbivore
carnivore	predator
prey	omnivore
phylum	invertebrate
vertebrate	

SECTION 2 — Symmetry

INTEGRATING MATHEMATICS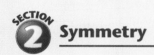

Key Ideas

◆ The bodies of complex animals all have either radial or bilateral symmetry.

◆ Animals with radial symmetry have body parts arranged around a central point. They do not have distinct front ends.

◆ Animals with bilateral symmetry have one line that divides them into two mirror images. These animals, which usually have a distinct front end, are generally more complex than radially symmetrical animals.

Key Terms
bilateral symmetry
radial symmetry

SECTION 3 — Sponges and Cnidarians

Key Ideas

◆ A sponge obtains food by straining water taken in through its pores. Sponges have no tissues or organs.

◆ Cnidarians, which include jellyfishes and hydras, are carnivores with stinging cells that help capture prey. Cnidarians have two body plans—polyp and medusa.

◆ Corals are cnidarians with hard skeletons around their soft bodies. Over time, the skeletons of corals form coral reefs.

Key Terms
larva
cnidarian
polyp
medusa

SECTION 4 — Worms

Key Ideas

◆ The three major worm phyla are flatworms, roundworms, and segmented worms.

◆ Most flatworms are parasites that obtain food from their hosts. Planarians are nonparasitic flatworms.

◆ Roundworms have a digestive system that is a tube open at both ends.

◆ Segmented worms have bodies made up of many segments. Segmented worms have a closed circulatory system in which blood is contained in blood vessels.

◆ Earthworms help farmers and gardeners by loosening and fertilizing the soil.

Key Terms

regeneration	parasite	host
anus		

USING THE INTERNET

ACTIVITY

www.science-explorer.phschool.com

Reviewing Content

For more review of key concepts, see the Interactive Student Tutorial CD-ROM.

Multiple Choice
Choose the letter of the best answer.

1. Organisms that make their own food are called
   a. omnivores.
   b. autotrophs.
   c. heterotrophs.
   d. carnivores.
2. Which of the following is *not* one of the major characteristics that biologists use to classify an animal?
   a. the structure of its body
   b. its height or length
   c. the development of its embryo
   d. its DNA
3. An animal with many lines of symmetry
   a. is bilaterally symmetrical.
   b. is radially symmetrical.
   c. has no symmetry.
   d. has line symmetry.
4. Which animal is a medusa?
   a. coral
   b. jellyfish
   c. planarian
   d. sea anemone
5. Which animal has a one-way digestive system?
   a. earthworm
   b. planarian
   c. sponge
   d. jellyfish

True or False
If the statement is true, write true. If it is false, change the underlined word or words to make the statement true.

6. <u>All</u> animals are made up of many cells.
7. <u>Sexual</u> reproduction produces offspring that are not exactly like either parent.
8. Fish have <u>radial symmetry</u>.
9. The bodies of <u>cnidarians</u> contain many pores.
10. The bodies of <u>roundworms</u> are segmented.

Checking Concepts

11. Explain the relationship among cells, tissues, and organs.
12. An oxygen molecule has just passed into a sponge's cell. Describe how it got there.
13. Compare a medusa and a polyp.
14. Are humans parasitic or free-living animals? Explain.
15. You dig up a handful of damp soil from the forest and examine it with a microscope. What kind of animal would probably be there in the greatest numbers? Explain.
16. **Writing to Learn** You are a small fish visiting a coral reef for the first time. What interesting sights would you see? Are there dangers to watch out for? In a paragraph, describe your adventures at the coral reef.

Thinking Visually

17. **Flowchart** The partially completed flowchart below shows how water travels through a sponge. Copy the flowchart onto a separate sheet of paper. Then complete it and add a title. (For more on flowcharts, see the Skills Handbook.)

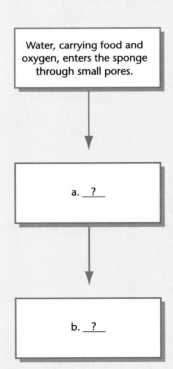

Water, carrying food and oxygen, enters the sponge through small pores.

↓

a. ?

↓

b. ?

Applying Skills

A scientist used a pesticide on one field and left a nearby field untreated. Next, she marked off five plots of equal size in each field. Then she dug up a cubic meter of soil beneath each plot, and counted the earthworms in the soil. The table below shows her data. Use the table to answer Questions 18–20.

Field with Pesticide		Untreated Field	
Plot	Worms per cubic meter	Plot	Worms per cubic meter
A	730	F	901
B	254	G	620
C	319	H	811
D	428	I	576
E	451	J	704

18. **Controlling Variables** Identify the manipulated and responding variables in this experiment.

19. **Calculating** Calculate the average number of worms per cubic meter in the treated field. Then do the same for the untreated field.

20. **Drawing Conclusions** How did this pesticide affect the population of worms in the soil?

Thinking Critically

21. **Comparing and Contrasting** Compare the ways in which a sponge, a planarian, and a roundworm digest their food.

22. **Predicting** The sand in a desert is bright orange. What color would sit-and-wait predators in that desert probably be? Explain.

23. **Relating Cause and Effect** If a pesticide killed off many of the earthworms in a garden, how might that affect the plants growing in that soil?

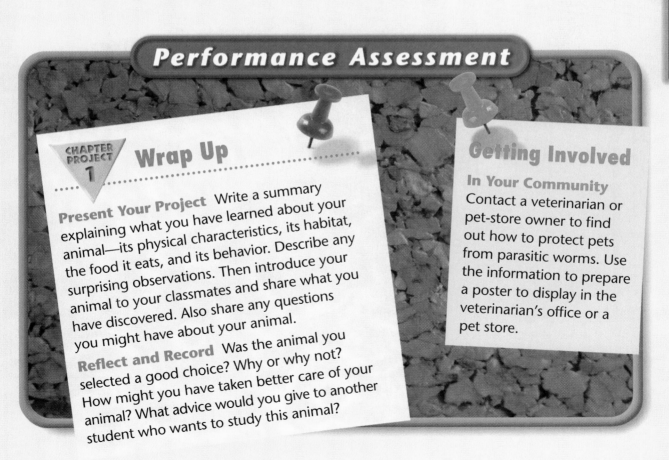

Performance Assessment

CHAPTER PROJECT 1
Wrap Up

Present Your Project Write a summary explaining what you have learned about your animal—its physical characteristics, its habitat, the food it eats, and its behavior. Describe any surprising observations. Then introduce your animal to your classmates and share what you have discovered. Also share any questions you might have about your animal.

Reflect and Record Was the animal you selected a good choice? Why or why not? How might you have taken better care of your animal? What advice would you give to another student who wants to study this animal?

Getting Involved

In Your Community Contact a veterinarian or pet-store owner to find out how to protect pets from parasitic worms. Use the information to prepare a poster to display in the veterinarian's office or a pet store.

CHAPTER

2 Mollusks, Arthropods, and Echinoderms

WHAT'S AHEAD

Going Through Changes

Look at the changes a treehopper insect goes through in its lifetime! In its white nymph stage, it doesn't look anything like an adult treehopper. Most of the animals you will read about in this chapter also change their form during their life cycles. In this project, you will view these kinds of changes firsthand as you observe mealworm development.

Your Goal To observe how different conditions affect mealworm development.

To complete this project successfully, you must
◆ compare mealworm development under two different conditions
◆ record your mealworm observations daily for several weeks
◆ draw conclusions about the effects of those conditions on development
◆ follow the safety guidelines in Appendix A

Get Started Find two containers, such as clean margarine tubs with lids, in which to keep the mealworms. Get some mealworm food, such as cornflakes, and a plastic spoon to transfer the food and count the mealworms. Choose two conditions, such as two different temperatures or food sources, and plan how to test the two conditions.

Check Your Progress You'll be working on this project as you study this chapter. To keep your project on track, look for Check Your Progress boxes at the following points.
Section 2 Review, page 61: Record your daily observations.
Section 3 Review, page 67: Sketch the stages of development.
Section 5 Review, page 76: Draw conclusions about mealworm development under each of the conditions.

Wrap Up At the end of the chapter (page 79), you will report on your results.

Treehoppers undergo dramatic changes in form during their lives. The whitish nymphs gradually turn into light green young adults. The young adults gradually change into dark green mature adults.

Mollusks

DISCOVER

How Can You Classify Shells?

1. Obtain an assortment of shells from your teacher. Examine each one carefully. Look at the shells and feel their surfaces.

2. Compare the outer surface of each shell to the inner surface.

3. Classify the shells into two or more groups based on the characteristics you observe.

Think It Over

Inferring How might it help an animal to have a shell?

GUIDE FOR READING

◆ What are the main characteristics of mollusks?

◆ What are the major groups of mollusks?

Reading Tip As you read, make a compare/contrast table to distinguish among the different mollusk groups.

▼ Wampum string and clamshell

From the shells of clams, Native Americans in the Northeast carved purple and white beads called wampum. They wove these beads into belts with complex designs that often had special, solemn significance. A wampum belt might record a group's history. When warring groups made peace, they exchanged weavings made of wampum. Iroquois women would honor a new chief with gifts of wampum strings.

The hard shells of clams provided the material for wampum, and the soft bodies within the shells were a major source of food for Native Americans who lived along the seacoast. Today, clams and similar animals, such as scallops and oysters, are still valuable sources of food for people in many parts of the world.

What Are Mollusks?

Clams, oysters, and scallops are all mollusks (phylum Mollusca). So are snails and octopuses. **Mollusks** are invertebrates with soft, unsegmented bodies that are often protected by hard outer shells. **In addition to soft bodies often covered with shells, mollusks have a thin layer of tissue called a mantle that covers their internal organs.** The mantle also produces the mollusk's shell. Most mollusks move with a muscular structure called a foot. The feet of different kinds of mollusks are adapted for various uses, such as crawling, digging, or catching prey.

Mollusks live nearly everywhere on Earth. Most live in water, from mountain streams to the deep ocean, but some live on land, usually in damp places.

Figure 1 Some mollusks, like the chambered nautilus, left, are protected by shells. Other mollusks, like the nudibranch, right, do not have shells. *Classifying What characteristics do these two organisms share?*

Like segmented worms, mollusks have bilateral symmetry. However, unlike segmented worms, the body parts of mollusks are not repeated. Instead, their internal organs, such as the stomach and reproductive organs, are all located together in one area. A mollusk's internal organs include a pair of **kidneys**, organs that remove the wastes produced by an animal's cells.

Most water-dwelling mollusks have **gills**, organs that remove oxygen from water. The gills are attached to the mantle and have a rich supply of blood vessels. Within these thin-walled blood vessels, oxygen from the surrounding water diffuses into the blood, while carbon dioxide diffuses out. The gills of most mollusks are covered by tiny, hairlike structures called cilia. The beating movement of these cilia makes water flow over the gills.

Many mollusks have an organ called a **radula** (RAJ oo luh) (plural *radulae*), which is a flexible ribbon of tiny teeth. Acting like sandpaper, the tiny teeth scrape food from a surface such as a leaf. A radula may have as many as 250,000 teeth. Biologists use the arrangement of teeth in the radula to help classify mollusks.

 Checkpoint How is the body structure of a mollusk different from that of a segmented worm?

Evidence of Early Mollusks

INTEGRATING EARTH SCIENCE Mollusks were living in Earth's oceans about 540 million years ago. Much evidence for this comes from fossil shells in limestone rocks. Some kinds of limestone are partially made from the shells of ancient, ocean-dwelling mollusks. After the mollusks died, their shells were broken into tiny pieces by waves and water currents. These shell pieces, along with the hard remains of other organisms, piled up on the ocean floor. These hard materials then underwent a chemical change in which they became cemented together to form limestone. During this process, some shells—or parts of shells—remained unbroken and eventually became fossils.

Snails and Their Relatives

Biologists classify mollusks into groups based on physical characteristics such as the presence of a shell, the type of shell, the type of foot, the arrangement of teeth in the radula, and the complexity of the nervous system. **The three major groups of mollusks are gastropods, bivalves, and cephalopods.**

The most numerous mollusks are the gastropods. **Gastropods**, which include snails and slugs, are mollusks that have a single shell or no shell at all. Most snails have a single, coiled shell, while many slugs have no shell. Gastropods usually creep along on a broad foot. Gastropods get their name, which means "stomach foot," from the fact that most of them have their foot on the same side of their body as their stomach. To learn more about the body of a gastropod, look at *Exploring a Snail.*

You can find gastropods nearly everywhere on Earth. They live in oceans, on rocky shores, in fresh water, and on dry land, too. Some snails even live in treetops.

Some gastropods are herbivores, while others are scavengers that feed on decaying material. Still others are carnivores. For example, the oyster drill is a snail that makes a hole in an oyster's shell by releasing acid and then boring a hole with its radula. The oyster drill then scrapes away the oyster's soft body.

Many snails have a tight-fitting plate or trapdoor on their foot that fits securely into the opening of their shell. When this kind of snail is threatened by a predator, it withdraws into its shell and tightly closes its trapdoor. Snails also pull back into their shells when conditions are dry and then come out when conditions are moist again. When they are sealed up in this way, gastropods can survive incredibly long times. In one museum the shells of two land snails, presumed to be dead, were glued to a piece of cardboard. Four years later, when someone put the cardboard in water, one of the snails crawled away!

☑ *Checkpoint* *How did gastropods get their name?*

Figure 2 The two shells of a bivalve are held together by hinges and strong muscles. Giant clams like this one are among the largest bivalves in the world.

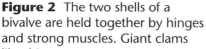
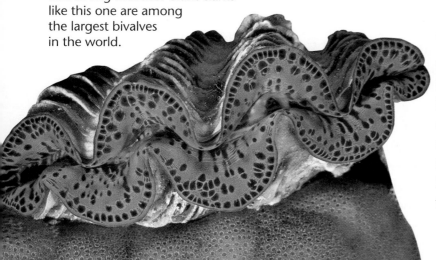

Two-Shelled Mollusks

Clams, oysters, scallops, and mussels are **bivalves**, mollusks that have two shells held together by hinges and strong muscles. Unlike other mollusks, bivalves do not have radulae. Instead, most are filter feeders; they strain their food from water. Bivalves use their gills to capture food as they breathe. Food particles stick to mucus

EXPLORING *a Snail*

Like other gastropods, a snail has a head with sense organs, and it has a wide, muscular foot. The snails shown here live in a pond.

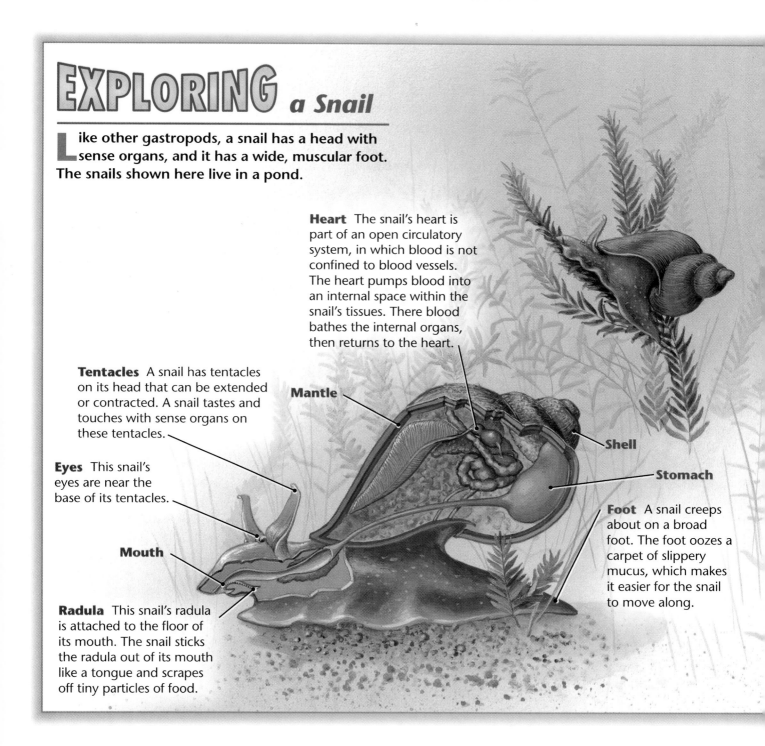

Heart The snail's heart is part of an open circulatory system, in which blood is not confined to blood vessels. The heart pumps blood into an internal space within the snail's tissues. There blood bathes the internal organs, then returns to the heart.

Tentacles A snail has tentacles on its head that can be extended or contracted. A snail tastes and touches with sense organs on these tentacles.

Eyes This snail's eyes are near the base of its tentacles.

Mouth

Radula This snail's radula is attached to the floor of its mouth. The snail sticks the radula out of its mouth like a tongue and scrapes off tiny particles of food.

Mantle

Shell

Stomach

Foot A snail creeps about on a broad foot. The foot oozes a carpet of slippery mucus, which makes it easier for the snail to move along.

that covers the gills. The cilia on the gills then move the food particles into the bivalve's mouth.

Bivalves are found in all kinds of watery environments. As adults, most bivalves stay in one place or move slowly. After their larval stage, for example, oysters and mussels attach themselves to an underwater surface. Clams, in contrast, are active; they use a thin foot to burrow down into the sand or mud. Scallops can also move from place to place. In fact, when startled, scallops clap their shells together and leap rapidly in the water over the sand.

Sometimes sand or grit becomes lodged between a bivalve's mantle and its shell, irritating the soft mantle. Just as you might put smooth tape around rough bicycle handlebars to protect your hands, the bivalve's mantle produces a smooth, pearly coat to cover the irritating object. Eventually a pearl forms around the grit. Some oysters make pearls so beautiful that they are used in jewelry.

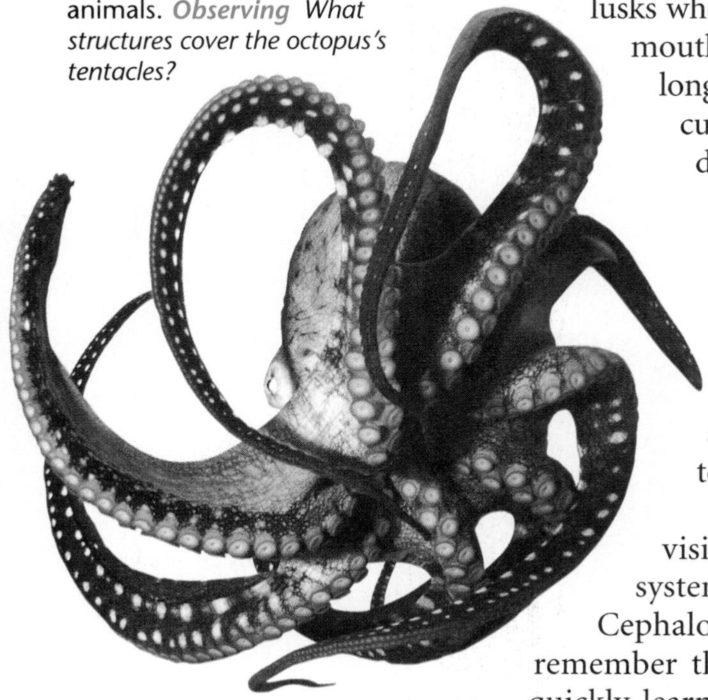

Mollusks with Tentacles

Octopuses, cuttlefish, nautiluses, and squids are **cephalopods**, mollusks whose feet are adapted to form tentacles around their mouths. Some octopuses have tentacles almost 5 meters long! While nautiluses have an external shell, squids and cuttlefish have a small shell within the body. Octopuses do not have shells.

Cephalopods capture food with their flexible, muscular tentacles. Sensitive suckers on the tentacles receive sensations of taste as well as touch. A cephalopod doesn't have to touch something to taste it; the suckers respond to chemicals in the water. For example, when an octopus feels beneath a rock, its tentacle may find a crab by taste before it touches it.

Cephalopods have large eyes and excellent vision. They also have the most complex nervous system, including a large brain, of any invertebrate. Cephalopods are highly intelligent animals that can remember things they have learned. In captivity, octopuses quickly learn when to expect deliveries of food and how to escape from their tanks.

INTEGRATING PHYSICS All cephalopods live in the ocean, where they swim by jet propulsion. They squeeze a current of water out of the mantle cavity through a tube, and like rockets, shoot off in the opposite direction. By turning the tube around, they can steer in any direction.

Figure 3 Octopuses live in coral reefs where they hide in holes when they are not hunting crabs and other small animals. *Observing What structures cover the octopus's tentacles?*

Section 1 Review

1. What characteristics do most mollusks have in common?
2. List the three main groups of mollusks. Describe the main characteristics of each group.
3. Explain how bivalves obtain food.
4. **Thinking Critically** **Predicting** Would gills function well if they had few blood vessels? Explain.

Science at Home

Visit a local supermarket with a family member and identify any mollusks that are being sold as food. Be sure to look in places other than the fish counter, such as the canned-foods section. Discuss the parts of the mollusks that are used for food and the parts that are not edible.

A Snail's Pace

I n this lab, you will use the skill of measuring to investigate how fast a snail moves in different water temperatures.

Problem

How do changes in environmental temperature affect the activity level of a snail?

Materials

freshwater snail	thermometer	ruler
plastic petri dish	graph paper	timer

spring water at three temperatures:
cool (9–13°C); medium (18–22°C);
warm (27–31°C)

Procedure

1. Create a data table for recording the water temperatures and the distance the snail travels at each temperature.

2. On one sheet of graph paper labeled *Snail,* trace a circle using the base of an empty petri dish. Divide and label the circle as shown in the illustration. On a second sheet of graph paper labeled *Data,* draw three more circles like the one in the illustration.

3. Place the petri dish over the circle on the Snail page, fill it with cool water, and record the water temperature. Then place the snail in the water just above the "S" in the circle. Be sure to handle the snail gently.

4. For five minutes, observe the snail. Record its movements by drawing a line that shows its path in the first circle on the Data page.

5. Find the distance the snail moved by measuring the line you drew. You may need to measure all the parts of the line and add them together. Record the distance in your data table.

6. Repeat Steps 3 through 5, first with medium-temperature water and then with warm water. Record the snail's paths in the second circle and third circle on the Data page.

7. Return the snail to your teacher when you are done. Wash your hands thoroughly.

8. For each temperature, compute the class average for distance traveled.

Analyze and Conclude

1. Make a bar graph showing the class average for each temperature. How does a snail's activity level change as temperature increases?

2. Do you think the pattern you found would continue at higher temperatures? Explain.

3. **Think About It** What factors in this lab were difficult to measure? How could you change the procedure to obtain more accurate measurements? Explain.

Design an Experiment

Design an experiment to measure the rate at which a snail moves in an aquarium with gravel on the bottom. Obtain your teacher's permission before trying your experiment.

SECTION
② Arthropods

DISCOVER · ACTIVITY

Will It Bend and Move?

1. Have a partner roll a piece of cardboard around your arm to form a tube that covers your elbow. Your partner should put three pieces of tape around the tube to hold it closed— one at each end and one in the middle.

2. With the tube in place, try to write your name on a piece of paper. Then try to scratch your head.

3. Keep the tube on your arm for 10 minutes. Observe how the tube affects your ability to do things.

Think It Over
Inferring Insects and many other animals have rigid skeletons on the outside of their bodies. Why do their skeletons need joints?

GUIDE FOR READING

◆ What are the major characteristics of arthropods?

◆ What are the main groups of arthropods?

Reading Tip Before you read, rewrite the headings in this section as questions. Answer the questions as you read.

On a moonless night at the edge of a wooded area, a moth flits from flower to flower, drinking nectar. Nearby, a hungry spider waits in its web that stretches, nearly invisible, between bushes. Suddenly, the moth gets caught by the spider web. The sticky threads of the web trap one of the moth's wings. As the trapped moth struggles to free itself, the spider rushes toward it. At the last second, the moth gives a strong flap, breaks free, and flutters away—safe! Next time, the moth may not be so lucky.

The hungry spider and lucky moth are both arthropods. Insects and spiders are probably the arthropods you are most familiar with, but the phylum also includes animals such as crabs, lobsters, centipedes, and scorpions. Scientists have identified about 875,000 different species of arthropods, and there are probably many more that have not yet been discovered. Earth has more species of arthropods than of all other animals combined.

◀ Spider awaiting prey

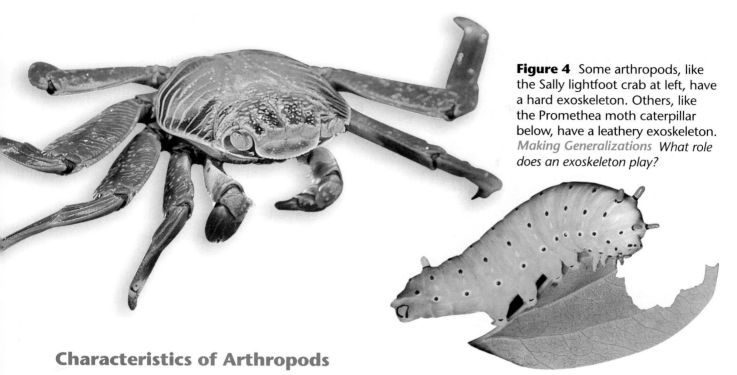

Figure 4 Some arthropods, like the Sally lightfoot crab at left, have a hard exoskeleton. Others, like the Promethea moth caterpillar below, have a leathery exoskeleton. *Making Generalizations What role does an exoskeleton play?*

Characteristics of Arthropods

Members of the **arthropod** phylum (phylum Arthropoda) share certain important characteristics. **An arthropod is an invertebrate that has an external skeleton, a segmented body, and jointed attachments called appendages.** Wings, mouthparts, and legs are all appendages. Jointed legs are such a distinctive characteristic that the arthropod phylum is named for it. *Arthros* means "joint" in Greek, and *podos* means "foot" or "leg."

Arthropods have additional characteristics in common, too. Arthropods have open circulatory systems—the blood leaves the blood vessels and bathes the internal organs. Most arthropods reproduce sexually. Unlike an earthworm, which has both male and female organs in its body, most arthropods are either male or female. Most arthropods have internal fertilization—sperm and egg unite inside the body of the female. This contrasts to external fertilization, which takes place outside an animal's body.

A Skeleton on the Outside If you were an arthropod, you would be completely covered by a waterproof shell. This waxy **exoskeleton,** or outer skeleton, protects the animal and helps prevent evaporation of water. Water animals are surrounded by water, but land animals need a way to keep from drying out. Arthropods were the first animals to move out of water and onto land, and their exoskeletons probably enabled them to do this.

INTEGRATING CHEMISTRY Arthropod exoskeletons are made of a material called **chitin** (KY tin). Chitin is made of long molecules that are built from many smaller building blocks, like links in a chain. Long-chain molecules like chitin are called polymers. Cotton fibers and rubber are polymers, too. For any

Figure 5 This rainforest cicada has just molted. You can see its old exoskeleton still hanging on the leaf just below it. *Applying Concepts* *Why must arthropods molt?*

Figure 6 Arthropod groups differ in the numbers of body sections, legs, and antennae, and in where they are found. *Interpreting Charts* *Which group of arthropods has no antennae?*

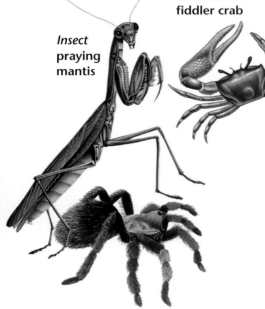

Crustacean **fiddler crab**

Insect **praying mantis**

Arachnid **tarantula**

polymer, the kinds, numbers, and the arrangement of its small building blocks determine its characteristics. Chitin's building blocks make it tough and flexible.

As an arthropod grows larger, its exoskeleton cannot expand. The growing arthropod is trapped within its exoskeleton, like a knight in armor that is too small for him. Arthropods solve this problem by occasionally shedding their exoskeletons and growing new ones that are larger. The process of shedding an outgrown exoskeleton is called **molting**. After an arthropod has molted, its new skeleton is soft for a time. During that time, the arthropod has less protection from danger than it does after its new skeleton has hardened.

Segmented Bodies Arthropods' bodies are segmented, something like an earthworm's. The segmented body plan is easiest to see in centipedes and millipedes, which have bodies made up of many identical-looking segments. You can also see segments on the tails of shrimp and lobsters.

In some groups of arthropods, several body segments become joined into distinct sections, with each section specialized to perform specific functions. Figure 6 shows the number of body sections and other physical characteristics that are typical of the three largest groups of arthropods.

Appendages Just as your fingers are appendages attached to your palms, many arthropods have jointed appendages attached to their bodies. The joints in the appendages give the animal flexibility and enable it to move. If you did the Discover activity, you saw how important joints are for allowing movement.

Arthropod appendages tend to be highly specialized tools. For example, the appendages attached to the head of a crayfish include mouthparts that it uses for crushing food. A crayfish also has two pairs of antennae. An

Comparisons of the Largest Arthropod Groups

Characteristic	Crustaceans	Arachnids	Insects
Number of body sections	2 or 3	2	3
Number of legs	5 or more pairs	4 pairs	3 pairs
Number of antennae	2 pairs	none	1 pair
Where found?	in water or damp places	mostly on land	mostly on land

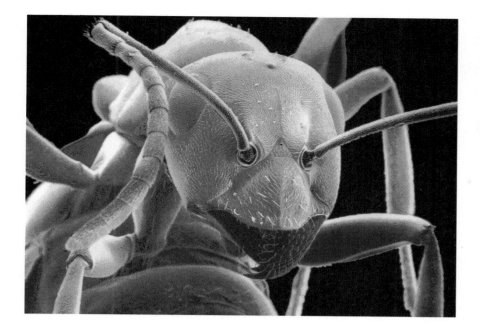

Figure 7 This wood ant's appendages include its antennae, legs, and mouthparts. It uses its mouthparts first to saw its food into small pieces and then to chew it.

antenna (plural *antennae*) is an appendage on the head that contains sense organs. A crayfish's antennae have organs for smelling, tasting, touching, and keeping balance. Legs are also appendages. Most of the crayfish's legs are adapted for walking, but the crayfish uses its first pair of legs, which have claws, for catching prey and defending against predators. The wings that most insects have are also appendages.

☑ *Checkpoint* *How do exoskeletons enable many arthropods to live on land?*

Origin of Arthropods

Since segmented worms and arthropods both have segmented bodies with appendages attached to some segments, many biologists have inferred that these two groups of animals have a common ancestor. However, DNA evidence indicates that arthropods and segmented worms may not be as closely related as previously thought.

Arthropods have been on Earth for about 540 million years. Like most other animal groups, arthropods first arose in the oceans. Today, however, they live almost everywhere. Some kinds of arthropods, like crayfish and crabs, are adapted to live in fresh or salt water. Very few insects, in contrast, live in salt water, but they live just about everywhere else.

Crustaceans

The major groups of arthropods are crustaceans, arachnids, centipedes, millipedes, and insects. If you've ever eaten shrimp cocktail or crab cakes, you've dined on crustaceans. A **crustacean** is an arthropod that has two or three body sections and usually

Pill bugs are crustaceans that roll up in a ball when they're disturbed. In this activity, you will find out whether they prefer a moist or dry environment.

1. Line a shoe box with aluminum foil. Tape down two paper towels side by side in the box. Tape a strip of masking tape between the two towels. Carefully moisten one of the paper towels. Keep the other towel dry.

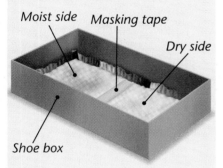

Moist side   Masking tape

Dry side

Shoe box

2. Put ten pill bugs on the masking tape. Then put a lid on the box.

3. After 5 minutes, lift the lid and quickly count the pill bugs on the dry towel, the moist towel, and the masking tape. Record your results in a data table.

4. Repeat Steps 2 and 3 two more times. Then average the results of the three trials. Wash your hands after handling the pill bugs.

Interpreting Data Do pill bugs prefer a moist or dry environment?

has three pairs of appendages for chewing. In addition, crustaceans always have five or more pairs of legs; each body segment has a pair of legs or modified legs attached to it. Crustaceans are the only arthropods that have two pairs of antennae. *Exploring a Crayfish* shows a typical crustacean.

Life Cycle Most crustaceans, such as crabs, barnacles, and shrimp, begin their lives as microscopic, swimming larvae. The bodies of these larvae do not resemble those of adults. Crustacean larvae develop into adults by **metamorphosis** (met uh MAWR fuh sis), a process in which an animal's body undergoes dramatic changes in form during its life cycle.

Environments Nearly every kind of watery environment is home to crustaceans, which usually obtain their oxygen through gills. Crustaceans thrive in freshwater lakes and rivers, and even in puddles that last a long time. You can find crustaceans in the deepest parts of oceans, floating in ocean currents, and crawling along coastlines. A few crustaceans live in damp areas on land, too. Some huge crabs even live in the tops of palm trees!

Feeding Crustaceans obtain food in many ways. Many eat dead plants and animals. Others are predators, eating animals they have killed. The pistol shrimp is a predator with an appendage that moves with such force that it stuns its prey. Krill, which are shrimplike crustaceans found in huge swarms in cold ocean waters, are herbivores that eat plantlike microorganisms. In turn, krill are eaten by predators such as fishes, penguins, seals, sea birds, and even by great blue whales, the world's largest animals.

✓ *Checkpoint* *An animal has an exoskeleton, two body sections, and eight legs. Is it a crustacean? Why or why not?*

Spiders and Their Relatives

Spiders, mites, and ticks are the arachnids that people most often encounter. To qualify as an **arachnid** (uh RAK nid), an arthropod must have only two body sections. The first section is a combined head and chest. The hind section, called the **abdomen**, contains the arachnid's reproductive organs and part of its digestive tract. Arachnids have eight legs, but no antennae. They breathe with organs called book lungs or with a network of tiny tubes that lead to openings on the exoskeleton.

Spiders Spiders are the most familiar, most feared, and most fascinating kind of arachnid. All spiders are predators, and most of them eat insects. Some spiders, such as tarantulas and wolf spiders, run down their prey, while others, such as golden garden spiders, spin webs and wait for their prey to become entangled.

EXPLORING *a Crayfish*

Crayfish are crustaceans that live in ponds, streams, or rivers, where they hide beneath rocks and burrow in the mud. Some build a tall mud "chimney" around their burrow entrance. Crayfish will eat nearly any animal or plant, dead or alive, including other crayfish.

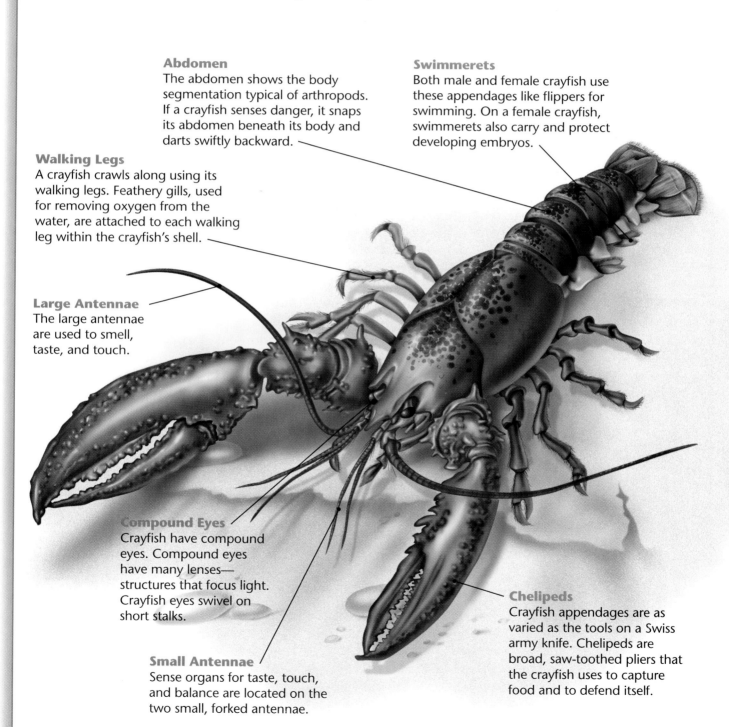

Abdomen
The abdomen shows the body segmentation typical of arthropods. If a crayfish senses danger, it snaps its abdomen beneath its body and darts swiftly backward.

Swimmerets
Both male and female crayfish use these appendages like flippers for swimming. On a female crayfish, swimmerets also carry and protect developing embryos.

Walking Legs
A crayfish crawls along using its walking legs. Feathery gills, used for removing oxygen from the water, are attached to each walking leg within the crayfish's shell.

Large Antennae
The large antennae are used to smell, taste, and touch.

Compound Eyes
Crayfish have compound eyes. Compound eyes have many lenses—structures that focus light. Crayfish eyes swivel on short stalks.

Small Antennae
Sense organs for taste, touch, and balance are located on the two small, forked antennae.

Chelipeds
Crayfish appendages are as varied as the tools on a Swiss army knife. Chelipeds are broad, saw-toothed pliers that the crayfish uses to capture food and to defend itself.

Spiders have hollow fangs, which are organs that inject venom into prey. Spider venom turns the tissues of the prey into mush. Later the spider uses its fangs like drinking straws, sucking in the mush. In spite of what some people might think, spiders rarely bite people. When they do, most spider bites are painful but not life-threatening. However, the bites of the brown recluse or the black widow may require hospital care.

Mites If chiggers have ever given you an itchy rash, you've had an unpleasant encounter with tiny arachnids called mites. Chiggers and many other mites are parasites. Ear mites, for example, give dogs and cats itchy ears. Mites are everywhere. Even the cleanest houses have microscopic dust mites. If you are allergic to dust, you may actually be allergic to the exoskeletons of dust mites. Mites also live in fresh water and in the ocean.

Ticks Ticks are parasites that live on the outside of a host animal's body. Nearly every kind of land animal has a species of tick that sucks its blood. Some ticks that attack humans can carry diseases. Lyme disease, for example, is spread by the bite of an infected deer tick.

Scorpions Scorpions, which live mainly in hot climates, are also arachnids. Usually active at night, scorpions hide in cool places during the day—under rocks and logs, or in holes in the ground, for example.

At the end of its abdomen, a scorpion has a spinelike stinger. The scorpion uses the stinger to inject venom into its prey, which is usually a spider or insect. Sometimes scorpions sting people. These stings, while painful, usually do not cause serious harm.

☑ *Checkpoint* *How do spiders obtain and digest their food?*

Figure 8 Arachnids are arthropods with two body sections, eight legs, and no antennae. **A.** A tick is a parasite that attaches itself to its prey to feed upon its blood. **B.** A scorpion is a carnivore that injects venom from a stinger at the end of its abdomen. **C.** The Honduran tarantula, a spider, uses its fangs to inject venom into a racer snake.

Centipedes and Millipedes

Centipedes and millipedes have highly segmented bodies, as you can see in Figure 9. Centipedes have one pair of legs attached to each segment, and some centipedes have over 100 segments. In fact, the word *centipede* means "hundred feet." Centipedes are swift predators with sharp jaws. They inject venom into the smaller animals that they catch for food.

Millipedes, which may have more than 80 segments, have two pairs of legs on each segment—more legs than any other arthropod. Though *millipede* means "thousand feet," they don't have quite that many legs. Most millipedes are herbivores that graze on partly decayed leaves. When they are disturbed, millipedes can curl up into an armored ball and squirt an awful-smelling liquid at a potential predator.

Figure 9 Centipedes and millipedes are arthropods with many body segments. Centipedes, left, are carnivores, while millipedes, right, are herbivores. *Comparing and Contrasting How can you tell the difference between these two organisms?*

Section 2 Review

1. Identify four characteristics that all arthropods share.
2. List the major groups of arthropods.
3. What characteristic distinguishes crustaceans from all other arthropods?
4. What are the main characteristics of arachnids?
5. **Thinking Critically Applying Concepts** Some seafood restaurants serve a dish called soft-shelled crab. What do you think happened to the crab just before it was caught? Why is that process important?

Check Your Progress

CHAPTER PROJECT 2

Construct a data table in your notebook. Each day, observe both groups of mealworms. Record how many mealworms in each group are still wormlike larvae, how many have formed motionless pupae, and how many, if any, have become adult insects. (*Hint:* You will learn about the stages of insect metamorphosis in Section 3. You may find it helpful to refer to *Exploring Insect Metamorphosis* on page 65 as you fill in your data table.)

3 Insects

What Kinds of Appendages Do Insects Have?

1. Your teacher will give you a collection of insects. Examine the insects carefully.

2. Note the physical characteristics of each insect's body covering.

3. Count the legs, wings, body sections, and antennae on each insect.

4. Carefully observe the appendages—antennae, mouthparts, wings, and legs. Contrast the appendages on different insects. Then return the insects to your teacher and wash your hands.

Think It Over

Observing Compare the legs and wings of two different species of insect. What kind of movements is each insect adapted to perform?

GUIDE FOR READING

◆ **What are the characteristics of insects?**

◆ **What is the overall impact of insects on humans?**

Reading Tip As you read, make an outline of this section using the headings as the main topics.

Monarch butterflies, with their beautiful orange and black wings, may seem delicate, but they are champion travelers. Every autumn, about 100 million of these butterflies fly south from southeastern Canada and the eastern United States, heading for the mountains of central Mexico. Some monarch butterflies fly thousands of kilometers before they reach their destination.

The monarch butterflies who make this long journey have never been to Mexico before. But somehow they find their way to the same trees where their ancestors, now dead, spent the previous winter. No one is certain how they are able to do this.

In the spring, the butterflies fly northward. After flying a few hundred miles, they stop, mate, lay eggs, and die. But their children—and later, their grandchildren and great-grandchildren—continue the northward journey. Eventually, monarch butterflies reach the area their ancestors left the previous fall.

Wintering monarch butterflies ▼

The Insect Body

The monarch butterfly is an **insect**, as is a dragonfly, cockroach, or bee. You can identify insects, like other arthropods, by counting their body sections and legs. **Insects are arthropods with three body sections, six legs, one pair of antennae, and usually one or two pairs of wings.** The three body regions are the head, thorax, and abdomen. An insect's **thorax,** or mid-section, is the section to which wings and legs are attached. Sense organs, such as the eyes and antennae, are located on an insect's head. The abdomen contains many of the insect's internal organs. You can see all three body sections on the grasshopper in Figure 11.

Like most crustaceans, insects usually have two large compound eyes, which contain many lenses. Compound eyes are especially keen at seeing movement. Most insects also have small simple eyes, which can distinguish between light and darkness.

Insects obtain oxygen through a system of tubes. These tubes lead to openings on the insect's exoskeleton. Air, which contains oxygen, enters the insect's body through these tubes and travels directly to the insect's body cells.

✔ *Checkpoint* *How are an insect's compound eyes different from its simple eyes?*

From Egg to Adult

Insects begin life as tiny, hard-shelled, fertilized eggs. After they hatch, insects begin a process of metamorphosis that eventually produces an adult insect. Each insect species undergoes one of two different types of metamorphosis.

Figure 10 Most insects, like this black fly, have compound eyes with many lenses. Because compound eyes are very effective at seeing movement, insects can quickly escape from potential predators.

Figure 11 A grasshopper's body, like that of every insect, consists of three sections. *Interpreting Diagrams* To which section are the grasshopper's legs attached?

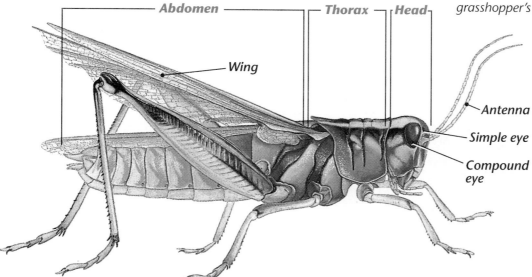

Abdomen — Thorax — Head

Wing

Antenna

Simple eye

Compound eye

The two types of insect metamorphosis are shown in *Exploring Insect Metamorphosis.* The first type, which is called **complete metamorphosis,** has four dramatically different stages: egg, larva, pupa, and adult. As you learned in Chapter 1, a larva is an immature form of an animal that looks significantly different from the adult. Insect larvae, such as the caterpillars of butterflies and moths, usually look something like worms. Larvae are specialized for eating and growing. After a time, the larva goes into the second stage of complete metamorphosis and becomes a **pupa** (plural *pupae*). During the pupal stage, the insect is enclosed in a protective covering and gradually changes from a larva to an adult. A butterfly in a chrysalis and a moth in a cocoon are examples of insect pupae. When it has completed its development, an adult insect emerges from the protective pupa. Beetles, butterflies, houseflies, and ants all undergo complete metamorphosis.

In contrast, the second type of metamorphosis, called **gradual metamorphosis,** has no distinctly different larval stage—an egg hatches into a stage called a **nymph,** which often resembles the adult insect. A nymph may molt several times before becoming an adult. Grasshoppers, termites, cockroaches, and dragonflies go through gradual metamorphosis.

☑ *Checkpoint* **List the stages of complete metamorphosis.**

How Insects Feed

The rule seems to be this: If it is living, or if it once was living, some kind of insect will eat it. Everyone knows that insects eat plants and parts of plants, such as leaves and nectar. But insects also eat products that are made from plants, such as paper. The next time you open a very old book, watch for book lice. These very small insects live in old books, chewing tiny crooked tunnels through the pages.

Insects feed on animals, too. Some, like fleas and mosquitoes, feed on the blood of living animals. Others, like dung beetles, feed on animal droppings. Still others, like burying beetles, feed on the decaying bodies of dead animals.

Insect mouthparts are adapted for a highly specific way of getting food. For example, a bee has a bristly tongue that laps nectar from flowers, and a mosquito has sharp mouthparts for jabbing and sucking blood.

Figure 12 This caterpillar feeds almost continuously. As a larva, it must store all the energy it will need for its pupal stage.

EXPLORING Insect Metamorphosis

Depending on the species, an insect develops into an adult through one of the two processes shown here. Fireflies undergo complete metamorphosis, while grasshoppers undergo gradual metamorphosis.

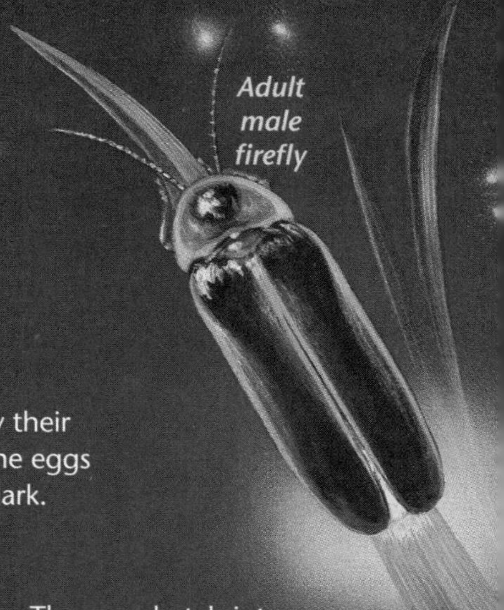

Adult male firefly

COMPLETE METAMORPHOSIS

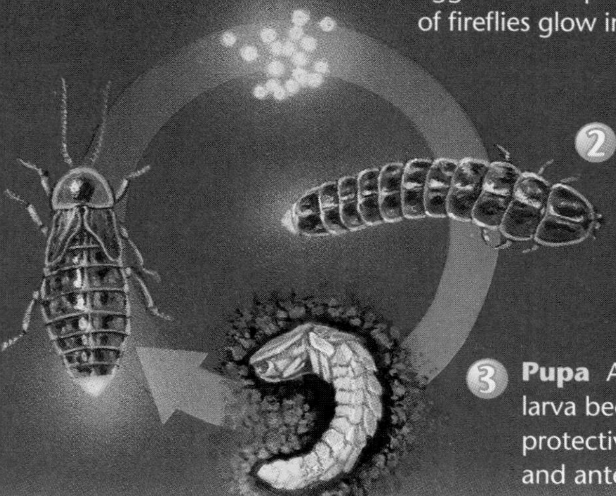

1 Egg Female fireflies lay their eggs in moist places. The eggs of fireflies glow in the dark.

2 Larva The eggs hatch into larvae that feed on snails and slugs. Firefly larvae are called glowworms because they give off light.

3 Pupa After a time, the firefly larva becomes a pupa. Inside the protective pupal case, wings, legs, and antennae form.

4 Adult When its development is complete, an adult firefly crawls out of its pupal case and unfurls its crumpled wings. After its exoskeleton hardens, the adult begins a life centered around feeding, flying into new areas, and mating. Adult fireflies flash their light to attract mates.

GRADUAL METAMORPHOSIS

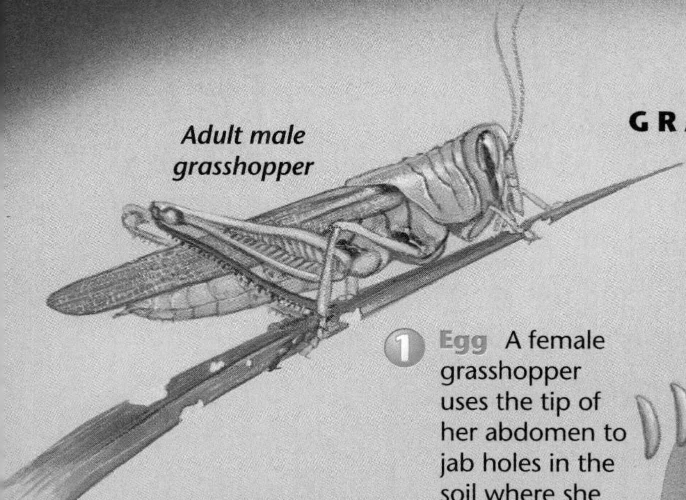

Adult male grasshopper

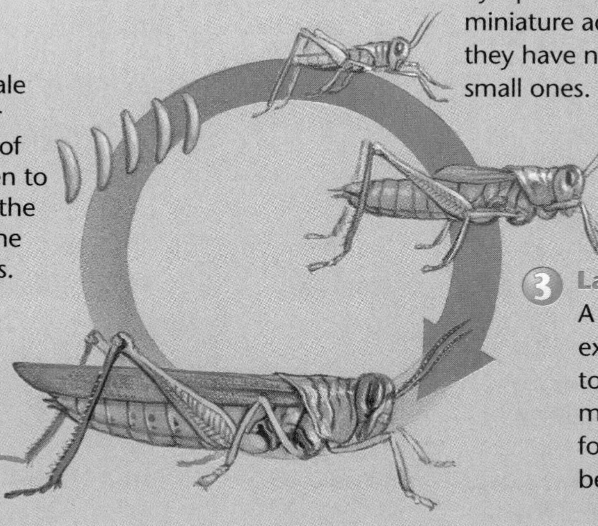

1 Egg A female grasshopper uses the tip of her abdomen to jab holes in the soil where she lays her eggs.

2 Nymph Eggs hatch into nymphs that look much like miniature adults, except that they have no wings, or only small ones.

3 Larger Nymph A nymph feeds until its exoskeleton becomes too tight, and then it molts. The nymph molts four or five times before becoming an adult.

4 Adult Most insects undergoing gradual metamorphosis emerge from the final molt equipped with full-sized wings. Once its wings have hardened, the adult flies off to mate and begin the cycle again.

Figure 13 The well-camouflaged thorn insect, left, and leaf insect, right, have very effective built-in defenses against predators. *Observing Why do you think the insect on the left is called a thorn insect?*

Social Studies
CONNECTION

In the fall of 1347, a ship sailed from a port on the Black Sea to the European island of Sicily. That ship carried insects that helped change the course of history. The insects were fleas, and their bite passed a deadly disease known as bubonic plague, or the Black Death, on to humans.

People who caught the plague usually died quickly. The Frenchman Jean de Venette wrote, "He who was well one day was dead the next." The Black Death rapidly spread all over Europe, killing about a third of the people. Because so many died, the plague caused serious economic problems and led to great social unrest.

In Your Journal

Imagine that the year is 1380. You lived through the plague epidemic and are now 45 years old. Write about how the plague epidemic has changed your village.

Defending Themselves

Insects have many defenses against predators, including a hard exoskeleton that helps protect them. Many insects can run quickly or fly away from danger, as you know if you've ever tried to swat a fly. Some insects, such as stinkbugs, smell or taste bad to predators. Other insects, such as bees and wasps, defend themselves with painful stings.

One of the most common defenses is **camouflage,** or protective coloration, in which the insect blends with its surroundings so perfectly that it is nearly invisible to a predator. Test yourself by trying to find the camouflaged insects in Figure 13. Walking sticks, many caterpillars, and grasshoppers are just a few insects that use camouflage as a defense.

Other insects are protected by their resemblance to different animals. The spots on the wings of certain moths, for example, resemble large eyes; predators who see these spots often avoid the moths, mistaking them for much larger animals.

✓ *Checkpoint* What are four ways in which insects protect themselves?

Insects and Humans

For every person alive today, scientists estimate that there are at least 200 million living insects. Many of those insects have an impact on people's lives. Some species of insects do major damage to crops. In addition, insects such as flies, fleas, and mosquitoes can carry microorganisms that cause diseases in humans. For example, when they bite humans, some mosquito species can transmit the microorganism that causes malaria.

The vast majority of insects, however, are harmless or beneficial to humans. Bees make honey, and the larvae of the silkworm moth spin the fibers used to make silk cloth. Some insects prey on harmful insects, helping to reduce those insect populations. And while some insects destroy food crops, many more insects, such as butterflies and flies, enable food crops and other plants to reproduce by carrying pollen from one plant to another. If insects were to disappear from Earth, you would never get a mosquito bite. But you wouldn't have much food to eat, either.

Figure 14 Bees and other pollinators are among the most beneficial of all insects. As a bee drinks nectar from a flower, pollen sticks to its body. When the insect carries that pollen to the next plant it eats from, it helps that plant to reproduce.

Controlling Insect Pests

INTEGRATING ENVIRONMENTAL SCIENCE People have tried to eliminate harmful insects by applying chemicals, called pesticides, to plants. However, pesticides also kill helpful insects, such as bees, and can harm other animals, including some birds. And after a time, insect populations become resistant to the pesticides—the pesticides no longer kill the insects.

Scientists are searching for other ways to deal with harmful insects. One method is the use of biological controls. Biological controls introduce natural predators or diseases into insect populations. For example, ladybug beetles can be added to fields where crops are grown. Ladybugs prey on aphids, which are insects that destroy peaches, potatoes, and other crop plants. Soil also can be treated with bacteria that are harmless to humans but cause diseases in the larvae of pest insects such as Japanese beetles. These biological controls kill only one or a few pest species. Because biological controls kill only specific pests, they are less damaging to the environment than insecticides.

Section 3 Review

1. List the characteristics that insects share.
2. Identify two ways in which insects benefit humans.
3. Compare and contrast complete and gradual metamorphosis.
4. **Thinking Critically** Inferring Honeybees sting predators that try to attack them. Hover flies, which do not sting, resemble honeybees. How might this resemblance be an advantage to the hover fly?

Check Your Progress
Continue observing the mealworms every day. Update the data table with your observations. As you observe the mealworms at different stages of development, make a sketch of a larva, a pupa, and an adult.

CHAPTER PROJECT 2

What's Living in the Soil?

The soil beneath a tree, in a garden, or under a rock is home to many organisms, including a variety of arthropods. Each of these patches of soil can be thought of as a miniature environment with its own group of living residents. In this lab, you will examine one specific soil environment.

Problem

What kinds of animals live in soil and leaf litter?

Skills Focus

observing, classifying, inferring

Materials

2-liter plastic bottle	large scissors
coarse steel wool	trowel
cheesecloth	large rubber band
gooseneck lamp	hand lens
large, wide-mouthed jar	small jar
fresh sample of soil and leaf litter	

Procedure

1. Select a location where your equipment can be set up and remain undisturbed for about 24 hours. At that location, place the small jar inside the center of the large jar as shown in the photograph.

2. Use scissors to cut a large plastic bottle in half. **CAUTION:** *Cut in a direction away from yourself and others.* Turn the top half of the bottle upside down to serve as a funnel.

3. Insert a small amount of coarse steel wool into the mouth of the funnel to keep the soil from falling out. Do not pack the steel wool too tightly. Leave spaces for small organisms to crawl through. Place the funnel into the large jar as shown in the photograph.

4. Using the trowel, fill the funnel with soil and surface leaf litter. When you finish handling the leaves and soil, wash your hands thoroughly.

5. Look closely to see whether the soil and litter are dry or wet. Record your observation.

6. Make a cover for your sample by placing a piece of cheesecloth over the top of the funnel. Hold the cheesecloth in place with a large rubber band. Immediately position a lamp about 15 cm above the funnel, and turn on the light. Allow this set-up to remain undisturbed for about 24 hours. **CAUTION:** *Hot light bulbs can cause burns. Do not touch the bulb.*

7. When you are ready to make your observations, turn off the lamp. Leave the funnel and jar in place while making your observations. Use a hand lens to examine each organism in the jar. **CAUTION:** *Do not touch any of the organisms.*

8. Use a data table like the one on the next page to sketch each type of organism and to record other observations. Be sure to include evidence that will help you classify the organisms. (*Hint:* Remember that some animals may be at different stages of metamorphosis.)

DATA TABLE				
Sketch of Organism	Number Found	Size	Important Characteristics	Probable Phylum

9. Examine the soil and leaf litter, and record whether this material is dry or wet.
10. When you are finished, follow your teacher's directions about returning the organisms to the soil.

Analyze and Conclude

1. Describe the conditions of the soil environment at the beginning and end of the lab. What caused the change?
2. What types of animals did you collect in the small jar? What characteristics did you use to identify each type of animal? Which types of animals were the most common?
3. Why do you think the animals moved down the funnel away from the soil?
4. **Apply** Using what you have learned about arthropods and other animals, make an inference about the role that each animal you collected plays in the environment.

More to Explore

What kinds of organisms might live in other soil types—for example, soil at the edge of a pond, dry sandy soil, or commercially prepared potting soil? Propose one or more ways to answer this question.

SECTION 4 The Sounds of Insects

DISCOVER ·······················ACTIVITY···

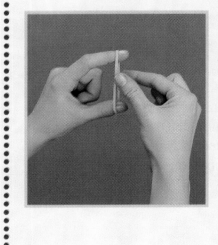

What Causes Sound?

1. Form a letter C with the index finger and thumb of one hand. Stretch a rubber band over the tips of your finger and thumb, as shown in the picture. Predict what will happen when you pluck the rubber band.

2. Pluck the rubber band so that it makes a sound. Observe the rubber band as it is making a sound. Note how the rubber band moves.

3. Repeat Step 2, but as soon as you pluck the rubber band, touch it so that it stops moving. Note what happens to the sound.

Think It Over
Inferring What is the relationship between sound and vibration?

GUIDE FOR READING

◆ How is sound produced?
◆ What function does sound serve for many insects?

Reading Tip As you read about the way in which sound is produced, refer to Figure 16.

Somewhere in your neighborhood, on this warm spring evening, a cricket is singing. With a flashlight in your hand, you quietly move toward the chirpy sound. When you're right on top of the sound, you turn on your light and see a black insect on the ground. Its wings are slightly raised, and are scraping against one another so fast that they look blurry. You have found a male cricket who is using sound to attract a mate. A female cricket may soon respond to his call.

How is Sound Produced?

The wings of the cricket vibrate—they move back and forth, faster than the eye can follow. When the cricket's wings stop moving, the chirping stops and all becomes quiet. Why is this so?

Figure 15 This male Borneo cricket can rub his wings together very quickly to make a chirping sound. He uses this chirping sound to call potential mates.

Figure 16 The vibration of a guitar string produces waves that consist of alternate areas in which air molecules are compressed and spread out. *Applying Concepts How does the sound of the guitar reach your ear?*

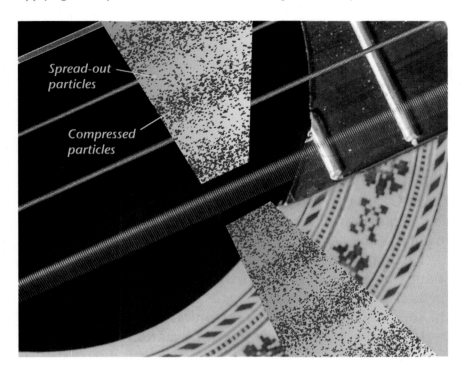

Spread-out particles

Compressed particles

All sound is produced by vibrations that create waves that move outward from the source. Figure 16 shows how the vibrations of a guitar string create sound. After you pull the string to the left and release it, the moving string bumps into air particles in its path. It shoves these particles together, compressing them, and pushes the compressed particles outward. This compressed area is followed by an area in which the air particles are spread out.

Since the guitar string keeps moving back and forth, over and over, it creates many alternating regions of compressed particles and spread-out particles. Together, the compressions and spread-out areas move outward in waves from the guitar string, as Figure 16 shows. The rapidly moving wings of a cricket produce sound in much the same way as a vibrating guitar string.

Sound waves must travel through a medium—a solid, a liquid, or a gas. The sound waves made by both the guitar strings and cricket wings travel through air, which is a gas. Sound can also travel through liquids, such as water, and through solids, such as wood. If you tap on your desk and lower your ear to the desk at the same time, you can hear sound vibrations traveling through solid material.

✔ *Checkpoint Through what medium does the sound of thunder travel?*

TRY THIS

Tune In

ACTIVITY

You can use a tuning fork to see how sound is caused by vibrations.

1. Hit the prongs of a tuning fork with a pencil and listen to the sound it makes. At the same time, look closely at the fork's prongs. What do you see?

2. Lightly touch the prongs of the fork. What do you feel?

Predicting Predict what will happen when you strike the prongs of the tuning fork and then plunge the prong tips into a glass of water. Give a reason to support your prediction. Then test your prediction.

Communicating by Sound

Insects make sound in a variety of ways. Many insects make sounds in the same way that guitars and other stringed instruments do. They rub a roughened part of their body against a sharp-edged part. The rough part is something like a guitar pick, and the sharp part is like the instrument's strings. Crickets chirp and katydids make their sandpapery songs with a rough patch on each wing.

Different species of insects use different parts of their bodies to produce sound. Large black beetles rub their hind wings against rough patches on their abdomen, making a faint screeching sound. Deathwatch beetles tap on the ground with their heads. Cicadas have thin sheets of tissue called tymbals on their abdomens. Tymbals produce sound by vibrating like the covering of a drum.

Hissing cockroaches are among the few insects that make sounds by forcing air out of their bodies. This is the same method that is used by humans and other vertebrates to produce the sounds with which they communicate.

Many insects use sound to attract mates. Usually it is the male that does the singing; that is the case with insects such as crickets, grasshoppers, and katydids. However, in some species the female makes the sound. For example, female mosquitoes attract males by using their wings to make distinctive, high-pitched vibrations.

Section 4 Review

1. Explain how beating a drum produces a sound.
2. What is communicated by the song of a grasshopper or cicada?
3. Describe two different ways in which insects produce sounds.
4. **Thinking Critically Applying Concepts** You are traveling in a spaceship in outer space, where there is no air. Another spaceship speeds past you. Does the spaceship make a sound? Why or why not?

Science at Home

You can use a spring toy like the one above to show your family how sound waves travel. Have a family member hold one end of the spring. Hold the other end in your hand. Gently stretch the spring so that it is fully extended and parallel to the floor. Start a wave moving by pushing on one end. Point out how the wave of compressed coils travels along the spring. Explain to your family how the wave is similar to a sound wave traveling through the air.

DISCOVER  ACTIVITY

How Do Sea Stars Hold On?

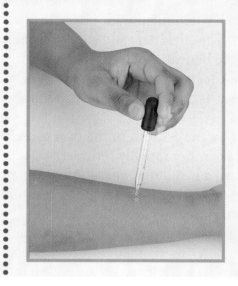

1. Sea stars use hundreds of tiny structures on their arms to cling to rocks and move across underwater surfaces. Use a plastic dropper to see how these structures work. Fill the dropper with water, and then squeeze out most of the water.

2. Squeeze one last drop of water onto the inside of your arm. Then, while squeezing the bulb, touch the tip of the dropper into the water drop. With the dropper tip against your skin, release the bulb.

3. Hold the dropper by the tube and lift it slowly, paying attention to what happens to your skin.

Think It Over
Predicting Besides moving and clinging to surfaces, what might sea stars use their suction structures for?

They look like stars, pincushions, coins, and cucumbers— are these creatures really animals? Sea stars, brittle stars, and basket stars have star-shaped bodies. Sea urchins look like living pincushions, while sand dollars are flat, round discs. Sea cucumbers, with green algae growing within their tissues, look like dill pickles—until they slowly start to crawl along the sand. All of these odd little animals belong to the same phylum.

The "Spiny Skinned" Animals

Biologists classify sea stars, sea urchins, sand dollars, and sea cucumbers as echinoderms (phylum Echinodermata). An **echinoderm** (ee KY noh durm) is a radially symmetrical invertebrate that lives on the ocean floor. *Echinoderm* means "spiny skinned." This name is appropriate because the skin of most of these animals is supported by a spiny internal skeleton, or **endoskeleton**, made of plates that contain calcium.

Adult echinoderms have a unique kind of radial symmetry in which body parts, usually in multiples of five, are arranged like spokes on a wheel. If you count the legs on a sea star or the body sections of a sea urchin, you will almost always get five or a multiple of five.

GUIDE FOR READING

◆ What characteristics are typical of echinoderms?

Reading Tip Before you read, look at *Exploring a Sea Star* on page 75 to note some echinoderm characteristics.

▼ Magnificent sea urchin

In addition to five-part radial symmetry and an endoskeleton, echinoderms also have an internal fluid system called a water vascular system. The **water vascular system** consists of fluid-filled tubes within the echinoderm's body. Portions of the tubes can contract, squeezing water into structures called tube feet, which are external parts of the water vascular system. The ends of tube feet are sticky and, when filled with water, they act like small, sticky suction cups. The stickiness and suction enable the tube feet to grip the surface beneath the echinoderm. Most echinoderms also use their tube feet to move along slowly and to capture food. If you turn a sea star upside down, you will see rows of moving tube feet.

Echinoderms crawl about on the bottom of the ocean, seeking food, shelter, and mates. Like other radially symmetrical animals, echinoderms do not have a head end where sense organs and nerve tissue are found. Instead, they are adapted to respond to food, mates, or predators coming from any direction.

Most echinoderms are either male or female. Eggs are usually fertilized right in the seawater, after the female releases her eggs and the male releases his sperm. The fertilized eggs develop into tiny, swimming larvae that eventually undergo metamorphosis and become adult echinoderms.

☑ *Checkpoint* *What is the function of an echinoderm's tube feet?*

Figure 17 This red sea star is in the process of regenerating two of its arms, possibly lost in a struggle with a predator.

Sea Stars

Sea stars are predators that eat mollusks, crabs, and even other echinoderms. A sea star uses its arms and tube feet, shown in *Exploring a Sea Star,* to capture prey. The sea star grasps a clam with all five arms. Then it pulls on the tightly closed shells with its tube feet. When the shells open, the sea star forces its stomach out through its mouth and into the opening between the clam's shells. Digestive chemicals break down the clam's tissues, and the sea star sucks in the partially digested body of its prey. Sea star behavior is quite impressive for an animal that doesn't have a brain.

If a sea star loses an arm, it can grow a replacement. The process by which an animal grows a new part to replace a lost one is called regeneration. Figure 17 shows a sea star with two partially regenerated arms. A few species of sea stars can even grow a whole animal from a single arm. Some sea stars reproduce by splitting into many parts. The arms pull the sea star apart in five different directions and five new sea stars regenerate!

EXPLORING *a Sea Star*

Sea stars, which are also called starfishes, usually have five arms. However, some have as many as fifty arms.

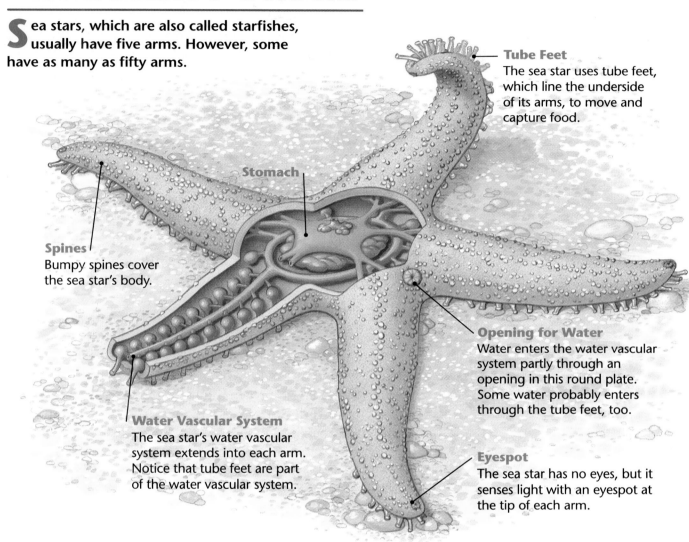

Tube Feet
The sea star uses tube feet, which line the underside of its arms, to move and capture food.

Stomach

Spines
Bumpy spines cover the sea star's body.

Water Vascular System
The sea star's water vascular system extends into each arm. Notice that tube feet are part of the water vascular system.

Opening for Water
Water enters the water vascular system partly through an opening in this round plate. Some water probably enters through the tube feet, too.

Eyespot
The sea star has no eyes, but it senses light with an eyespot at the tip of each arm.

Other Echinoderms

Brittle stars are close relatives of sea stars. Like sea stars, brittle stars have five arms, but their arms are long and slender, with flexible joints. Like sea stars, brittle stars can regenerate lost arms. Brittle stars' tube feet, which have no suction cups, are used for catching food but not for moving. Instead, brittle stars propel themselves along the ocean bottom by moving their giant arms against the ground. They are among the most mobile of all the echinoderms.

Unlike sea stars and brittle stars, sand dollars and sea urchins have no arms. Sand dollars look like large coins. Their flat bodies are covered with very short spines that help them burrow into sand.

Movable spines cover and protect the bodies of sea urchins, making them look like pincushions or round brushes. The spines cover a central shell that is made of plates joined together. Sea urchins move by using bands of tube feet that extend out between the spines. With the five strong teeth that can be projected from their mouths, sea urchins can scrape algae, chew seaweed, and crush pieces of coral and the shells of small mollusks. Some sea urchins use their teeth and spines to dig themselves into rock crevices to hide from predators.

As you might expect from their name, sea cucumbers look a little bit like leathery-skinned cucumbers—but you won't see one in a tossed salad. These strange animals, which live on the sandy or rocky ocean floor, can be red, brown, blue, or green. Their bodies are soft, flexible, and muscular. Sea cucumbers have rows of tube feet on their underside, enabling them to crawl slowly along the ocean bottom. At one end of a sea cucumber is a mouth surrounded by tentacles. The sea cucumber, which is a filter feeder, can lengthen its tentacles to sweep food toward its mouth, and then pull the tentacles back into its tough skin.

Figure 18 The blue-and-red sea cucumber (A), spiny brittle stars (B), and sand dollar (C) are all echinoderms. *Observing What type of symmetry do these organisms exhibit?*

Section 5 Review

1. Identify the main characteristics of echinoderms.
2. Define *regeneration* and explain how it applies to sea stars.
3. Compare and contrast sea urchins and sea stars.
4. **Thinking Critically** Inferring How are tube feet adapted to slow, rather than rapid, movement?

Check Your Progress

CHAPTER PROJECT 2

Continue to examine the mealworm containers every day and record your data. In your notebook, record any differences between the two groups of mealworms. Begin to draw conclusions about how the different conditions affected metamorphosis. When you have finished working with the insects, return them to your teacher.

SECTION 1 — Mollusks

Key Ideas

◆ Most mollusks have shells, soft bodies, a mantle covering internal organs, and a muscular foot.

◆ Mollusks are classified based on the presence of a shell, the type of shell, the type of foot, the arrangement of teeth in the radula, and the complexity of the nervous system.

◆ Major groups of mollusks include gastropods, bivalves, and cephalopods.

Key Terms

mollusk	kidney
gill	radula
gastropod	bivalve
cephalopod	

SECTION 2 — Arthropods

Key Ideas

◆ Arthropods have an exoskeleton, jointed appendages, and a segmented body.

◆ Major groups of arthropods include crustaceans, arachnids, centipedes, millipedes, and insects.

◆ Crustaceans are the only arthropods with two pairs of antennae.

◆ Arachnids have two body sections, eight legs, and no antennae.

Key Terms

arthropod	exoskeleton	chitin
molting	antenna	crustacean
metamorphosis	arachnid	abdomen

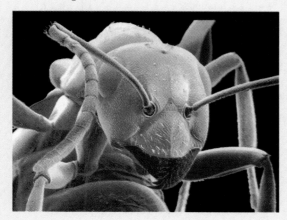

SECTION 3 — Insects

Key Ideas

◆ Insects are arthropods with three body sections, six legs, one pair of antennae, and usually one or two pairs of wings.

◆ An insect undergoing complete metamorphosis goes through four distinct stages—egg, larva, pupa, and adult. An insect undergoing gradual metamorphosis hatches from an egg to a nymph; the nymph may molt several times before becoming an adult.

◆ While some insects are harmful to humans, the vast majority are harmless or beneficial.

Key Terms

insect	thorax
complete metamorphosis	pupa
gradual metamorphosis	nymph
camouflage	

SECTION 4 — The Sounds of Insects

INTEGRATING **PHYSICS**

Key Ideas

◆ Sound is generated by something that vibrates. Sound travels in waves through solids, liquids, and gases.

◆ Many insects use sound to attract mates.

SECTION 5 — Echinoderms

Key Ideas

◆ Echinoderms are characterized by an endoskeleton, five-part radial symmetry, and a water vascular system.

◆ Echinoderms include sea stars, sea urchins, brittle stars, and sea cucumbers.

Key Terms

echinoderm	endoskeleton
water vascular system	

USING THE INTERNET

ACTIVITY

www.science-explorer.phschool.com

Reviewing Content

For more review of key concepts, see the Interactive Student Tutorial CD-ROM.

Multiple Choice

Choose the letter of the best answer.

1. Mollusks with tentacles are known as
   a. cephalopods.
   b. gastropods.
   c. bivalves.
   d. sea stars.
2. Which of these is true of the legs of arthropods?
   a. They always number six.
   b. They are always attached to the abdomen.
   c. They are rigid.
   d. They are jointed.
3. At which stage of its development is a moth enclosed in a cocoon?
   a. egg
   b. larva
   c. pupa
   d. adult
4. Sound can travel through
   a. solids only.
   b. liquids only.
   c. gases only.
   d. solids, liquids, and gases.
5. A sea star is a(n)
   a. mollusk.
   b. arthropod.
   c. echinoderm.
   d. sponge.

True or False

If the statement is true, write true. If it is false, change the underlined word or words to make the statement true.

6. All <u>arthropods</u> have an exoskeleton.
7. All <u>sea urchins</u> have two pairs of antennae.
8. An insect's midsection is called an <u>abdomen</u>.
9. Many insects use <u>sound</u> to attract mates.
10. All echinoderms have an <u>endoskeleton</u>.

Checking Concepts

11. Explain how a snail uses its radula.
12. How is a cephalopod's way of moving different from that of most mollusks?
13. Describe five things that a crayfish can do with its appendages.
14. How is the process by which a spider digests its food similar to that of a sea star?
15. How are centipedes different from millipedes?
16. Identify some ways in which insects harm people.
17. How are insects different from other arthropods?
18. How does sound travel from its source?
19. How is an echinoderm's radial symmetry different from that of a jellyfish?
20. **Writing to Learn** Imagine that you are a lobster that has just molted. Using vivid, precise words, describe a dangerous situation that you might encounter before your new exoskeleton has hardened.

Thinking Visually

21. **Concept Map** The concept map below shows the classification of arthropods. Copy the map and complete it. (For more on concept maps, see the Skills Handbook.)

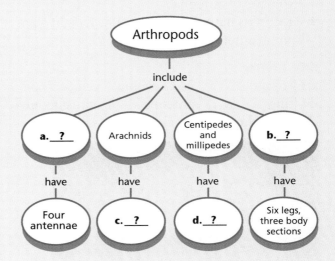

Applying Skills

The following information appeared in a book on insects. Use it to answer Questions 22–25.

"A hummingbird moth beats its wings an average of 85 times per second, and it flies at a speed of about 17.8 kilometers per hour (kph). A bumblebee's wings beat about 250 times per second, and it flies about 10.3 kph. A housefly's wings beat about 190 times per second, and it flies about 7.1 kph."

22. Creating Data Tables Make a data table to organize the wing-beat rate and flight speed information above.

23. Graphing Construct two bar graphs: one showing the three insect wing-beat rates and another showing the flight speeds.

24. Interpreting Data Which of the three insects has the highest wing-beat rate? Which insect flies the fastest?

25. Drawing Conclusions On the basis of the data, do you see any relationship between the rate at which an insect beats its wings and the speed at which it flies? Explain. What factors besides wing-beat rate might affect an insect's flight speed?

Thinking Critically

26. Applying Concepts Explain why the development of a lion, which grows larger as it changes from a tiny cub to a 200-pound adult, is not metamorphosis.

27. Comparing and Contrasting Compare and contrast bivalves and cephalopods.

28. Making Judgments Do you think that pesticides should be used to kill harmful insects? Support your ideas with facts.

29. Relating Cause and Effect Sea stars sometimes get caught in fishing nets. At one time, in an attempt to protect clams from their natural predators, workers on fishing boats cut the sea stars into pieces and threw the pieces back in the water. What do you think happened to the sea star population? Explain.

30. Classifying Your friend said he found a dead insect that had two pairs of antennae and eight legs. Is this possible? Why or why not?

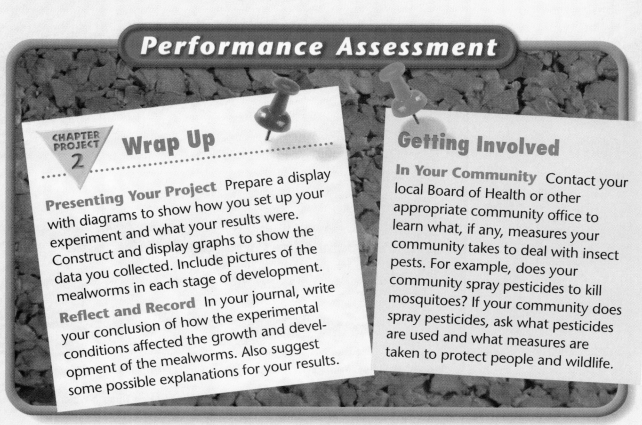

Performance Assessment

CHAPTER PROJECT 2 — Wrap Up

Presenting Your Project Prepare a display with diagrams to show how you set up your experiment and what your results were. Construct and display graphs to show the data you collected. Include pictures of the mealworms in each stage of development.

Reflect and Record In your journal, write your conclusion of how the experimental conditions affected the growth and development of the mealworms. Also suggest some possible explanations for your results.

Getting Involved

In Your Community Contact your local Board of Health or other appropriate community office to learn what, if any, measures your community takes to deal with insect pests. For example, does your community spray pesticides to kill mosquitoes? If your community does spray pesticides, ask what pesticides are used and what measures are taken to protect people and wildlife.

This three-horned chameleon has just invited a cricket to lunch.

WHAT'S AHEAD

PROJECT 3

Animal Adaptations

The chameleon sits still on a twig, as if frozen. Only its eyes move as it sights a cricket resting nearby. Suddenly, the chameleon's long tongue shoots out and captures the unsuspecting cricket, pulling the insect into its mouth. Watch any animal for a few minutes and you will see many ways in which it is adapted for life in its environment. How does the animal capture food, escape from predators, or obtain oxygen? To help answer these questions, you will create models of three different animals—a fish, an amphibian, and a reptile—and show how each is adapted to the environment in which it lives.

Your Goal To construct three-dimensional models of a fish, an amphibian, and a reptile that show how each is adapted to carry out an essential life function in its environment.

To complete the project successfully, you must
◆ select one important adaptation to show
◆ build a three-dimensional model of each animal, showing how it carries out the function you selected
◆ include a poster that explains how each animal's adaptation is suited to its environment
◆ follow the safety guidelines in Appendix A

Get Started Pair up with a classmate and share what you already know about fishes, amphibians, and reptiles. Discuss the following questions: Where do these organisms live? How do they move around? How do they protect themselves? Begin thinking about the characteristics that you would like to model.

Check Your Progress You'll be working on this project as you study this chapter. To keep your project on track, look for Check Your Progress boxes at the following points:

Section 2 Review, page 93: Select a fish to model, and assemble your materials.
Section 3 Review, page 100: Make a model of an amphibian.
Section 4 Review, page 110: Model a reptile. Begin your poster.

Wrap Up At the end of the chapter (page 117), you will display your models and poster.

SECTION 4 Reptiles

Discover **How Do Snakes Feed?**
Sharpen Your Skills **Drawing Conclusions**
Skills Lab **Soaking Up Those Rays**

SECTION 5 *Integrating Earth Science* 🌐 **Vertebrate History in Rocks**

Discover **What Can You Tell From an Imprint?**

Chapter 3 **B ◆**

SECTION 1 What Is a Vertebrate?

DISCOVER

How Is an Umbrella Like a Skeleton?

1. Open an umbrella. Turn it upside down and examine how it is made.

2. Now fold the umbrella, and watch how the braces and ribs collapse against the central pole.

3. Think of what would happen if you removed the ribs from the umbrella and then tried to use it during a rainstorm.

Think It Over

Inferring What is the function of the ribs of an umbrella? How are the ribs of the umbrella similar to the bones in your skeleton? How are they different?

GUIDE FOR READING

◆ **What main characteristic is shared by all vertebrates?**

◆ **How do vertebrates differ in the way in which they control body temperature?**

Reading Tip As you read, write a definition, in your own words, of each boldfaced science term.

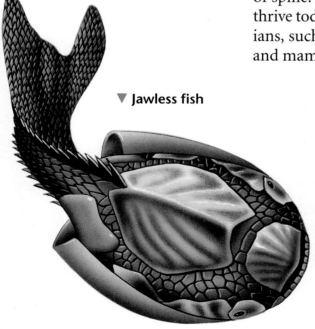

▼ Jawless fish

Look backward in time, into an ocean 530 million years ago. There you see a strange-looking creature, about as long as your middle finger. The creature is swimming with a side-to-side motion, like a flag flapping in an invisible wind. Its tail-fin is broad and flat. Tiny armorlike plates cover its small body. Its eyes are set wide apart. If you could see inside the animal, you would notice that it has a backbone. You are looking at one of the earliest vertebrates, at home in an ancient sea.

Recall from Chapter 1 that vertebrates are animals with a backbone, which is also called a vertebral column, spinal column, or spine. Fishes were the first vertebrates to appear, and they still thrive today in Earth's waters. Other vertebrates include amphibians, such as frogs, and reptiles, such as snakes, as well as birds and mammals.

The Chordate Phylum

Vertebrates are a subgroup in the phylum Chordata. Members of this phylum, called **chordates** (KAWR daytz), share these characteristics: at some point in their lives, they have a notochord, a nerve cord, and slits in their throat area. The phylum name comes from the **notochord,** a flexible rod that supports the animal's back. Some chordates, like the lancelet in Figure 1, keep the notochord all their lives. Others, such as tunicates, have a notochord as larvae, but not as adults. In vertebrates, part or all of the notochord is

82 ◆ B

replaced by a backbone. A few vertebrates have backbones made of **cartilage,** a connective tissue that is softer than bone, but flexible and strong. Most vertebrates have backbones made of hard bone.

Besides a notochord, all chordates have a nerve cord that runs down their back—your spinal cord is such a nerve cord. The nerve cord is the connection between the brain and the nerves, on which messages travel back and forth. Many other groups of animals—crustaceans and worms, for example—have nerve cords, but their nerve cords do not run down their backs.

In addition, chordates have slits in their throat area called pharyngeal (fayr uhn JEE uhl) slits. Fishes keep these slits as part of their gills for their entire lives, but in many vertebrates, including humans, pharyngeal slits disappear before birth.

Figure 1 This lancelet exhibits all the typical characteristics of a chordate. It has a notochord that helps support its body, pharyngeal slits that help it to breathe, and a nerve cord.

✓ *Checkpoint* *What characteristics do all chordates share?*

The Backbone and Endoskeleton

A vertebrate's backbone runs down the center of its back. The backbone is formed by many similar bones, called **vertebrae** (singular *vertebra*), lined up in a row, like beads on a string. Joints between the vertebrae give the vertebral column flexibility. You are able to bend over and tie your sneakers partly because your backbone is flexible. Each vertebra has a hole in it that allows the spinal cord to pass through it. The spinal cord fits into the vertebrae like fingers fit into rings.

A vertebrate's backbone is part of an endoskeleton, or internal skeleton. The endoskeleton supports and protects the body, helps give it shape, and gives muscles a place to attach. In addition to the backbone, the vertebrate's endoskeleton includes

Figure 2 The bodies of all vertebrates are supported by an endoskeleton with a backbone. *Comparing and Contrasting What are two ways in which the cow and chicken skeletons are similar? What are two ways in which they are different?*

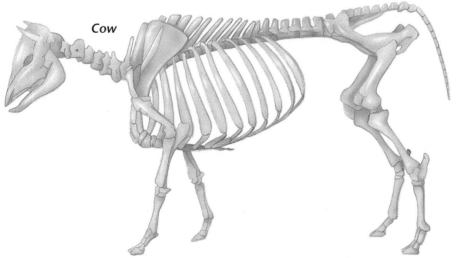

Cow

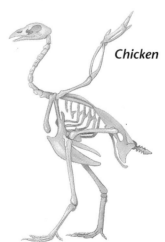

Chicken

Bead-y Bones

You can use a string and 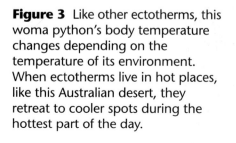 beads to model the structure of a vertebrate's backbone.

1. Tie a large knot at one end of a piece of string.

2. Slide beads onto the string one by one. Stop when there is just enough string left to tie another large knot.

3. Tie a large knot in the unknotted end of the string.

4. Try to bend the string of beads at different places.

Making Models What does the string represent in your model? What do the beads represent?

the skull and ribs. The skull protects the brain and sense organs. The ribs attach to the vertebrae and protect the heart, lungs, and other internal organs. Many vertebrates also have arm and leg bones adapted for a variety of movements.

A vertebrate's endoskeleton has several important characteristics. For one thing, unlike an arthropod's exoskeleton, it grows as the animal grows. It also forms an internal frame that supports the body against the downward pull of gravity, while allowing easy movement. Because of these endoskeleton characteristics, vertebrates can grow bigger than animals with exoskeletons or no skeletons at all.

☑ *Checkpoint* *What functions does a vertebrate's skeleton perform?*

Maintaining Body Temperature

One characteristic that distinguishes the major groups of vertebrates from each other is the way in which they control their body temperature. **Most fishes, amphibians, and reptiles have a body temperature that is close to the temperature of their environment. In contrast, birds and mammals have a stable body temperature that is typically much warmer than their environment.** Fishes, amphibians, and reptiles are ectotherms. An **ectotherm** is an animal whose body does not produce much internal heat—its body temperature changes depending on the temperature of its environment. For example, when a turtle is lying in the sun on a riverbank, it has a higher body temperature than when it is swimming in a cool river. Ectotherms are sometimes called "coldblooded," but this term is misleading because the blood of ectotherms is often quite warm.

Figure 3 Like other ectotherms, this woma python's body temperature changes depending on the temperature of its environment. When ectotherms live in hot places, like this Australian desert, they retreat to cooler spots during the hottest part of the day.

In contrast to a turtle, a beaver would have the same body temperature whether it was in cool water or on warm land. The beaver is a mammal, and mammals and birds are endotherms. An **endotherm** is an animal whose body controls and regulates its temperature by controlling the internal heat it produces. An endotherm's body temperature usually does not change much, even when the temperature of its environment changes.

Endotherms also have other adaptations, such as fur or feathers and sweat glands, for maintaining their body temperature. Fur and feathers keep endotherms warm on cool days. On hot days, on the other hand, some endotherms sweat. As the sweat evaporates, the animal is cooled. Because endotherms can keep their body temperatures stable, they can live in a greater variety of environments than ectotherms can.

Evolution of Vertebrates

The first tiny chordates swam in Earth's waters long before vertebrates appeared. If you look at Figure 5 on the next page, you will see that the pattern of vertebrate evolution looks something like a branching tree. Fossil evidence indicates that the earliest vertebrates were fishes, which first appeared about 530 million years ago. Amphibians, which appeared on Earth about 380 million years ago, are descended from fishes. Then, about 320 million years ago, amphibians gave rise to reptiles. Both mammals and birds, which you will learn about in Chapter 4, are descended from reptiles. Mammals appeared about 220 million years ago. Birds, which were the latest group of vertebrates to arise, appeared about 150 million years ago.

Figure 4 Though Antarctic winter temperatures can fall to −50°C, a dense coat keeps adult emperor penguins warm. A thick, fluffy baby coat keeps a penguin chick warm until it gets its adult coat.
Inferring Do you think the emperor penguin is an ectotherm or an endotherm?

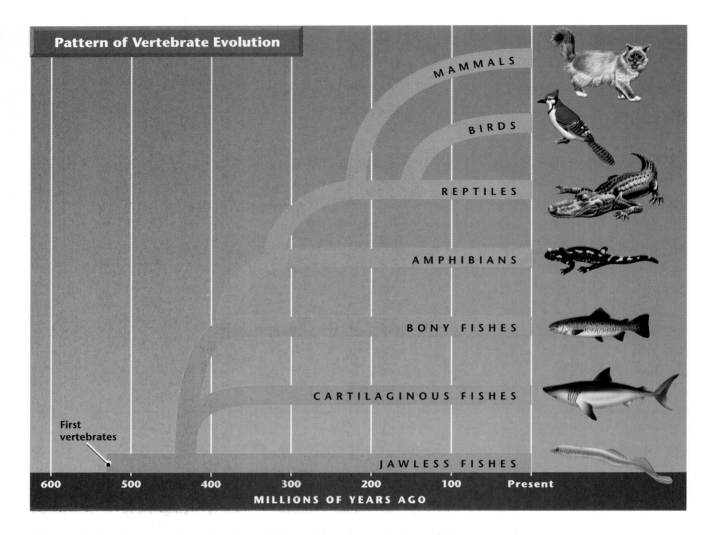

Pattern of Vertebrate Evolution

MAMMALS

BIRDS

REPTILES

AMPHIBIANS

BONY FISHES

CARTILAGINOUS FISHES

First vertebrates

JAWLESS FISHES

| 600 | 500 | 400 | 300 | 200 | 100 | Present |

MILLIONS OF YEARS AGO

Figure 5 The diagram shows the branching pattern of vertebrate evolution. The first vertebrates, the jawless fishes, arose about 530 million years ago. *Interpreting Diagrams About how much time passed between the time when fishes first appeared and the time that birds arose?*

Section 1 Review

1. What are three functions of a backbone?
2. Explain how ectotherms and endotherms differ in the way they control their body temperature. Give two examples of each.
3. What two groups of present-day vertebrates are the descendants of reptiles?
4. Thinking Critically Making Generalizations Would you expect ectotherms or endotherms to be more active at night? Explain your answer.

Science at Home

Have members of your family feel the tops of the vertebrae running down the center of their backs. Then have them feel the hard skull beneath the skin on their foreheads. In addition, if you have fish with bones for dinner, examine the fish skeleton with your family after dinner, pointing out the backbone. Show where the spinal cord runs through the vertebrae. Discuss the functions of the backbone and skull.

 Fishes

DISCOVER ·· ACTIVITY

How Does Water Flow Over a Fish's Gills?

1. Closely observe a fish in an aquarium for a few minutes. Note how frequently the fish opens its mouth. Water moves through the fish's mouth across its gills.

2. Notice the flaps on each side of the fish's head behind its eyes. Observe how the flaps open and close.

3. Observe the movements of the mouth and the flaps at the same time. Note any relationship between the movements of these two structures.

Think It Over

Observing What do the flaps on the sides of the fish do when the fish opens its mouth? What role do you think these two structures play in a fish's life?

In the warm waters of a coral reef, a fish called a moray eel hovers in the water, barely moving. A smaller fish, a wrasse, swims up to the moray and begins to eat tiny parasites that are attached to the moray's skin. Like a vacuum cleaner on a rug, the wrasse moves slowly over the moray eel, eating dead skin and bacteria as well as parasites. The wrasse even cleans inside the moray's mouth and gills. Both fishes benefit from this cleaning. The moray gets rid of parasites and other unwanted materials, and the wrasse gets a meal.

Both the wrasse and the moray it cleans belong to the vertebrate group known as fishes. A **fish** is an ectothermic vertebrate that lives in the water and has fins, which are structures used for moving. In addition, most fishes obtain oxygen through gills and have scales. Scales are thin, overlapping plates that cover the skin of a fish. They are made of a hard substance similar to that of your fingernails.

Fishes make up the largest group of vertebrates—nearly half of all vertebrate species are fishes. In addition, fishes have been swimming in Earth's waters for more than 500 million years—longer than any other kind of vertebrate.

GUIDE FOR READING

◆ How do fish use their gills?

◆ What are the three groups of fishes?

Reading Tip As you read about the different groups of fishes, make a table that compares and contrasts the characteristics of the groups.

▲ Small wrasse cleaning a moray eel

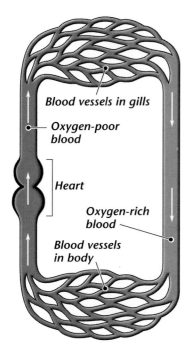

Figure 6 Trace the path of blood through a fish's one-loop circulatory system. *Interpreting Diagrams* *Where does the blood pick up oxygen?*

Labels in figure: Blood vessels in gills; Oxygen-poor blood; Heart; Oxygen-rich blood; Blood vessels in body

Communicating

Put on your goggles. Observe a preserved fish. Note its size, shape, and the number and locations of its fins. Lift the gill cover and observe the gill with a hand lens. Make a diagram of your observations, and include a written description. Wash your hands.

Ask a classmate to check your work to make sure it clearly communicates what you observed. Then make any necessary improvements.

Obtaining Oxygen

Fishes get their oxygen from water. As a fish cruises along, it automatically opens its mouth, as you observed in the Discover activity, and takes a gulp of water. The water, which contains oxygen, moves through openings in the fish's throat region that lead to the gills. Gills, which look like tiny feathers, are red because of the many blood vessels within them. **As water flows over the gills, oxygen moves from the water into the fish's blood, while carbon dioxide, a waste product, moves out of the blood and into the water.** After flowing over the gills, water leaves the fish by flowing out through slits beneath the gill covers.

From the gills, the blood travels throughout the fish's body, supplying the body cells with oxygen. Like all vertebrates, fishes have a closed circulatory system, in which blood flows through blood vessels to all regions of the body. The heart of a fish pumps blood in one continuous loop—from the heart to the gills, from the gills to the rest of the body, and back to the heart. Trace this path in Figure 6.

Moving and Feeding

Fins help fish swim. A typical fin, such as those on the angelfish in Figure 7, consists of a thin membrane stretched across bony supports. Like a wide canoe paddle, a fin provides a large surface to push against the water. If you've ever swum wearing a pair of swim fins and noticed how much faster you move through the water, you understand the great advantage of the large surface of a fin.

Because fishes spend most of their time hunting for food or feeding, most of their movements are related to eating. The bodies of most fishes are adapted for efficient feeding. Some carnivores, such as barracuda, have sharp and pointed teeth—good for stabbing smaller fishes. Insect-eating fish, such as trout, have short, blunt teeth with which they grip and crush their prey. Filter feeders, such as basking sharks, use comblike structures on their gills to filter tiny animals and plants from the water.

A fish's highly developed nervous system and sense organs help it find food and avoid predators. Fishes can see much better in water than you can. Keen senses of touch, smell, and taste also help fishes capture food. A shark can smell and taste even a tiny amount of blood—as little as one drop in 115 liters of water! Some fishes have taste organs in unusual places; a catfish, for example, tastes with its whiskers.

☑ *Checkpoint* *How does having fins help a fish?*

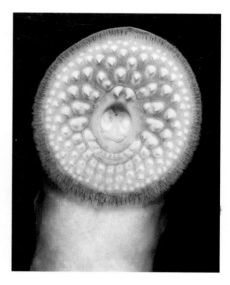

Figure 7 A fish's fins act as paddles to propel it through the water. You can clearly see the bone structure of a fin on the skeleton of an angelfish.

How Fishes Reproduce

Most fishes have external fertilization. Recall from Chapter 2 that in external fertilization, the eggs are fertilized outside of the female's body. The male hovers close to the female and spreads a cloud of sperm over the eggs as she releases them. Sharks and guppies, in contrast, have internal fertilization, in which the eggs are fertilized inside the female's body. The young fish then develop inside her body. When they are mature enough to live on their own, she gives birth to them.

Fishes Without Jaws

Biologists classify fishes into three major groups: jawless fishes, cartilaginous fishes, and bony fishes. They are distinguished from one another by the structure of their mouths and the types of skeletons they have. Jawless fishes were the earliest vertebrates. Today there are only about 60 species. Modern jawless fishes are unlike other fishes in that they have no scales. Their skeletons are made of cartilage, and they do not have pairs of fins. Most remarkably, they cannot bite like other fishes because their mouths do not have jaws! How can a fish without a jaw eat? The mouths of jawless fishes have structures for scraping, stabbing, and sucking.

Hagfishes and lampreys are the only kinds of jawless fishes. Hagfishes look like large, slimy worms. They crawl into the bodies of dead or dying fishes and use their sandpapery tongue to consume their decaying tissues. Many lampreys are parasites of other fishes. They attach their mouths to healthy fishes and then suck in the tissues and blood of their victims. If you look at the lamprey's mouth in Figure 8, you can probably imagine the damage it can do.

Figure 8 Lampreys are fish with eel-shaped bodies. They use their sharp teeth and suction-cup mouth to feed on other fish. *Classifying To what group of fishes do lampreys belong?*

Cartilaginous Fishes

Sharks, rays, and skates are cartilaginous (cahrt uhl AJ uh nuhs) fishes. As the group's name suggests, the skeletons of these fishes are made of cartilage, just like the skeletons of jawless fishes. However, unlike lampreys and hagfishes, cartilaginous fishes have jaws and pairs of fins. Pointed, toothlike scales cover their bodies, giving them a texture that is rougher than sandpaper. Cartilaginous fishes are all carnivores. Rays and skates live on the ocean floor, where they filter feed or hunt mollusks, crustaceans, and small fishes.

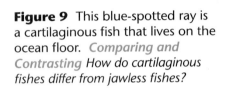

Figure 9 This blue-spotted ray is a cartilaginous fish that lives on the ocean floor. *Comparing and Contrasting How do cartilaginous fishes differ from jawless fishes?*

A Shark's Body Most shark bodies are streamlined so they can move quickly through the water. A shark's mouth is usually on the bottom part of its head. It contains jagged teeth arranged in rows. Most sharks use only the first couple of rows for feeding— the remaining rows are replacements. If a shark loses a front-row tooth, a tooth behind it moves up to replace it.

Always on the Move Most sharks cannot pump water over their gills. Instead they rely on swimming or currents to keep water moving across their gills. When sharks sleep, they position themselves in currents that send water over their gills.

Sharks spend most of their time hunting for food. They will attack and eat nearly anything that smells like food. Because they see poorly, sometimes they swallow strange objects. For example, one shark was found to have a raincoat, three overcoats, and an automobile license plate in its stomach.

☑ *Checkpoint Why must sharks always keep water moving over their gills?*

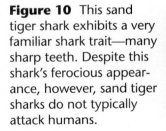

Figure 10 This sand tiger shark exhibits a very familiar shark trait—many sharp teeth. Despite this shark's ferocious appearance, however, sand tiger sharks do not typically attack humans.

Bony Fishes

Most familiar kinds of fishes, such as trout, tuna, and goldfish, have skeletons made of hard bone. Their bodies are covered with scales, and a pocket on each side of the head holds the fish's gills. Each gill pocket is covered by a flexible flap that opens to release water. To learn more about the major characteristics of bony fishes, look closely at the perch in *Exploring a Bony Fish*.

Swim Bladders and Buoyancy If you drop a brick into water, it sinks to the bottom. A wooden block, in contrast, floats on the surface. Unlike the brick or the block, fishes neither sink nor float on the surface.

INTEGRATING PHYSICS

EXPLORING *a Bony Fish*

In a quiet, shady area near the bank of a stream or pond, you might find some yellow perch swimming along. These freshwater fish, which like slow-moving water, travel in groups called schools.

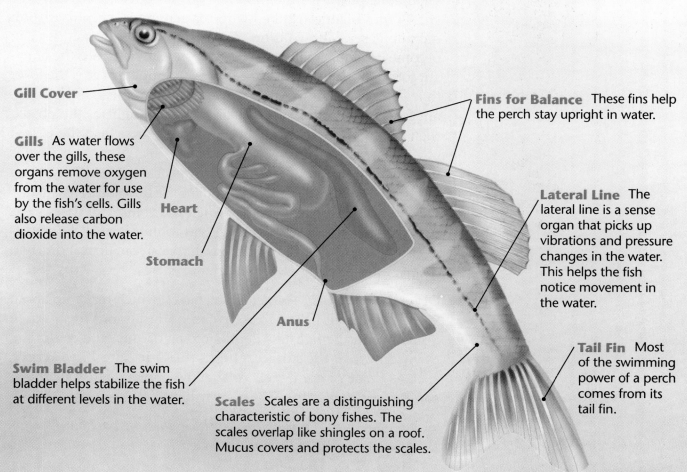

Gill Cover

Gills As water flows over the gills, these organs remove oxygen from the water for use by the fish's cells. Gills also release carbon dioxide into the water.

Heart

Stomach

Anus

Swim Bladder The swim bladder helps stabilize the fish at different levels in the water.

Scales Scales are a distinguishing characteristic of bony fishes. The scales overlap like shingles on a roof. Mucus covers and protects the scales.

Fins for Balance These fins help the perch stay upright in water.

Lateral Line The lateral line is a sense organ that picks up vibrations and pressure changes in the water. This helps the fish notice movement in the water.

Tail Fin Most of the swimming power of a perch comes from its tail fin.

Figure 11 The photographs show just a few species of bony fishes. *Making Generalizations What characteristics do all of these fish have in common?*

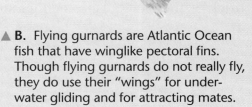

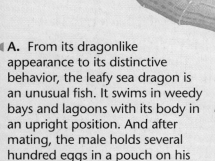

◄ **A.** From its dragonlike appearance to its distinctive behavior, the leafy sea dragon is an unusual fish. It swims in weedy bays and lagoons with its body in an upright position. And after mating, the male holds several hundred eggs in a pouch on his belly until they are ready to hatch.

▲ **B.** Flying gurnards are Atlantic Ocean fish that have winglike pectoral fins. Though flying gurnards do not really fly, they do use their "wings" for under-water gliding and for attracting mates.

Instead, they swim at different depths in the water. Most bony fishes have an organ called a **swim bladder**, an internal gas-filled sac that helps the fish stabilize its body at different depths.

A swim bladder is filled with oxygen, nitrogen, and carbon dioxide gases. The volume of gases in the swim bladder can become larger or smaller. This change in volume affects the buoyant force on the fish. **Buoyant force** (BOI uhnt force) is the force that water exerts upward on any underwater object. If the buoyant force on an object is greater than the weight of the object, then the object floats. If the buoyant force is less than the weight of the object, the object sinks. A brick sinks because it weighs more than the buoyant force pushing upward against it; a wooden block floats because it weighs less than the buoyant force.

A fish has greater buoyancy when the volume of gases in its swim bladder is large than when the gas volume is small. By adjusting its buoyancy as it moves in the water, a fish can float at different depths without using a large amount of energy.

Diversity of Bony Fishes Bony fishes, which make up about 95 percent of all fish species, live in both salt and fresh water. Some live in the lightless depths of the oceans, and seldom, if ever, come near the surface. Others thrive in light-filled waters, such as those of coral reefs or shallow ponds. Figure 11 shows some of the great variety of bony fishes.

☑ *Checkpoint* *If a pencil floats, how does the buoyant force on the pencil compare to the pencil's weight?*

D. Balloonfish are spiny puffer fish that live in warm waters all over the world. When a balloonfish is threatened, it swallows large amounts of water or air to make itself into a spiny ball. Few predators would dare take a bite! ▼

▲ **C.** These brightly colored anemone fish swim safely through the tentacles of a sea anemone. The sea anemone's tentacles can be fatal to other fishes, but they don't harm the anemone fish. Each type of anemone fish prefers to live in one specific type of anemone.

Food for People

INTEGRATING ENVIRONMENTAL SCIENCE People used to think of oceans and rivers as having a limitless supply of fish. Recently, though, overfishing has drastically reduced populations of the Atlantic codfish, Pacific salmon, and many other fish species. Some countries are trying to stop overfishing. The United States, Canada, and other countries have recently set limits on the amounts of certain kinds of fish that can be caught. In addition, some fishes, such as catfish, are being raised in "fish farms." This practice reduces the demand for fish caught in rivers and oceans.

Section 2 Review

1. Could a fish obtain oxygen if it could not open its mouth? In explaining your answer, describe the role of the fish's gills.
2. How is a shark's skeleton different from a perch's?
3. Describe the ways in which two different fishes are adapted to obtain food.
4. **Thinking Critically Predicting** How might a shark's hunting be affected if it were unable to smell?

Check Your Progress

CHAPTER PROJECT 3

By now you should have decided on the adaptation that you want to model. Select a specific fish in which to model this adaptation. Reference books, software, and magazine articles can help you make this choice. Then assemble your materials and build your model. *(Hint:* You might want to go to a pet store to observe how fish and other vertebrates move.)

Home Sweet Home

For an artificial environment to work, it must meet the needs of the organisms that live in it. In this lab, you will build an aquarium for guppies, whose natural environment is warm, fresh water.

Problem

How does an aquarium enable fish to survive?

Skills Focus

making models, posing questions

Materials

gravel	metric ruler	guppies
snails	guppy food	dip net
tap water	thermometer	water plants
aquarium filter	aquarium heater	

rectangular aquarium tank (15 to 20 liters) with cover

Procedure

1. Wash the aquarium tank with lukewarm water—do not use soap. Then place it on a flat surface in indirect sunlight.
2. Rinse the gravel and spread it over the bottom of the tank to a depth of about 3 cm.
3. Fill the tank about two-thirds full with tap water. Position several water plants in the tank by gently pushing their roots into the gravel. Wash your hands after handling the plants.
4. Add more water until the level is about 5 cm from the top.

5. Place the filter in the water and turn it on. Insert an aquarium heater into the tank, and turn it on. Set the temperature to 25°C. **CAUTION:** *Do not touch electrical equipment with wet hands.*
6. Allow the water to "age" by letting it stand for 2 days. Aging allows the chlorine to evaporate.
7. When the water has aged and is at the proper temperature, add guppies and snails to the tank. Include one guppy and one snail for each 4 liters of water. Cover the aquarium. Wash your hands after handling the animals.
8. Observe the aquarium every day for 2 weeks. Feed the guppies a small amount of food daily. Look for evidence that the fish and snails have adapted to their new environment. Also look for the ways they carry out their life activities, such as feeding and respiration. Record your observations.
9. Use a dip net to keep the gravel layer clean and to remove any dead plants or animals.

Analyze and Conclude

1. How does the aquarium meet the following needs of the organisms living in it: (a) oxygen supply, (b) proper temperature, and (c) food?
2. What happens to the oxygen that the fish take in from the water in this aquarium? How is that oxygen replaced?
3. **Apply** How is an aquarium like a guppy's natural environment? How is it different?

More to Explore

Write a plan for adding a different kind of fish to the aquarium. Include a list of questions that you would need to have answered before you could carry out your plan. Get the approval of your teacher before going ahead with your plan.

SECTION 3 Amphibians

DISCOVER ··· ACTIVITY

What's the Advantage of Being Green?

1. Count out 20 dried yellow peas and 20 green ones. Mix them up in a paper cup.

2. Cover your eyes. Have your partner gently scatter the peas onto a large sheet of green paper.

3. Uncover your eyes. Have your partner keep time while you pick up as many peas, one at a time, as you can find in 15 seconds.

4. When 15 seconds are up, count how many peas of each color you picked up.

5. Repeat Steps 2 through 4, but this time you scatter the peas and keep time while your partner picks up the peas.

6. Compare your results with those of your partner and your classmates.

Think It Over

Inferring Many frogs are green, and the environment in which they live is mostly green. What advantage does a frog have in being green?

If you walk through a damp, wooded area in the Northeast, you may be surrounded by them. But chances are good that you'll never see one. During the day, they hide in holes in the ground and cracks in rocks. At night they scramble over the decaying leaves on the forest floor, searching for food. Some climb to the tops of bushes and rocks to find their prey. What are these creatures that roam by night? They are red-backed salamanders.

Most of these slender, long-tailed animals are only as long as your longest finger. They may be small, but there are a lot of them. Some northeastern woodlands probably have more red-backed salamanders than all birds and mammals combined.

GUIDE FOR READING

◆ What is the life cycle of an amphibian like?

◆ How are amphibians adapted for movement on land?

Reading Tip Before you begin to read, write two or three things you already know about amphibians. After you have read this section, add three things you have learned.

Figure 12 Red-backed salamanders are the most common amphibians in some damp northeastern woodlands.

Chapter 3 **B ◆ 95**

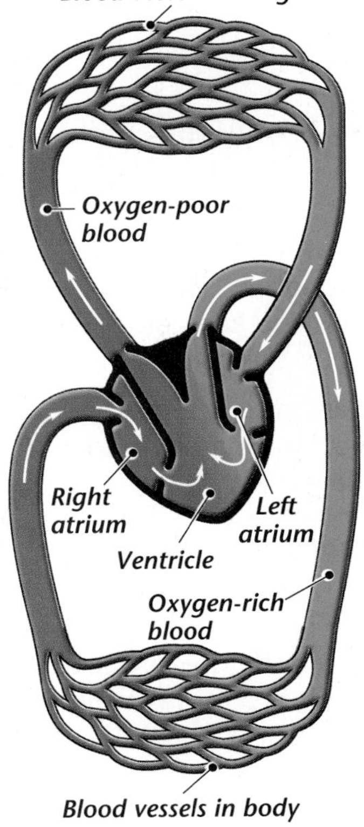

Blood vessels in lungs

Oxygen-poor
blood

Right
atrium

Ventricle

Left
atrium

Oxygen-rich
blood

Blood vessels in body

Figure 13 An adult amphibian's circulatory system has two loops. One loop runs from the heart to the lungs and back, and the second runs from the heart to the body and back.

Figure 14 The throat of this "peeper" inflates as he calls out to potential mates.

Gills to Lungs

The red-backed salamander is one kind of amphibian; frogs and toads are others. An **amphibian** is an ectothermic vertebrate that spends its early life in water. The word *amphibian* means "double life," and amphibians have exactly that. **After beginning their lives in the water, most amphibians spend their adulthood on land, returning to water to reproduce.**

Most amphibians lay their eggs in water. Amphibian eggs hatch into larvae that swim and have gills for obtaining oxygen. As they undergo metamorphosis and become adults, most amphibians lose their gills and acquire lungs. Adult amphibians also obtain oxygen and get rid of carbon dioxide through their thin, moist skin.

Amphibian Circulation

The circulatory system of a tadpole—the larval form of a frog or toad—has a single loop, like that of a fish. In contrast, the circulatory system of many adult amphibians has two loops. In the first loop, blood flows from the heart to the lungs and skin, and picks up oxygen. This oxygen-rich blood then returns to the heart. In the second loop, the blood flows to the rest of the body, delivering oxygen-rich blood to the cells.

As you read about the heart, trace the path of blood through the amphibian's circulatory system shown in Figure 13. The hearts of most amphibians have three inner spaces, or chambers. The two upper chambers of the heart, called **atria** (singular *atrium*), receive blood. One atrium receives oxygen-rich blood from the lungs, and the other receives oxygen-poor blood from the rest of the body. From the atria, blood moves into the lower chamber, the **ventricle**, which pumps blood out to the lungs and body. Oxygen-rich and oxygen-poor blood mix in the ventricle.

Checkpoint Compare the functions of the atria and ventricle.

Reproduction and Development

On spring evenings near a lake or pond, you can usually hear a loud chorus of "peepers," male frogs calling to attract mates. Most frogs and toads have external fertilization—a female frog releases eggs that are then fertilized by the male's sperm. In contrast, most salamanders have internal fertilization—the eggs are fertilized before they are laid.

Amphibian eggs are coated with clear jelly that keeps moisture in and helps protect them from infection. Inside each fertilized egg, a tiny embryo develops. In a few days, larvae wriggle out of the jelly and begin a free-swimming, fishlike life.

Most amphibian parents don't take care of their eggs after fertilization, but some do. For example, in one species of South American river toad, the male presses the fertilized eggs into the skin of the female's back. Skin grows over the eggs, and the young go through the tadpole stage beneath their mother's skin, safe from predators. Tiny frogs eventually hatch out of her skin.

Most amphibians undergo metamorphosis. Trace the process of frog metamorphosis in Figure 15. Hind legs appear first, accompanied by changes in the skeleton, circulatory system, and digestive system. Later the front legs appear. At about the same time, the tadpole loses its gills and starts to breathe with its lungs.

Unlike the tadpoles of frogs and toads, the larvae of salamanders resemble the adults. Most salamander larvae undergo a metamorphosis in which they lose their gills. However, the changes are not as dramatic as those that happen during frog and toad metamorphosis.

Figure 15 During its metamorphosis from tadpole to adult, a frog's body undergoes a series of dramatic changes. *Applying Concepts How do these changes prepare a frog for living on land?*

Language Arts
CONNECTION

When a tadpole becomes an adult frog, it moves to an unfamiliar location—a land environment that is very different from the watery one in which it has been living. While real tadpoles need no instructions for how to accomplish this move, you are about to write an imaginary guidebook for tadpoles that prepares them for their move onto land.

In Your Journal

First, brainstorm what types of information might be useful to the tadpole, such as how solid ground is different from water and where a frog might find food. Then choose four or five of your ideas and write a brief suggestion for each. Write in a lively way, using descriptive language.

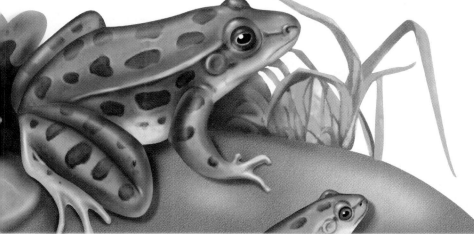
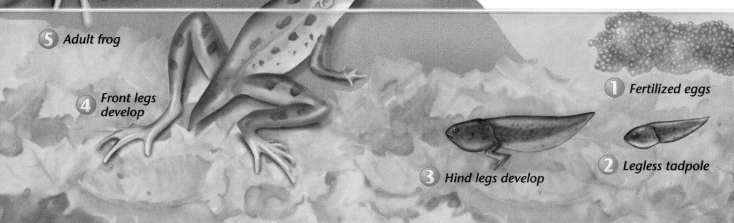

5 *Adult frog*

4 *Front legs develop*

3 *Hind legs develop*

2 *Legless tadpole*

1 *Fertilized eggs*

Webbing Through Water

ACTIVITY

How does having webbed feet make it easier to swim?

1. Fill a sink or pail with water.

2. Spread your fingers and put your hand into the water just far enough so that only your fingers are underwater. Drag your fingers back and forth through the water.

3. Take your hand out of the water and dry it. Put a small plastic bag over your hand. Secure it around your wrist with a rubber band.

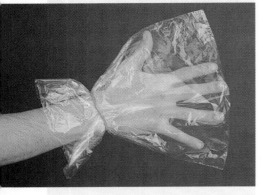

4. Repeat Step 2. Note any difference in the way in which your fingers push the water.

Making Models Use your model to explain how a frog's webbed feet help it move through water.

Getting Around on Land

Because it is not supported by water's buoyancy, a land animal needs a strong skeleton to support its body against the pull of gravity. In addition, a land animal needs some way of moving. Fins work in water, but they don't work on land. **Most adult amphibians have strong skeletons and muscular limbs adapted for movement on land.** Amphibians were the first vertebrates to have legs.

The eyes of amphibians are adapted to life on land. A transparent membrane helps keep them from drying out. Amphibians also have eyelids. Unlike fishes and tadpoles, whose wide-open eyes are always bathed in water, adult amphibians can close their eyes.

Frogs and Toads

When most people hear the word *amphibian,* they first think of frogs and toads—amphibians that are adapted for hopping and leaping. This kind of movement requires powerful hind-leg muscles and a skeleton that can absorb the shock of landing. The feet of frogs and toads have other adaptations, too. The webbed feet and long toes of bullfrogs form swim fins that help the frogs dart through the water. Tree frogs have toe pads with adhesive suckers that provide secure holds as the frogs leap from twig to twig.

It is usually easy to distinguish a frog from a toad. The skin of a frog is smooth and very moist, while that of a toad is drier and bumpy. Many toads have large lumps behind their eyes. These are actually skin glands that ooze a poisonous liquid when the toad is attacked by a predator such as a raccoon.

Although most tadpoles are herbivores, most adult frogs and toads are predators that feed on insects or other small animals. Insects don't usually see the frogs and toads that prey on them, because many frogs and toads are colored in such a way that they blend in with their environment. Green frogs, such as the one shown in *Exploring a Frog,* are brownish-green, making them hard to see in the ponds and meadows where they live. If you did the Discover activity, you learned that it is hard to see something green against a green background. Besides concealing frogs and toads from prey, their coloring also helps protect them from enemies.

☑ *Checkpoint* How can you tell a frog from a toad?

Salamanders

Salamanders are amphibians that keep their tails as adults. Their bodies are long and usually slender. Unlike frogs and toads, the

EXPLORING a Frog

Green frogs are common throughout the eastern United States and southeastern Canada.

Eyes A frog's large eyes give it excellent vision and allow it to see predators while it floats in the water.

Mouth The mouth has teeth and nostril openings. The frog's tongue is attached at the front of its mouth—it flips out to catch insects.

Lungs In the lungs, oxygen enters the blood and carbon dioxide is released into the air.

Skin A frog's skin is smooth and moist. It absorbs some oxygen through its skin.

Ears A frog's ears look like small drumheads located behind its eyes.

Kidney

Heart Like all amphibians, a green frog has a three-chambered heart.

Stomach

Hind Legs Long hind legs and powerful leg muscles make the green frog an excellent leaper.

legs of salamanders are not adapted for jumping. Rather, salamanders stalk and ambush the small invertebrates that they eat. Most salamanders return to water each year to breed and lay their eggs. The eggs hatch into larvae that swim, feed, and soon grow into adults.

Some kinds of salamanders live in water all of their lives, while many other kinds live almost entirely on land. Some salamanders that live only on land do not have lungs. They rely on their thin, moist skins to obtain oxygen from air and to remove carbon dioxide from their blood. These lungless salamanders do not even return to water to reproduce. They lay their eggs in moist places on land, and they look like miniature adults when they hatch, not like larvae with gills.

Figure 16 This young red-spotted newt is among the many amphibians in danger from poisons in its environment.

Amphibians in Danger

INTEGRATING ENVIRONMENTAL SCIENCE All over the world, populations of amphibians are decreasing. One reason is the destruction of amphibian habitats. An animal's **habitat** is the specific environment in which it lives. When a swamp is filled in or a forest is cut, an area that was moist becomes drier. Few amphibians can survive in dry, sunny areas. But habitat destruction does not account for the whole problem, because amphibians are declining even in areas where their habitats have not been damaged.

Because their skins are very thin and their eggs lack shells, amphibians are especially sensitive to changes in the environment. Poisons in the environment, such as insecticides and other chemicals, can pollute the waters that are essential to the life of an amphibian. Even small amounts of these chemicals can weaken adult amphibians, kill amphibian eggs, or cause tadpoles to be deformed.

The decline in amphibians may be a warning that other animals are also in danger. The environmental changes that are hurting amphibians may eventually affect other animals, including humans. To try to save amphibians and prevent harm to other animals, scientists are working to understand what is causing amphibian numbers to decline.

Section 3 Review

1. Why is it said that amphibians have a double life?
2. Compare an adult amphibian's skeleton and method of moving to those of a fish.
3. How has forest destruction affected amphibians? Why has it had this effect?
4. **Thinking Critically** Relating Cause and Effect A lungless salamander cannot survive if its skin dries out. Explain why.

Check Your Progress
CHAPTER PROJECT 3
At this point, you should have chosen an amphibian to model. Make sure that you are modeling the same type of adaptation that you did for the fish. (*Hint:* Before you begin constructing your model, make a sketch of what it will look like.)

SECTION 4 Reptiles

DISCOVER •••••••••••••••••••••••••••••••••••• ACTIVITY

How Do Snakes Feed?

1. To model how a snake feeds, stretch a sock cuff over a grapefruit "prey" by first pulling on one side and then on the other. Work the grapefruit down into the "stomach." A snake's jawbones can spread apart like the sock cuff.

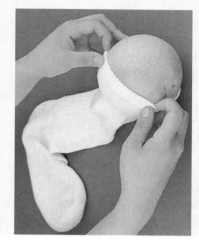

2. Remove the grapefruit and put a rubber band around the sock about 8 cm below the opening. The rubber band represents the firmly joined jawbones of a lizard. Now try to repeat Step 1.

Think It Over

Inferring What is the advantage of having jawbones like a snake's?

The king cobra of Southeast Asia, which can grow to more than 4 meters, is the world's longest venomous snake. When it encounters a predator, a king cobra flattens its neck and rears up. Its ropelike body sways back and forth, and its tongue flicks in and out.

A king cobra's fearsome behavior in response to a predator contrasts with the gentle way it treats its eggs. King cobras are one of the only snakes that build nests. The female builds a nest of grass and leaves on the forest floor. She lays her eggs inside the nest and guards them until they hatch.

Protection from Drying Out

Like other reptiles, king cobras lay their eggs on land rather than in water. A **reptile** is an ectothermic vertebrate that has lungs and scaly skin. In addition to snakes, lizards, turtles, and alligators are also reptiles.

GUIDE FOR READING

◆ What are some adaptations that allow reptiles to live on dry land?

◆ How is a reptile's egg different from an amphibian's egg?

Reading Tip As you read, write brief summaries of the information under each heading.

◀ King cobra

Unlike amphibians, reptiles can spend their entire lives on dry land. Reptiles were the first vertebrates that were well adapted to live on land, and they were the dominant land animals for about 160 million years. About 7,000 kinds of reptiles are alive today, but they are only a tiny fraction of a group that once dominated the land.

You can think of a land animal as a pocket of water held within a bag of skin. To thrive on land, an animal must have adaptations that keep the water within the "bag" from evaporating in the dry air. **The eggs, skin, and kidneys of reptiles are adapted to conserve water.**

An Egg With a Shell The eggs of reptiles are fertilized internally. While they are still inside the body of the female, fertilized eggs are covered with membranes and a shell. **Unlike an amphibian's egg, a reptile's egg has a shell and membranes that protect the developing embryo and help keep it from drying out.** Reptile eggs look much like bird eggs, except that their shells are soft and leathery, instead of rigid. Tiny holes, or pores, in the shell let oxygen in and carbon dioxide out. Since their eggs conserve water, reptiles—unlike amphibians—can lay their eggs on dry land.

Look carefully at Figure 17 to see how the membranes of a reptile's egg are arranged. One membrane holds the liquid that surrounds the embryo. Like bubble wrap that cushions breakable objects, the liquid keeps the embryo from getting crushed. The liquid also keeps the embryo moist. A second membrane holds the yolk, which provides the embryo with the food its cells must have to grow. A third membrane holds the embryo's wastes.

Figure 17 The egg from which this turtle is hatching provided it with food, moisture, and protection when it was an embryo. *Relating Cause and Effect List the parts of the egg that help keep the embryo from drying out.*

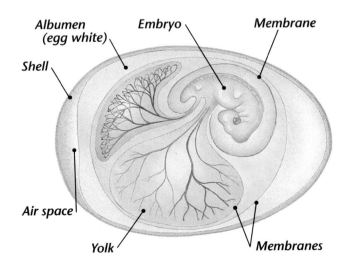

Albumen (egg white)
Embryo
Membrane
Shell
Air space
Yolk
Membranes

Skin and Kidneys Unlike amphibians, which have thin, moist skin, reptiles have dry, tough skins covered with scales. This scaly skin protects reptiles and helps keep water in their bodies. Another adaptation that helps keep water inside a reptile's body is its kidneys, which are organs that filter wastes from the blood. The wastes are then excreted in a watery fluid called **urine**. The kidneys of reptiles concentrate the urine so that they lose very little water.

☑ *Checkpoint* *List two functions of a reptile's skin.*

Obtaining Oxygen from the Air

Reptiles get their oxygen from the air. Like you, most reptiles breathe entirely with lungs. Like adult amphibians, reptiles have two loops in which their blood circulates through their bodies. In the first loop, the blood travels from the heart to the lungs and back to the heart. In the thin, moist surfaces of lung tissue, the oxygen moves into the blood and carbon dioxide moves out. In the second loop, blood travels from the heart to the tissues of the body. In the tissues, oxygen moves out of the blood and carbon dioxide moves into it. Then the blood returns to the heart. Like amphibians, the hearts of most reptiles have three chambers—two atria and one ventricle—and some mixing of oxygen-rich and oxygen-poor blood occurs.

Lizards

Most reptiles alive today are either lizards or snakes. These two groups of reptiles are closely related and share some important characteristics. Both have skin covered with overlapping scales. As lizards and snakes grow, they shed their skins, replacing the worn scales with a new coat. Most lizards and snakes live in warm areas.

Figure 18 The skin color of this chameleon can change in response to factors in its environment, such as changes in temperature.

EXPLORING a Lizard

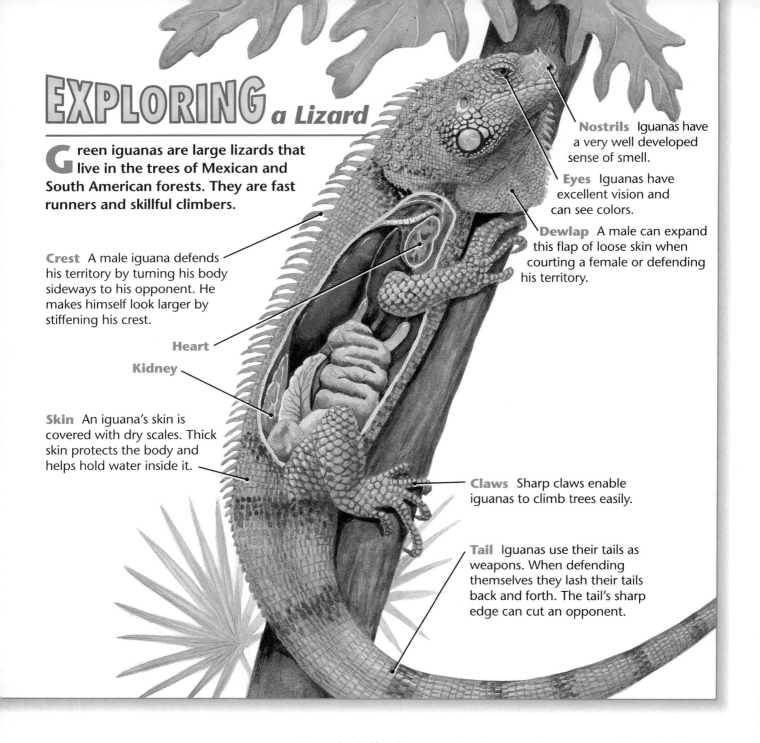

Green iguanas are large lizards that live in the trees of Mexican and South American forests. They are fast runners and skillful climbers.

Crest A male iguana defends his territory by turning his body sideways to his opponent. He makes himself look larger by stiffening his crest.

Heart

Kidney

Skin An iguana's skin is covered with dry scales. Thick skin protects the body and helps hold water inside it.

Nostrils Iguanas have a very well developed sense of smell.

Eyes Iguanas have excellent vision and can see colors.

Dewlap A male can expand this flap of loose skin when courting a female or defending his territory.

Claws Sharp claws enable iguanas to climb trees easily.

Tail Iguanas use their tails as weapons. When defending themselves they lash their tails back and forth. The tail's sharp edge can cut an opponent.

Lizards differ from snakes in one obvious way. Lizards have four legs, usually with claws on the toes. Many lizards have long tails, slender bodies, movable eyelids, and external ears.

A few lizards, including the iguana shown in *Exploring a Lizard,* are herbivores that eat leaves. Most lizards, however, are carnivores that capture food by jumping at it. While large lizards will eat large prey such as frogs and ground-dwelling birds, most small lizards are insect-hunters. Chameleons, which are found in Africa and India, have a sticky tongue adapted for snaring insects. This elastic tongue shoots out rapidly, extending as long as the chameleon's head and body put together!

Snakes

Snakes are able to live in almost every sort of habitat, from deserts to swamps. They are similar to lizards, but streamlined, both externally and internally. Snakes have no legs, eyelids, or external ears, and most snakes have only one lung.

Snakes on the Move If you've ever seen a snake slither across the ground, you know that when it moves, its long, thin body bends into curves. Snakes move by contracting, or shortening, bands of muscles that are connected to their ribs and backbones. Alternate contractions of muscles on the right and left sides produce a slithering side-to-side motion.

How Snakes Feed All snakes are carnivores, and some eat large prey. If you did the Discover activity, you learned that a snake's jawbones can spread widely apart. In addition, the bones of a snake's skull can move to let the snake swallow an animal much larger in diameter than itself. Most snakes, however, feed on small rodents, such as mice.

Snakes capture their prey in different ways. The sharp-tailed snakes of western North America, which eat only slugs, have long, curved front teeth for hooking their slippery prey. Some West Indian boas are bat hunters that wait in ambush at the entrances to caves where bats live. At twilight, when the bats fly out of the cave to feed, the snakes snatch them out of the air.

Some snakes, such as rattlesnakes and copperheads, have venom glands attached to hollow teeth called fangs. When these snakes bite a prey animal, venom flows down inside the fangs. The venom enters the flesh of the prey and kills it quickly.

☑ *Checkpoint* **How do snakes move?**

Figure 19 A wide variety of snakes live on Earth, some adapted to almost every habitat. **A.** The temple viper from Thailand has one of the strongest venoms of any snake. **B.** Although the kingsnake is not venomous, it is quite aggressive—a kingsnake will even attack and eat a rattlesnake. *Making Generalizations How are snakes different from lizards?*

Soaking Up Those Rays

I n this lab, you will examine and interpret data associated with an ectotherm.

Problem

How do some lizards control their body temperatures in the extreme heat of a desert environment?

Materials

paper   pencil

Procedure

1. The data in the diagram below were collected by scientists studying how lizards control their body temperature. Examine the data.
2. Copy the data table on the next page into your notebook.
3. Organize the data in the diagram by filling in the table, putting the appropriate information in each column. Begin by writing a brief description of each type of lizard behavior.
4. Complete the data table using the information in the diagram.

Analyze and Conclude

1. How did the lizard's body temperature vary from 6 A.M. until 8 P.M.?
2. What are the three sources of heat that caused the lizard's body temperature to rise during the day?
3. During the hottest part of the day, what were the air and ground temperatures? Why do you think the lizard's temperature remained below 40°C?
4. Predict what the lizard's body temperature would have been from 8 P.M. to 6 A.M. Explain your prediction.

6 A.M.–7 A.M.
Emerging from burrow
Air temperature **20°C**
Ground temperature **28°C**
Body temperature **25°C**

7 A.M.–9 A.M.
Basking (lying on ground in sun)
Air temperature **27°C**
Ground temperature **29°C**
Body temperature **32.6°C**

9 A.M.–12 noon
Active (moving about)
Air temperature **27°C**
Ground temperature **30.8°C**
Body temperature **36.6°C**

DATA TABLE

Activity	Description of Activity	Time of Day	Air Temperature (°C)	Ground Temperature (°C)	Body Temperature (°C)
1. Emerging					
2. Basking					
3. Active					
4. Retreat					
5. Stilting					
6. Retreat					

5. Based on what you learned from the data, explain why it is misleading to say that an ectotherm is a "coldblooded" animal.

6. Predict what would happen to your own body temperature if you spent a brief period outdoors in the desert at noon. Predict what your temperature would be if you spent time in a burrow at 7 P.M. Explain your predictions.

7. **Think About It** Why is it helpful to organize data in a data table before you try to interpret the data?

More to Explore

Make one or more bar graphs of the temperature data. Explain what the graphs show you. How do these graphs help you interpret the data?

12 noon–2:30 P.M.
Retreat to burrow
Air temperature **40.3ºC**
Ground temperature **53.8ºC**
Body temperature **39.5ºC**

2:30 P.M.–6 P.M.
Stilting (belly off ground)
Air temperature **34.2ºC**
Ground temperature **47.4ºC**
Body temperature **39.5ºC**

6 P.M.–9 P.M.
Retreat to burrow
Air temperature **25ºC**
Ground temperature **26ºC**
Body temperature **25ºC**

Figure 20 Turtles vary greatly in their feeding habits. **A.** The green sea turtle lives entirely at sea and is a carnivore. **B.** The Galapagos tortoise lives on land, where it eats mainly cacti.

Turtles

A turtle is a reptile whose body is covered by a protective shell, which is made from the turtle's ribs and backbone. As you can see in Figure 20, the bony plates of the shell are covered by large scales made from the same material as the skin's scales. Some turtle shells can cover the whole body—a box turtle can draw its head, legs, and tail inside its shell for protection. Turtles like the snapping turtle have much smaller shells. Soft-shelled turtles, as their name suggests, have shells that are as soft as pancakes. Soft-shelled turtles lie in stream beds, concealed from predators, with only their nostrils and eyes above the sand.

The feeding habits of turtles are quite diverse. The largest turtles, the leatherbacks, are carnivores. Leatherbacks, which can weigh over 500 kilograms, are sea turtles that feed mainly on venomous jellyfishes. The stinging cells of the jellyfish can kill other animals, but the leatherback's tough skin seems to be unharmed by them. The giant Galapagos tortoises, on the other hand, are herbivores that feed mainly on cacti. They carefully scrape the prickly spines off before swallowing the cactus. Turtles have sharp-edged beaks instead of teeth. The razor-sharp beaks of soft-shelled turtles can chop fishes in two.

Figure 21 Alligators, left, and crocodiles, right, are the largest reptiles still living on Earth. They are similar in many ways, including appearance. *Comparing and Contrasting How can you tell the difference between an alligator and a crocodile?*

Alligators and Crocodiles

If you walk along a lake in Florida, you just might see an alligator swimming silently in the water. Most of its body lies beneath the surface, but you can see its large, bulging eyes above the surface. Alligators, crocodiles, and their relatives are the largest living reptiles. The American alligator can grow to be more than 5 meters long.

How do you tell an alligator from a crocodile? Look for teeth—but use binoculars and stay far away! Alligators have broad, rounded snouts, with only a few teeth visible. In comparison, crocodiles have pointed snouts, and you can see most of their teeth. Both alligators and crocodiles spend much of their days resting in the sun or lying in the water.

Alligators and crocodiles are carnivores that hunt mostly at night. They have several adaptations to help them capture prey. They use their strong, muscular tails to swim rapidly through the water. Their jaws are equipped with many large, sharp, and pointed teeth. Their jaw muscles are extremely strong when biting down. Although alligators will eat dogs, raccoons, and deer, they usually do not attack humans.

Unlike most other reptiles, crocodiles and alligators care for their eggs and newly hatched young. After laying eggs in a nest of rotting plants, the female stays near the nest. From time to time she comes out of the water and crawls over the nest to keep it moist. After the tiny alligators or crocodiles hatch, the female scoops them up in her huge mouth. She carries them from the nest to a nursery area in the water where they will be safer. For as long as a year, she will stay near her young, which make gulping quacks when they're alarmed. When their mother hears her young quack, she rushes toward them.

☑ *Checkpoint* *How are alligators and crocodiles adapted for catching prey?*

Sharpen your Skills

Drawing Conclusions

ACTIVITY

Scientists incubated, or raised, eggs of one alligator species at four different temperatures. When the alligators hatched, the scientists counted the numbers of males and females. The table below shows the results.

Incubation Temperature	Number of Females	Number of Males
29.4°C	80	0
30.6°C	19	13
31.7°C	13	38
32.8°C	0	106

Use the data to answer these questions.
1. What effect does incubation temperature have on the sex of the alligators?
2. Suppose a scientist incubated 50 eggs at 31°C. About how many of the alligators that hatched would be males? Explain.

Extinct Reptiles—The Dinosaurs

Millions of years ago, huge turtles and fish-eating reptiles swam in the oceans. Flying reptiles soared through the skies. And from about 225 million years ago until 65 million years ago, reptiles were the major form of vertebrate life on land. Snakes and lizards basked on warm rocks. And there were dinosaurs of every description. Unlike today's reptiles, dinosaurs may have been endothermic. Some dinosaurs, such as the *Brachiosaurus* in Figure 22, were the largest land animals that have ever lived.

Dinosaurs were the earliest vertebrates that had legs positioned directly beneath their bodies. This adaptation allowed them to move more easily than animals, such as salamanders, whose legs stick out to the sides of their bodies. Most herbivorous dinosaurs, such as *Brachiosaurus,* walked on four legs; most carnivores, such as the huge *Tyrannosaurus rex,* ran on two legs.

Dinosaurs became extinct about 65 million years ago, long before humans appeared on Earth. Several theories try to explain their disappearance, but no one is sure why they became extinct. A change in climate from warm to cool probably played a role. One leading theory suggests that a huge meteorite, a chunk of rock sailing through space, crashed into Earth. The impact sent up thick clouds of dust that blocked out the sun. The decrease in sunlight not only made Earth cooler, it also decreased plant growth, thus limiting food supplies. Dust from massive volcanic eruptions may also have blocked out sunlight. The dinosaurs were unable to survive in these changed conditions and died out.

Today, it's only in movies that dinosaurs shake the ground with their footsteps. But in a way, dinosaurs still exist. Birds may be descended from certain small dinosaurs. Some biologists think that birds are dinosaurs with feathers.

Figure 22 *Brachiosaurus* grew to be over 22.5 meters long—longer than two school buses put together. *Observing What adaptation is demonstrated by the legs of* Brachiosaurus *and many other dinosaurs?*

Section 4 Review

1. Describe three adaptations that enabled reptiles to live on land.
2. Explain how the structure of a reptile's egg protects the developing embryo.
3. Explain how snakes are able to eat large prey.
4. **Thinking Critically** **Making Generalizations** If some dinosaurs had been endotherms, what advantage might they have had over other reptiles?

Check Your Progress

CHAPTER PROJECT 3

Assemble the materials you need in order to build your reptile model. Make sure that your model clearly shows how the animal is adapted for the same function as your fish and amphibian. Begin preparing a written explanation of the adaptations that your three models demonstrate. Your written explanation should include labeled diagrams.

SECTION 5 Vertebrate History in Rocks

What Can You Tell From an Imprint?

1. Flatten some modeling clay into a thin sheet on a piece of paper.

2. Firmly but gently press two or three small objects into different sections of the clay. The objects might include such things as a key, a leaf, a feather, a pencil, a postage stamp, a flower, or a raisin. Don't let anyone see the objects you are using.

3. Carefully remove the objects from the clay, leaving only the objects' imprints.

4. Exchange your sheet of imprints with a partner. Try to identify the objects that made the imprints.

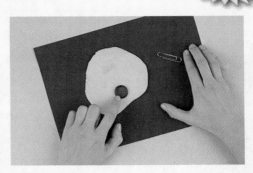

Think It Over

Observing In general, what types of objects made the clearest imprints? If those imprints were fossils, what could you learn about the objects by looking at their "fossils"? What couldn't you learn?

Millions of years ago, in an ancient pond, some fish died and their bodies settled into the mud on the bottom. Soon heavy rains fell, and more mud washed into the pond, covering the fish. The fish's soft tissues decayed, but their bones remained. After many thousands of years, the mud hardened into rock, and the fish bones became the fossils shown here.

GUIDE FOR READING

◆ What can scientists learn from studying fossils?

Reading Tip Predict what you will learn in this section. Then read to see whether your prediction is correct.

◀ Fossilized fish

Fossils in Sedimentary Rock

A **fossil** is the hardened remains or other evidence of a living thing that existed a long time in the past. Sometimes a fossil is an imprint in rock, such as an animal's footprint or the outline of a leaf. Other fossils are the remains of bones or other parts of living things—a chemical process has taken place in which the organism's tissues have become replaced by hard minerals. Because most living tissues decay rapidly, only a very few organisms become preserved as fossils.

Fossils occur most frequently in the type of rock known as sedimentary rock. **Sedimentary rock** is made of hardened layers of sediments—particles of clay, sand, mud, or silt. Have you ever

Discovering Vertebrate Fossils

People have been discovering fossils since ancient times. However, it is only within the last few centuries that people have understood that fossils are the remains of extinct organisms. Here are some especially important fossil discoveries.

1822
Dinosaur Tooth

In a quarry near Lewes, England, Mary Ann Mantell discovered a strange-looking tooth embedded in stone. Her husband Gideon drew the picture of the tooth shown here. The tooth belonged to the dinosaur *Iguanodon*.

| 1675 | 1725 | 1775 | 1825 |

1677
Dinosaur-Bone Illustration

Robert Plot, the head of a museum in England, published a book that had an illustration of a huge fossilized thighbone. Plot thought that the bone belonged to a giant human, but it probably was the thighbone of a dinosaur.

1811
Sea Reptile

Along the cliffs near Lyme Regis, England, 12-year-old Mary Anning discovered the fossilized remains of the giant sea reptile now called *Ichthyosaurus*. Mary became one of England's first professional fossil collectors.

washed a dirty soccer ball and seen sand and mud settle on the bottom of the sink? If you washed a dozen soccer balls, the sink bottom would be covered with a layer of sediment. Sediments build up in many ways. For example, wind can blow a thick layer of sand onto dunes. Sediments can also form when muddy water stands in an area for a long time. Muddy sediment in the water will eventually settle to the bottom and build up.

Over a very long time, layers of sediments can be pressed and cemented together to form rock. As sedimentary rock forms, traces of living things that have been trapped in the sediments are sometimes preserved as fossils.

☑ *Checkpoint* **What are two ways in which fossils form?**

In Your Journal

If you could interview the discoverer of one of these fossils, what questions would you ask about the fossil and how it was found? Write a list of those questions in your journal. Then use reference materials to try to find the answers to some of them.

1902
Tyrannosaurus

A tip from a local rancher sent Barnum Brown, a fossil hunter, to a barren, rocky area near Jordan, Montana. There Brown found the first relatively complete *Tyrannosaurus rex* skeleton.

1991
Dinosaur Eggs in China

Digging beneath the ground, a farmer on Green Dragon Mountain in China uncovered what may be the largest nest of fossil dinosaur eggs ever found. A paleontologist chips carefully to remove one of the eggs from the rock.

| 1875 | 1925 | 1975 | 2025 |

1861
Bird Bones

A worker in a stone quarry in Germany discovered *Archaeopteryx*, a feathered, birdlike animal that also had many reptile characteristics.

1964
Deinonychus

In Montana, paleontologist John Ostrom discovered the remains of a small dinosaur, *Deinonychus*. This dinosaur was probably a predator who could move rapidly. This fossil led scientists to hypothesize that dinosaurs may have been endotherms.

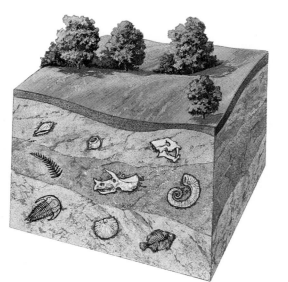

Figure 23 The diagram shows fossils in layers of sedimentary rocks. *Interpreting Diagrams* *Which rock layer probably contains the oldest fossils? Explain.*

Interpretation of Fossils

What information can scientists learn from fossils? **Paleontologists** (pay lee uhn TAHL uh jihsts), the scientists who study extinct organisms, examine fossil structure and make comparisons to present-day organisms. **By studying fossils, paleontologists can infer how a species changed over time.** One important piece of information that paleontologists can learn from a fossil is its approximate age.

One method for estimating a fossil's age takes advantage of the process in which sediments form. Think about sediments settling out of water—the lowest layers are deposited first, and newer sediments settle on top of the older layers. Therefore, fossils in higher layers of rock are often younger than fossils in lower layers.

However, rock layers can become tilted or even turned upside down. Natural events such as earthquakes and human events such as construction can change the position of rock layers. Therefore, a fossil's position in rock is not always a reliable indication of its age. Scientists must usually rely on other methods to help determine a fossil's age. For example, fossils—and the rocks in which they are found—contain some radioactive chemical elements. These radioactive elements decay, or change into other chemical elements, over a known period of time. The more there is of the decayed form of the element, the older the fossil.

Paleontologists have used fossil evidence to piece together the history of the major groups of vertebrates. As new fossils are found, paleontologists will reinterpret the fossil evidence and possibly revise their ideas about when different animal groups first appeared and how the groups may be related to one another.

Section 5 Review

1. How can paleontologists use fossils to determine how a species changed over time?
2. Describe how sedimentary rock forms.
3. Describe the process by which a leaf becomes fossilized.
4. **Thinking Critically** **Inferring** Fossil A is found in a rock layer 200 meters below the surface of the ground. Fossil B is found in the same rock formation, but at a depth of 150 meters. Which fossil is probably older? What additional evidence would help verify the fossils' ages?

Science at Home

Does your family store newspapers or magazines in a stack? With someone in your family, check the dates of the newspapers in the stack. Going from the top of the pile to the bottom, are the newspapers in any particular order? If the oldest newspapers are on the bottom and the newest on top, you can relate this to the way in which sediments are laid down. Ask family members to imagine that two fossils were trapped in different newspapers. Explain which fossil would probably be older, and why.

1 What Is a Vertebrate?

Key Ideas

◆ Vertebrates have a backbone that is part of an endoskeleton. The endoskeleton supports, protects, and gives shape to the body.

◆ Most fishes, amphibians, and reptiles are ectotherms. Mammals and birds are endotherms.

Key Terms

chordate   notochord   cartilage
vertebra   ectotherm   endotherm

2 Fishes

Key Ideas

◆ A fish is an ectothermic vertebrate that lives in the water, has fins, usually has scales, and obtains oxygen through gills.

◆ Major groups of fishes include jawless fishes, cartilaginous fishes, and bony fishes.

Key Terms

fish
swim bladder
buoyant force

3 Amphibians

Key Ideas

◆ An amphibian is a moist-skinned, ectothermic vertebrate. Most amphibians spend their early lives in water and adulthood on land, returning to water to reproduce.

◆ Major groups of amphibians include frogs, toads, and salamanders.

◆ Adult amphibians have strong skeletons and muscular limbs adapted for moving on land.

Key Terms

amphibian   atrium   ventricle
habitat

4 Reptiles

Key Ideas

◆ A reptile is an ectothermic vertebrate that has lungs and scaly skin. Reptiles can spend their entire lives on dry land.

◆ The leathery eggs, scaly skin, and the kidneys of reptiles are adapted to conserving water.

◆ Major groups of reptiles include lizards, snakes, turtles, and alligators and crocodiles.

Key Terms
reptile
urine

5 Vertebrate History in Rocks

INTEGRATING EARTH SCIENCE

Key Ideas

◆ Sedimentary rock forms from hardened layers of sediments such as clay, mud, or sand.

◆ Fossils are found primarily in sedimentary rock.

◆ Paleontologists study fossils to infer how organisms, including vertebrates, have changed over time. Scientists are always reinterpreting fossil evidence.

Key Terms

fossil   sedimentary rock   paleontologist

USING THE INTERNET   **ACTIVITY**

Reviewing Content

 For more review of key concepts, see the Interactive Student Tutorial CD-ROM.

Multiple Choice

Choose the letter of the best answer.

1. Which fishes do not have jaws, scales, or paired fins?
   a. sharks
   b. lampreys and hagfishes
   c. sturgeons
   d. ocean sunfish
2. A bony fish uses a swim bladder to
   a. propel itself through water.
   b. regulate its buoyancy.
   c. remove wastes.
   d. pump water over its gills.
3. Adult frogs must return to the water to
   a. catch flies.
   b. obtain all their food.
   c. reproduce.
   d. moisten their gills.
4. Which of the following animals breathes with lungs?
   a. shark   b. lamprey
   c. larval salamander   d. lizard
5. Fossils are rare because
   a. there were few living things in ancient times.
   b. scientists have only searched for fossils in Africa and the United States.
   c. most fossils have sunk to the ocean floor.
   d. the bodies of dead organisms decay rapidly.

True or False

If the statement is true, write true. If it is false, change the underlined word or words to make the statement true.

6. Birds and mammals are <u>endotherms</u>.
7. If a shark loses a <u>fin</u>, another one will move into its place.
8. <u>Buoyant force</u> is the force that pushes upward against an underwater object.
9. Amphibians usually begin their lives <u>on land</u>.
10. Paleontologists are scientists who study <u>fishes</u>.

Checking Concepts

11. Describe the main characteristics of chordates.
12. How do fish reproduce?
13. Describe the life cycle of a frog.
14. How is an amphibian's circulatory system different from that of a fish?
15. Explain how the structure of a reptile's egg protects the embryo inside.
16. Compare and contrast lizards and snakes.
17. Why does a snake move in a wavelike pattern rather than in a straight line?
18. What may have caused the dinosaurs to become extinct?
19. Describe two methods that scientists use to determine the age of a fossil.
20. **Writing to Learn** Write a description of an hour in the life of a shark. Before you begin to write, list the events you want to include, and arrange those events in the sequence in which you want them to occur. As you write, use words such a *then* and *a moment later* to let your readers know that the shark is progressing from one activity to another.

Thinking Visually

21. **Compare/Contrast Table** Copy the table comparing fish groups onto a separate sheet of paper. Then complete the table and add a title. (For more on compare/contrast tables, see the Skills Handbook.)

Kind of Fish	Kind of Skeleton	Jaws?	Scales	Example
Jawless Fishes	a. ?	no	b. ?	c. ?
d. ?	e. ?	f. ?	toothlike scales	shark
Bony Fishes	bone	g. ?	h. ?	i. ?

Applying Skills

A scientist performed an experiment on five goldfish to test the effect of water temperature on "breathing rate"—the rate at which the fish open and close their gill covers. The graph shows the data that the scientist obtained at four different temperatures. Use the graph to answer Questions 22–24.

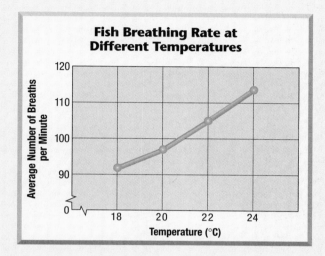

Fish Breathing Rate at Different Temperatures

Average Number of Breaths per Minute (y-axis: 90, 100, 110, 120)

Temperature (°C) (x-axis: 18, 20, 22, 24)

22. **Controlling Variables** Identify the manipulated variable and the responding variable in this experiment.
23. **Interpreting Data** How does the breathing rate at 18°C compare to the breathing rate at 22°C?
24. **Drawing Conclusions** Based on the data shown in the graph, what is the relationship between water temperature and goldfish breathing rate?

Thinking Critically

25. **Comparing and Contrasting** Compare the ways a tadpole and an adult frog obtain oxygen.
26. **Applying Concepts** Imagine that you are in the hot desert sun with a wet paper towel. You must keep the towel from drying out. What strategy can you copy from reptiles to keep the towel wet?

Performance Assessment

CHAPTER PROJECT 3 **Wrap Up**

Present Your Project Present your models of animal adaptations. Display the models in a creative and interesting way—for example, show the models in action and show details of the animals' habitats. Display your poster that describes the adaptations you chose.

Reflect and Record In your journal, record what you learned by doing this project. List all the adaptations you learned about from your classmates' presentations. How did constructing a three-dimensional model help you understand the characteristics of these three vertebrate groups?

Getting Involved

In Your Community Find out what fishes people catch in your area, as a hobby and for food. Then learn the laws and regulations that govern sport fishing in your state or community. Also find out whether fishing is prohibited in any local waterways and why. Prepare a fact sheet to summarize the information you find. Make copies of the fact sheet that could be posted in stores that sell fishing supplies.

CHAPTER
4 Birds and Mammals

WHAT'S AHEAD

SECTION
1 Birds

Discover **What Are Feathers Like?**
Skills Lab **Looking at an Owl's Leftovers**
Try This **Eggs-amination**

Integrating Physics 🌐

SECTION
2 The Physics of Bird Flight

Discover **What Lifts Airplanes and Birds Into the Air?**
Try This **It's Plane to See**

SECTION
3 What Is a Mammal?

Discover **What Are Mammals' Teeth Like?**
Try This **Insulated Mammals**
Sharpen Your Skills **Classifying**
Real-World Lab **Keeping Warm**

118 ◆ **B**

Bird Watch

One of the best ways to learn about animals is to watch them in action. In this project, you'll watch birds and other animals that visit a bird feeder. You may be surprised at how much you will discover. How do birds eat? Which ones eat first? How do different birds interact? What happens if a squirrel arrives on the scene? Careful observation and record keeping will reveal answers to these questions. They may also raise new questions for you to answer.

Your Goal To make detailed observations of the birds that appear at a bird feeder.

To complete this project successfully, you must
◆ observe the feeder regularly for at least two weeks, and identify the kinds of birds that visit the feeder
◆ make detailed observations of how the birds at your feeder eat
◆ describe the most common kinds of bird behavior
◆ follow the safety guidelines in Appendix A

Get Started Begin by meeting with some classmates to share your knowledge about the birds in your area. What kinds of birds can you expect to see? What types of foods do birds eat? Brainstorm how you could find out more about the birds that live in your area.

Check Your Progress You'll be working on this project as you study this chapter. To keep your project on track, look for Check Your Progress boxes at the following points.
Section 1 Review, page 129: Identify birds (and mammals) that come to the feeder. Observe how the animals interact.
Section 2 Review, page 132: Observe how birds feed.
Section 4 Review, page 146: Interpret your bird-feeding data, and prepare your graphs.

Wrap Up At the end of this chapter (page 149), you will share what you have learned about birds and their behavior.

This broad-tailed hummingbird enjoys a sip of nectar from a beardtongue flower.

SECTION 1 Birds

DISCOVER •••••••••••••••••••••••••••••••••••ACTIVITY••••

What Are Feathers Like?

1.  Examine a feather. Observe its overall shape and structure. Use a hand lens to examine the many hairlike barbs that project out from the feather's central shaft.

2. With your fingertip, gently stroke the feather from bottom to top. Observe whether the barbs stick together or separate.

3. Gently separate two barbs in the middle of the feather. Rub the separated edges with your fingertip.

4. Use a hand lens to examine the feather, including the edges of the two separated barbs. Draw a diagram of what you observe.

5. Now rejoin the two separated barbs by gently pulling outward from the shaft. Then wash your hands.

Think It Over

Observing Once barbs have been separated, is it easy to rejoin them? How might this be an advantage to the bird?

GUIDE FOR READING

◆ **What characteristics do birds have in common?**

◆ **How are birds adapted to their environments?**

Reading Tip Before you read, look at *Exploring a Bird* on page 123 and make a list of unfamiliar terms. As you read, write definitions for the terms.

One day in 1861, in a limestone quarry in what is now Germany, Hermann von Meyer was inspecting rocks. Meyer, who was a fossil hunter, spotted something dark in one of the rocks. It was the blackened fossil imprint of a feather! Excited, Meyer began searching for a fossil of an entire bird. Though it took a month, he eventually found what he was looking for—a skeleton surrounded by the clear imprint of many feathers. The fossil was given the scientific name *Archaeopteryx* (ahr kee AHP tur iks), meaning "ancient, winged thing."

Paleontologists estimate that *Archaeopteryx* lived about 145 million years ago. *Archaeopteryx* didn't look much like the birds you know. It looked more like a reptile with wings. While no modern bird has any teeth, *Archaeopteryx* had a mouthful of them. No modern bird has a long, bony tail, either, but *Archaeopteryx* did. However, unlike any reptile, extinct or modern, *Archaeopteryx* had feathers— its wings and tail were covered with them. Paleontologists think that *Archaeopteryx* and today's birds descended from some kind of reptile, possibly from a dinosaur.

Figure 1 The extinct bird *Archaeopteryx* may have looked like this.

Figure 2 John James Audubon painted this little blue heron in 1832.
(© Collection of the New York Historical Society)

What Is a Bird?

Modern **birds** all share certain characteristics. **A bird is an endothermic vertebrate that has feathers and a four-chambered heart, and lays eggs.** Birds have scales on their feet and legs, evidence of their descent from reptiles. In addition, most birds can fly.

The flight of birds is an amazing feat that people watch with delight and envy. All modern birds—including ostriches, penguins, and other flightless birds—evolved from ancestors that could fly.

The bodies of birds are adapted for flight. For example, the bones of a bird's forelimbs form wings. In addition, many of a bird's bones are nearly hollow, making the bird's body extremely lightweight. Flying birds have large chest muscles that move the wings. Finally, feathers are a major adaptation that help birds fly.

☑ *Checkpoint* *List four ways in which birds are adapted for flight.*

Feathers

The rule is this: If it has feathers, it's a bird. Feathers probably evolved from reptiles' scales. Both feathers and reptile scales are made of the same tough material as your fingernails.

Birds have different types of feathers. If you've ever picked up a feather from the ground, chances are good that it was a contour feather. A **contour feather** is one of the large feathers that give shape to a bird's body. The long contour feathers that extend beyond the body on the wings and tail are called flight feathers. When a bird flies, these feathers help it balance and steer.

In Figure 3, you can see that a contour feather consists of a central shaft and many hairlike projections, called barbs, that are arranged parallel to each other. If you examined a contour feather in the Discover activity, you know that you can "unzip" its flat surface by pulling apart the barbs. When birds fly, their feathers sometimes become "unzipped." To keep their flight feathers in good condition, birds often pull the feathers through their bills in an action called preening. Preening "zips" the barbs back together again, smoothing the ruffled feathers.

INTEGRATING PHYSICS In addition to contour feathers, birds have short, fluffy **down feathers** that are specialized to trap heat and keep the bird warm. Down feathers are found right next to a bird's skin, at the base of contour feathers. Down feathers are soft and flexible, unlike contour feathers. Down feathers mingle and overlap, trapping air. Air is a good **insulator**—a material that does not conduct heat well and therefore helps prevent it from escaping. By trapping a blanket of warm air next to the bird's skin, down feathers slow the rate at which the skin loses heat. In effect, down feathers cover a bird in lightweight long underwear.

☑ *Checkpoint* *Why do you think quilts and jackets are often stuffed with down feathers?*

Food and Body Temperature

Birds have no teeth. To capture, grip, and handle food, birds primarily use their bills. Each species of bird has a bill shaped to help it feed quickly and efficiently. For example, the pointy, curved bill of a hawk acts like a meathook. A hawk holds its prey with its claws and uses its sharp bill to pull off bits of flesh. In contrast, the straight, sharp bill of a woodpecker is a tool for chipping into wood. When a woodpecker chisels a hole in a tree and finds a tasty insect, the woodpecker spears the insect with its long, barbed tongue.

After a bird eats its food, digestion begins. Each organ in a bird's digestive system is adapted to process food. Many birds have an internal storage tank, or **crop,** that allows them to store food inside the body after swallowing it. Find the crop in *Exploring a Bird,* and notice that it is connected to the stomach.

Figure 3 Birds are the only animals that have feathers. **A.** Down feathers act as insulation to trap warmth next to a bird's body. **B.** Contour feathers, like this one from a Steller's jay, give a bird its shape and help it to fly. *Observing Where do you see down feathers and contour feathers on the family of Emperor geese above?*

The first part of the stomach is long and has thin walls. Here food is bathed in chemicals that begin to break it down. Then the partially digested food moves to a thick-walled, muscular part of the stomach called the **gizzard,** which squeezes and grinds the partially digested food. Remember that birds do not have teeth—their gizzard performs the grinding function of teeth. The gizzard may contain small stones that the bird has swallowed. These stones help with the grinding by rubbing against the food and crushing it.

EXPLORING *a Bird*

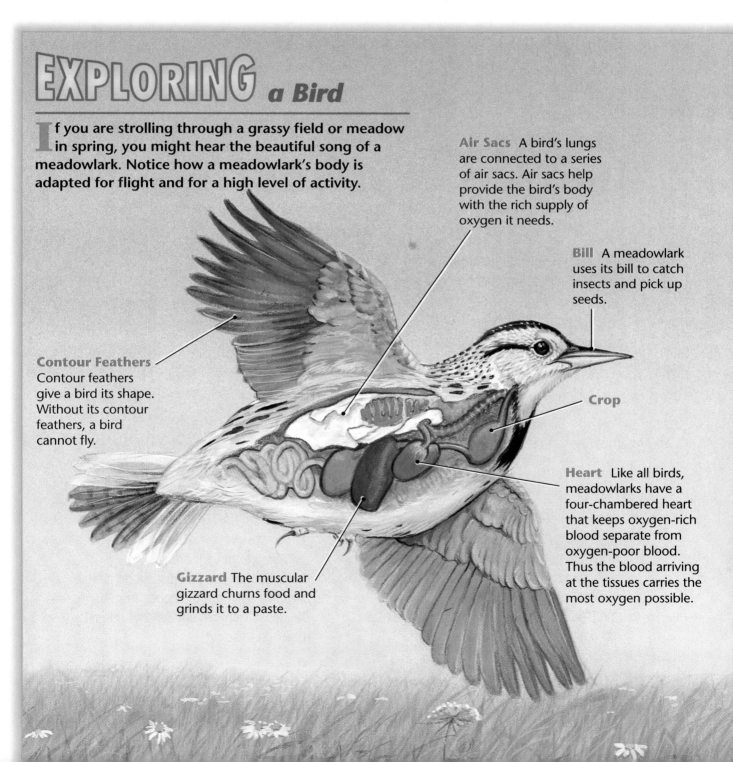

If you are strolling through a grassy field or meadow in spring, you might hear the beautiful song of a meadowlark. Notice how a meadowlark's body is adapted for flight and for a high level of activity.

Air Sacs A bird's lungs are connected to a series of air sacs. Air sacs help provide the bird's body with the rich supply of oxygen it needs.

Bill A meadowlark uses its bill to catch insects and pick up seeds.

Contour Feathers Contour feathers give a bird its shape. Without its contour feathers, a bird cannot fly.

Crop

Heart Like all birds, meadowlarks have a four-chambered heart that keeps oxygen-rich blood separate from oxygen-poor blood. Thus the blood arriving at the tissues carries the most oxygen possible.

Gizzard The muscular gizzard churns food and grinds it to a paste.

Like all animals, birds use the food they eat for energy. Because birds are endotherms, they need a lot of energy to maintain their body temperature. It also takes an enormous amount of energy to power the muscles used in flight. Each day an average bird eats food equal to about a quarter of its body weight. When people say, "You're eating like a bird," they usually mean that you're eating very little. But if you were actually eating as a bird does, you would be eating huge meals. You might eat 100 hamburger patties in one day!

Drawing Conclusions

LOOKING AT AN OWL'S LEFTOVERS

I n this lab, you will gather evidence and draw conclusions about an owl's diet.

Problem

What can you learn about owls' diets from studying the pellets that they cough up?

Materials

owl pellet   hand lens   dissecting needle
metric ruler   forceps

Procedure

1. An owl pellet is a collection of undigested materials that an owl coughs up after a meal. Write a hypothesis describing what items you expect an owl pellet to contain. List the reasons for your hypothesis.
2. Use a hand lens to observe the outside of an owl pellet. Record your observations.

3. Use one hand to grasp the owl pellet with forceps. Hold a dissecting needle in your other hand, and use it to gently separate the pellet into pieces. **CAUTION:** *Dissecting needles are sharp. Never cut material toward you; always cut away from your body.*
4. Using the forceps and dissecting needle, carefully separate the bones from the rest of the pellet. Remove any fur that might be attached to bones.

Delivering Oxygen to Cells

Cells must receive plenty of oxygen to release the energy contained in food. Flying requires much energy. Therefore, birds need a highly efficient way to get oxygen into their body and to their cells. Birds have a system of air sacs in their body that connects to the lungs. The air sacs enable birds to extract much more oxygen from each breath of air than other animals can.

The circulatory system of a bird is also efficient at getting oxygen to the cells. Unlike amphibians and most reptiles,

Shrew	House mouse	Meadow vole	Mole	Rat

Upper jaw has at least 18 teeth; teeth are brown. Skull length is 23 mm or less.	Upper jaw has 2 biting teeth and extends past lower jaw. Skull length is 22 mm or less.	Upper jaw has 2 biting teeth that are smooth, not grooved. Skull length is more than 23 mm.	Upper jaw has at least 18 teeth. Skull length is 23 mm or more.	Upper jaw has 2 biting teeth. Upper jaw extends past lower jaw. Skull length is 22 mm or more.

5. Group similar bones together in separate piles. Observe the skulls, and draw them. Record the number of skulls, their length, and the number, shape, and color of the teeth.

6. Use the chart on this page to determine what kinds of skulls you found. If any skulls do not match the chart exactly, record which animal the skulls resemble most.

7. Try to fit together any of the remaining bones to form complete or partial skeletons. Sketch your results.

8. Wash your hands thoroughly with soap when you are finished.

Analyze and Conclude

1. How many animals' remains were in the pellet? What data led you to that conclusion?

2. Combine your results with those of your classmates. Which three animals were eaten most frequently? How do these results compare to your hypothesis?

3. Owls cough up about two pellets a day. Based on your class's data, what can you conclude about the number of animals an owl might eat in one month?

4. **Think About It** In this lab, you were able to examine only the part of the owl's diet that it did not digest. How might this fact affect your confidence in the conclusions you reached?

More to Explore

Design a study that might tell you how an owl's diet varies at different times of the year. Give an example of a conclusion you might expect to draw from such a study.

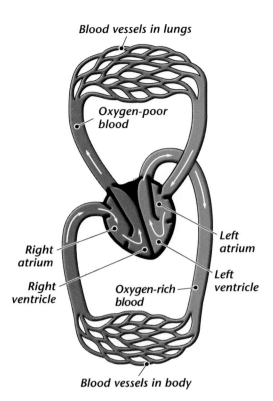

Blood vessels in lungs

Oxygen-poor blood

Right atrium

Right ventricle

Oxygen-rich blood

Left atrium

Left ventricle

Blood vessels in body

Figure 4 Birds have hearts with four chambers. Notice how the left side of the heart is completely separate from the right side. This separation prevents oxygen-rich blood from mixing with oxygen-poor blood. *Comparing and Contrasting* Contrast a bird's circulatory system with that of an amphibian, as shown on page 96, Figure 13. How do the circulatory systems differ?

whose hearts have three chambers, birds have hearts with four chambers—two atria and two ventricles. Trace the path of blood through a bird's two-loop circulatory system in Figure 4. The right side of a bird's heart pumps blood to the lungs, where the blood picks up oxygen. Oxygen-rich blood then returns to the left side of the heart, which pumps it to the rest of the body. The advantage of a four-chambered heart is that there is no mixing of oxygen-rich and oxygen-poor blood. Therefore, blood that arrives in the body's tissues has plenty of oxygen.

Nervous System and Senses

In order to fly, birds must have very quick reactions. To appreciate why, imagine how quickly you would have to react if you were a sparrow trying to land safely on a tree branch. You approach the tree headfirst, diving into a maze of tree branches. As you approach, you only have an instant to find a place where you can land safely and avoid crashing into those branches. If birds had slow reactions, they would not live very long.

A bird can react so quickly because of its well-developed brain and finely-tuned senses of sight and hearing. The brain of a bird controls such complex activities as flying, singing, and finding food. Most birds have keener eyesight than humans. A flying vulture, for example, can spot food on the ground from a height of more than one and a half kilometers. Some birds have excellent hearing, too. How could keen hearing help an owl search for prey in a dark forest?

Reproducing and Caring for Young

Like reptiles, birds have internal fertilization and lay eggs. Bird eggs are similar to reptile eggs, except that their shells are harder. In most bird species, the female lays the eggs in a nest that has been prepared by one or both parents.

Bird eggs will only develop at a temperature close to the body temperature of the parent bird. A parent bird usually incubates the eggs by sitting on them to keep them warm. In some species, incubating the eggs is the job of one parent. Female robins, for example, incubate their delicate blue eggs. In other species, such as pigeons, the parents take turns incubating the eggs.

Birds differ in the length of time that it takes for their chicks to develop until hatching. Sparrow eggs take only about 12 days. Chicken eggs take about 21 days, and albatross eggs take about 80 days. In general, the larger the bird species, the longer its incubation time.

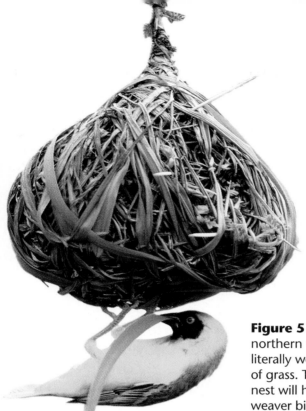

Figure 5 This masked northern weaver bird is literally weaving a nest out of grass. The finished baglike nest will have only a small, weaver bird-sized hole in it. The small entrance helps keep the eggs and young safe from predators.

Eggs-amination

Like reptile eggs, bird eggs protect the developing embryo, provide food for it, and keep it from drying out.

ACTIVITY

1. Look at the surface of a chicken egg with a hand lens. Then gently crack the egg into a bowl. Do not break the yolk.

2. Note the membrane attached to the inside of the shell. Then look at the blunt end of the egg. What do you see?

3. Fill one part of the eggshell with water. What do you observe?

4. Find the egg yolk. What is its function?

5. Look for a small white spot on the yolk. This marks the spot where the embryo would have developed if the egg had been fertilized.

6. Wash your hands with soap.

Observing Draw a labeled diagram of the egg that names each structure and describes its function.

When it is ready to hatch, a chick pecks its way out of the eggshell. Some newly hatched chicks, such as bluebirds and robins, are featherless, blind, and so weak they can barely lift their heads to beg for food. Other chicks, such as ducks, chickens, and pheasants, are covered with down and can run about soon after they have hatched. Most parent birds feed and protect their young at least until they are able to fly.

✓ *Checkpoint* *How do bird eggs differ from reptile eggs?*

Diversity of Birds

With almost 10,000 species, birds are the most diverse land-dwelling vertebrates. **In addition to adaptations for flight, birds have adaptations—such as the shapes of their legs, claws, and bills—for living in widely diverse environments.** For example, the long legs and toes of wading birds, such as herons and cranes, make wading easy, while the toes of perching birds, such as goldfinches and mockingbirds, can automatically lock onto a branch or other perch. The bills of ducks enable them to filter tiny plants and animals from water. Birds also have adaptations for flying, finding mates, and caring for their young. You can see a variety of bird adaptations in *Exploring Birds* on the next page.

EXPLORING Birds

Every bird has adaptations that help it live in its environment. Note how the bill and feet of each of these birds are adapted to help the bird survive.

▲ **Bee-Eaters**
This rainbow bee-eater feeds on bees and other insects, which it catches as it flies. Bee-eaters, which are found in Africa, Europe, Australia, and Asia, help control insect pests such as locusts.

▲ **Long-Legged Waders**
The roseate spoonbill is found in the southern United States and throughout much of South America. The spoonbill catches small animals by sweeping its long, flattened bill back and forth underwater.

▲ **Woodpeckers**
The pileated woodpecker is the largest woodpecker in North America—adults average about 44 centimeters in length. This woodpecker feeds on insects it finds in holes it has chiseled into trees.

Ostriches
The ostrich, found in Africa, is the largest living bird. It cannot fly, but it can run at speeds greater than 60 kilometers per hour. Its speed helps it escape from predators. ▼

Birds of Prey
The American kestrel, a small falcon, catches its food by hovering in the air and scanning the ground. When it sees prey, such as an insect, the kestrel swoops down and grabs it. Kestrels are found worldwide.
▼

◄ **Owls**
Owls are predators that hunt mostly at night. Sharp vision and keen hearing help owls find prey in the darkness. Razor-sharp claws and great strength allow larger owls, like this eagle owl, to prey on animals as large as deer.

▲ **Perching Birds**
There are over 5,000 species of perching birds. They represent more than half of all the bird species in the world. The painted bunting, a seed-eating bird, lives in the southern United States and northern Mexico.

Why Birds Are Important

A walk through the woods or a park would be dull without birds. You wouldn't hear their musical songs, and you wouldn't see them flitting gracefully from tree to tree. But people benefit from birds in practical ways, too. Birds and their eggs provide food, while feathers are used to stuff pillows and clothing.

 INTEGRATING ENVIRONMENTAL SCIENCE Birds also play an important role in the environment. Nectar-eating birds, like hummingbirds, carry pollen from one flower to another, thus enabling some flowers to reproduce. Seed-eating birds, like painted buntings, carry the seeds of plants to new places. This happens when the birds eat the fruits or seeds of a plant, fly to a new location, and then eliminate some of the seeds in digestive wastes. In addition, birds are some of the chief predators of pest animals. Hawks and owls eat many rats and mice, while many perching birds feed on insect pests.

Section 1 Review

1. What characteristics do modern birds share with reptiles? How are birds different from reptiles?
2. Choose two different bird species and describe how they are adapted to obtain food in their environment.
3. Predict how the size of crop harvests might be affected if all birds disappeared from Earth.
4. **Thinking Critically** **Comparing and Contrasting** Compare contour feathers with down feathers, noting both similarities and differences.

Check Your Progress

CHAPTER PROJECT 4

By now you should have set up your bird feeder. As you begin making observations, use a field guide to identify the species of birds. Count and record the number of each species that appears. Also observe the birds' behaviors. How long do birds stay at the feeder? How do birds respond to other birds and mammals? Look for signs that some birds are trying to dominate others.

SECTION 2 The Physics of Bird Flight

What Lifts Airplanes and Birds Into the Air?

1. Cut a strip of notebook paper 5 centimeters wide and 28 centimeters long. Insert about 5 centimeters of the paper strip into the middle of a book. The rest of the paper strip should hang over the edge.

2. Hold the book up so that the paper is below your mouth.

3. Blow gently across the top of the paper and watch what happens to the paper. Then blow harder.

Think It Over
Predicting If a strong current of air flowed across the top of a bird's outstretched wing, what might happen to the bird?

GUIDE FOR READING

◆ How is a bird able to fly?

Reading Tip Before you read, look at Figure 6 on page 131. Then predict how a bird's wing is similar to that of an airplane.

From ancient times, people have dreamed of soaring into the air like birds. When people first started experimenting with flying machines, they tried to glue feathers to their arms or to strap on feathered wings. Many failures, crash-landings, and broken bones later, these people had learned that feathers by themselves weren't the secret of flight. If an object is to fly, it must be lightweight. Another key to flying—for birds and insects as well as for airplanes—lies in the shape of wings and the way in which air moves across them.

How Air Moves Across a Wing

All objects on land are surrounded by an invisible ocean of air. Air is a mixture of gas molecules that exert pressure on the objects they surround. You see the results of air pressure when

▼ Owl in flight

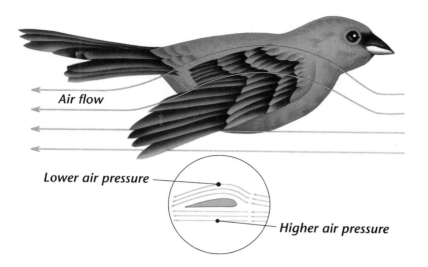

Figure 6 Air moves faster across a wing's upper surface than across its lower surface. The fast-moving air exerts less pressure than the slow-moving air. *Relating Cause and Effect* How does this difference in pressure help a bird to fly?

Air flow

Lower air pressure

Higher air pressure

you blow up a balloon. The pressure of the air molecules pushing on the sides of the balloon makes the balloon expand.

Moving air exerts less pressure than air that is not moving. The faster air moves, the less pressure it exerts. In the Discover activity, the air blowing across the top of the paper was in motion. The moving air above the paper exerted less pressure than the air beneath it, so the paper rose.

Like the paper, a wing is surrounded by air molecules that exert pressure on the wing's surfaces. The lower surface of a wing—whether it belongs to a bird, an insect, or an airplane—is flatter than the upper surface. This difference between the shapes of the upper and lower surfaces of a wing helps birds, insects, and airplanes to fly. In Figure 6, you can see that the curved upper surface of a wing is a little longer than the flatter lower surface. When the wing moves forward, air travels the longer distance over the upper wing in the same amount of time as it takes to travel the shorter distance beneath the wing. Therefore, the air moves faster over the upper surface.

Because fast-moving air exerts less pressure than air that is moving slowly, the air above the wing exerts less pressure than the air beneath the wing. **The difference in pressure above and below the bird's wing produces an upward force that causes the wing to rise.** That upward force is called **lift**.

☑ *Checkpoint* *How is the air pressure above a moving wing different from the air pressure below the wing?*

Birds in Flight

Wing shape alone does not enable a bird to fly—it must have some way of getting off the ground. To do this, a bird pushes off with its legs. The bird must also move forward, since lift depends

TRY THIS

It's Plane to See

Use this activity to **ACTIVITY** discover how wing shape is important for flight.

1. Work with a partner to design a paper airplane with wings shaped like those of a bird. You can use any of these materials: paper, tape, glue, paper clips, string, rubber bands, and staples. Draw a sketch of your design.

2. Construct your "birdplane" and make one or two trial flights. If necessary, modify your design and try again.

3. Compare your design with those of other groups. Which designs were most successful?

Making Models In what ways was the flight of your airplane like the flight of a bird? In what ways was it different?

on air moving over its wings. So, at the same time that the bird pushes off from the ground, it sharply pulls its wings down. This downstroke provides the power that pushes the bird forward and upward.

Once they are in the air, birds fly in a variety of ways. All birds flap their wings at least part of the time. Flapping requires a lot of energy. Most small birds, such as sparrows, depend heavily on flapping flight. Canada geese and many other birds that travel long distances also use flapping flight.

Unlike flapping flight, soaring and gliding flight involve little wing movement. Birds soar and glide with their wings extended, as shown in Figure 7. When soaring, birds rise up into the sky on currents of warm air. In contrast, when gliding, birds coast downward through the air. Because they require less wing movement, soaring and gliding use less energy than flapping.

Sometimes birds fly with a combination of soaring and gliding. They "take the elevator up" by flying into a current of warm, rising air. The birds stretch their wings out and circle round and round within the column of rising air. High in the atmosphere the column of warm air grows cooler and ceases to rise. At this point the soaring bird "gets off the elevator" and begins gliding downward until it reaches the next "up elevator" of rising air. Predatory birds that spot their food from the air, such as hawks, often soar and glide.

The peregrine falcon, a predatory bird, is one of the fastest fliers. It catches its prey—often other birds such as pigeons—in flight. When it is pursuing prey, a peregrine's speed may reach 300 kilometers per hour. But it is not always useful for birds to fly fast. Birds that are migrating, or traveling long distances, take it slow but steady, usually flying 30 to 70 kilometers per hour. You will learn more about bird migrations in Chapter 5.

Figure 7 As it glides above the ocean's surface, this gannet searches for a school of mackerel or herring. When its search is successful, it will dive into the water to claim its catch.

Section 2 Review

1. How is lift related to air pressure?
2. Explain how a bird takes off from the ground and begins to fly.
3. Compare and contrast flapping flight, soaring, and gliding.
4. **Thinking Critically Relating Cause and Effect** If a bird loses too many contour feathers, it can no longer fly. Relate this to the feathers' role in giving shape to a bird's wing.

Check Your Progress

CHAPTER PROJECT 4

As you continue your bird-feeder observations, pay careful attention to the way in which two or three different kinds of birds feed. Note the shapes of their beaks and how they use their beaks to pick up and crack seeds. Note how each bird's head moves during feeding. Also note whether certain birds prefer particular kinds of seeds. Write your detailed observations in your notebook.

DISCOVER ....ACTIVITY..

What Are Mammals' Teeth Like?

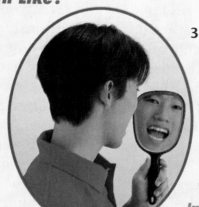

1. 🖐 Wash your hands before you begin. Then, with a small mirror, examine the shapes of your teeth. Observe the incisors (the front teeth); the pointed canine teeth; the premolars that follow the canine teeth; and the molars, which are the large teeth in the rear of your jaws.

2. Compare and contrast the structures of the different kinds of teeth.

3. Use your tongue to feel the cutting surfaces of the different kinds of teeth in your mouth.

4. Bite off a piece of cracker and chew it. Observe the teeth that you use to bite and chew. Wash your hands when you are finished.

Think It Over

Inferring What is the advantage of having teeth with different shapes?

High in the Himalaya Mountains of Tibet, several yaks inch their way, single file, along a narrow cliff path. The cliff plunges thousands of meters to the valley below, so one false step can mean disaster. But the sure-footed yaks, carrying heavy loads of grain, slowly but steadily cross the cliff and make their way through the mountains.

Yaks, which are related to cows, have large lungs and a complex system of chest muscles that enables them to breathe deeply and rapidly. These structures allow yaks to obtain the oxygen necessary to survive at high altitudes. People who live in the mountains of central Asia have depended on yaks for thousands of years. Not only do yaks carry materials for trade, they also pull plows and provide milk. Mountain villagers weave blankets from yak hair and make shoes and ropes from yak hides.

The yak is a member of the group of vertebrates called **mammals,** a diverse group that share many characteristics. **All mammals are endothermic vertebrates with a four-chambered heart, and skin covered with fur or hair. The young of most mammals are born alive, and every young mammal is fed with milk produced in its mother's body.** In addition, mammals have teeth of different shapes that are adapted to their diets.

GUIDE FOR READING

◆ What characteristics do all mammals share?

Reading Tip As you read this section, write one or two sentences summarizing the information under each heading.

▼ Himalayan yak

Today there are about 6,000 different species of mammals. There are mammals that you may never have seen, such as kangaroos and wildebeests, as well as familiar mammals such as dogs, cats, bats, and mice.

Mammals First Appear

Two hundred and seventy million years ago, before dinosaurs appeared, and long before birds appeared, there was a group of animals that had a blend of reptilian and mammalian characteristics. They were more like reptiles than mammals, but they resembled mammals in some ways, such as in the shapes of their teeth. These mammal-like reptiles, which became extinct about 160 million years ago, were the ancestors of the true mammals.

The earliest mammals were small, mouse-sized animals that lived in habitats dominated by dinosaurs. These early mammals may have been nocturnal, or active mainly at night, presumably the time when the dinosaurs were inactive or asleep. It was only after the dinosaurs disappeared, about 65 million years ago, that large mammals first evolved.

Most mammals, such as kangaroos and giraffes, became specialized to live on land. Other mammals, such as dolphins, became adapted to life in Earth's waters, while still others, the bats, became adapted to flight.

Fur and Hair

All mammals have fur or hair at some point in their lives. Like a bird's down feathers, thick fur provides lightweight insulation

Figure 8 The amount of fur or hair covering a mammal's body varies greatly. **A.** Hippopotamuses live in hot regions such as Africa year-round and have little hair. **B.** Gray wolves live in the northern half of North America and have thick fur coats during the cold winter months. During the summer, however, their coats are thinner. *Comparing and Contrasting Compare the function of a mammal's fur or hair to that of down feathers.*

that prevents body heat from escaping. Fur and hair help mammals maintain a stable body temperature in cold weather. Each strand of hair or fur is composed of dead cells strengthened with the same tough material that strengthens feathers. Hair grows from living cells located below the surface of the skin.

The amount of hair that covers the skin of a mammal varies a great deal from group to group. Some mammals, such as whales and manatees, have only a few bristles. Others, including dogs and weasels, have thick, short fur. The fur of sea otters is thickest of all—on some areas of its body, a sea otter can have 150,000 hairs per square centimeter! Human bodies are covered with hair, but in places the hairs are spaced widely apart.

In general, animals that live in cold regions have thicker coats of fur than animals in warmer environments, as you can see by contrasting the hippopotamus and wolf in Figure 8. Mammals such as wolves and rabbits that live in places where cold and warm seasons alternate usually grow thicker coats in winter than in summer.

Fur is not the only adaptation that allows mammals to live in cold climates. Mammals also have a layer of fat beneath their skins. Fat, like fur and feathers, is an insulating material that keeps heat in the body. Recall that mammals are endotherms, which means that their bodies produce enough heat to maintain a stable body temperature regardless of the temperature of their environment.

☑ *Checkpoint* **What is the major function of fur or hair?**

Insulated Mammals

In this activity, you will discover whether or not fat is an effective insulator.

1. Put on a pair of rubber gloves.
2. Spread a thick coating of solid white shortening on the outside of one of the gloves. Leave the other glove uncoated.
3. Put both hands in a bucket or sink filled with cold water.

Inferring Which hand got cold faster? Explain how this activity relates to mammalian adaptations.

Teeth

Endotherms need a lot of energy to maintain their body temperature, and that energy comes from food. Mammals' teeth are adapted to chew their food, breaking it into small bits that make digestion easier. Unlike reptiles and fishes, whose teeth usually all have the same shape, most mammals have teeth with four different shapes. **Incisors** are flat-edged teeth used to bite off and cut parts of food. **Canines** are sharply pointed teeth that stab food and tear into it. **Premolars** and **molars** grind and shred food into tiny bits.

The size, shape, and hardness of a mammal's teeth reflect its diet. For example, the canines of carnivores are especially large and sharp. Large carnivores, such as lions and tigers, use their canines as meat hooks that securely hold the prey while the carnivore kills it. The molars of herbivores, such as deer and woodchucks, have upper surfaces that are broad and flat—ideal for grinding and mashing plants.

Figure 9 Lions have sharp, pointed teeth. Note the especially long canine teeth. *Inferring What kind of diet do lions eat?*

Getting Oxygen to Cells

To release energy, food molecules must combine with oxygen inside cells. Therefore, a mammal needs an efficient way to get oxygen into the body and to the cells that need it.

Like reptiles and birds, all mammals breathe with lungs—even mammals such as whales that live in the ocean. Mammals breathe in and out because of the combined action of rib muscles and a large muscle called the **diaphragm** located at the bottom of the chest. The lungs have a huge, moist surface area where oxygen can dissolve and then move into the bloodstream.

Like birds, mammals have a four-chambered heart and a two-loop circulation. One loop pumps oxygen-poor blood from the heart to the lungs and then back to the heart. The second loop pumps oxygen-rich blood from the heart to the tissues of the mammal's body, and then back to the heart.

Checkpoint *How do mammals take air into their bodies?*

Nervous System and Senses

The nervous system and senses of an animal receive information about its environment and coordinate the animal's movements. The brains of mammals enable them to learn, remember, and behave in complex ways. Squirrels, for example, feed on

nuts. In order to do this, they must crack the nutshell to get to the meat inside. Squirrels learn to use different methods to crack different kinds of nuts, depending on where the weak points in each kind of shell are located.

The senses of mammals are highly developed and adapted for the ways that individual species live. Tarsiers, which are active at night, have huge eyes that enable them to see in the dark. Humans, monkeys, gorillas, and chimpanzees are able to see objects in color. This ability is extremely useful because these mammals are most active during the day when colors are visible.

Most mammals hear well. Bats even use their sense of hearing to navigate. Bats make high-pitched squeaks that bounce off objects. The echoes give bats information about the shapes of objects around them and about how far away the objects are. Bats use their hearing to fly at night and to capture flying insects.

Most mammals have highly developed senses of smell. Many mammals, including dogs and cats, use smell to track their prey. By detecting the scent of an approaching predator, antelopes use their sense of smell to protect themselves.

Movement

One function of a mammal's nervous system is to direct and coordinate complex movement. No other group of vertebrates can move in as many different ways as mammals can. Like most mammals, camels and leopards have four limbs and can walk and run. Other four-limbed mammals have specialized ways of moving. For example, kangaroos hop, gibbons swing by their arms from branch to branch, and flying squirrels glide down from high perches. Moles use their powerful front limbs to burrow through the soil. Bats, in contrast, are adapted to fly through the air—their front limbs are wings. Whales, dolphins, and other sea mammals have no hind limbs—their front limbs are flippers adapted for swimming in water.

Sharpen your Skills

Classifying

Unlike humans, birds and bats both fly. Does this mean that bats are more closely related to birds than to humans? Use the diagrams below to find out. The diagrams show the front-limb bones of a bird, a bat, and a human. Examine them carefully, noting similarities and differences. Then decide which two animals are more closely related. Give evidence to support your classification.

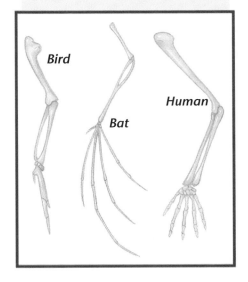

Figure 10 Mammals, like these springboks, have large brains. A springbok's brain processes complex information about its environment and then quickly decides on an appropriate action.

Reproducing and Caring for Young

Like reptiles and birds, mammals have internal fertilization. Although a few kinds of mammals lay shelled eggs, the young of most mammals develop within their mothers' bodies and are never enclosed in an eggshell. All mammals, even those that lay eggs, feed their young with milk produced in **mammary glands**. In fact, the word *mammal* comes from the term *mammary*.

Young mammals are usually quite helpless for a long time after being born. Many are born without a coat of insulating fur. Their eyes are often sealed and may not open for weeks. For example, black bear cubs are surprisingly tiny when they are born. The blind, nearly hairless cubs have a mass of only 240 to 330 grams—about as small as a grapefruit. The mass of an adult black bear, in contrast, ranges from about 120 to 150 kilograms—about 500 times as large as a newborn cub!

Young mammals usually stay with their mother or both parents for an extended time. After black bear cubs learn to walk, they follow their mother about for the next year, learning how to be a bear. They learn things that are important to their survival, such as which mushrooms and berries are good to eat and how to rip apart a rotten log and find good-tasting grubs within it. During the winter, when black bears go through a period of inactivity, the young bears stay with their mother. The following spring, she will usually force them to live independently.

Figure 11 This young giraffe is feeding on milk produced by its mother, as do all young mammals.

Section 3 Review

1. List five characteristics that all mammals share.
2. Name three ways in which mammals are similar to birds. Then list three ways in which they are different.
3. Relate the shape of any mammal's teeth to its diet.
4. Explain how a keen sense of hearing is an advantage to a bat.
5. **Thinking Critically Making Generalizations** What characteristics enable mammals to live in colder environments than reptiles can?

Science at Home

With a family member, examine the nutrition facts listed on a container of whole milk. What types of nutrients does whole milk contain? Discuss why milk is an ideal source of food for young, growing mammals.

KEEPING WARM

ny time you wear a sweater or socks made of wool, you are using a mammalian adaptation to keep yourself warm. Suppose a manufacturer claims that its wool socks keep your feet as warm when the socks are wet as when they are dry. In this investigation, you will test that claim.

Problem

Do wool products provide insulation from the cold? How well does wool insulate when it is wet?

Skills Focus

controlling variables, interpreting data

Materials

tap water, hot
beaker, 1 L
clock or watch
a pair of wool socks
tap water, room temperature
3 containers, 250 mL, with lids

scissors
3 thermometers
graph paper

Procedure

1. Put one container into a dry woolen sock. Soak a second sock with water at room temperature, wring it out so it's not dripping, and then slide the second container into the wet sock. Both containers should stand upright. Leave the third container uncovered.
2. Create a data table in your notebook, listing the containers in the first column. Provide four more columns in which to record the water temperatures during the experiment.

3. Use scissors to carefully cut a small "X" in the center of each lid. Make the X just large enough for a thermometer to pass through.
4. Fill a beaker with about 800 mL of hot tap water. Then pour hot water nearly to the top of each of the three containers. **CAUTION:** *Avoid spilling hot water on yourself or others.*
5. Place a lid on each of the containers, and insert a thermometer into the water through the hole in each lid. Gather the socks around the thermometers above the first two containers so that the containers are completely covered.
6. Immediately measure the temperature of the water in each container, and record it in your data table. Take temperature readings every 5 minutes for at least 15 minutes.

Analyze and Conclude

1. Graph your results using a different color to represent each container. Graph time in minutes on the horizontal axis and temperature on the vertical axis.
2. Compare the temperature changes in the three containers. Relate your findings to the insulation characteristics of mammal skin coverings.
3. **Apply** Suppose an ad for wool gloves claims that the gloves keep you warm even if they get wet. Do your findings support this claim? Why or why not?

Design an Experiment

Design an experiment to compare how wool's insulating properties compare with those of other natural materials (such as cotton) or manufactured materials (such as acrylic). Obtain your teacher's approval before conducting your experiment.

Animals and Medical Research

In laboratories around the world, scientists search for cures for cancer, AIDS, and other diseases. Scientists use millions of animals each year in research—mostly to test drugs and surgical procedures. Finding treatments could save millions of human lives. However, these experiments can hurt and even kill animals.

The Issues

Why Is Animal Testing Done? If you have ever used an antibiotic or other medicine, animal testing has helped you. The United States Food and Drug Administration requires that new medicines be tested on research animals before they can be used by humans. Through testing, researchers can learn whether a drug works and what doses are safe. Because of animal research, many serious diseases can now be treated or prevented. New treatments for AIDS, cancer, and Alzheimer's disease will also depend on animal testing.

Which Animals Are Used for Testing?
Most often mice, rats, and other small mammals are used. These animals reproduce rapidly, so scientists can study many generations in a year. Since apes and monkeys are similar to humans in many ways, they are often used to test new treatments for serious diseases. In other cases, researchers use animals that naturally get diseases common to humans. Cocker spaniels, for example, often develop glaucoma, an eye disease that can cause blindness. Surgeons may test new surgical treatments for the disease on cocker spaniels.

What Happens to Research Animals? In a typical laboratory experiment, a group of animals will first be infected with a disease. Then they will be given a drug to see if it can fight off the disease. In many cases, the animals suffer, and some die. Some people are concerned that laboratory animals do not receive proper care.

What Are the Alternatives? Other testing methods do exist. For example, in some cases, scientists can use computer models to test drugs or surgical treatments. Another testing method is to mix drugs with animal cells grown in petri dishes. Unfortunately, neither computer models nor cell experiments are as useful as tests on living animals.

You Decide

1. Identify the Problem
In a sentence, describe the controversy over using animals in medical research.

2. Analyze the Options
Review the different positions. Is animal testing acceptable? Is it acceptable for some animals but not for others? Is animal research never acceptable? List the benefits and drawbacks of each option.

3. Find a Solution
Suppose you are a scientist who has found a possible cure for a type of cancer. The drug needs to be tested on research animals first, but you know that testing could harm the animals. What would you do? Support your opinion with sound reasons.

SECTION 4 Diversity of Mammals

DISCOVER .... ACTIVITY

How Is a Thumb Useful?

1. Tape the thumb of your writing hand to your palm so that you cannot move your thumb. The tape should keep your thumb from moving but allow your other fingers to move freely.

2. Pick up a pencil with the taped hand and try to write your name.

3. Keep the tape on for 5 minutes. During that time, try to use your taped hand to do such everyday activities as lifting a book, turning the pages, and untying and retying your shoes.

4. Remove the tape and repeat all the activities you tried to do when your thumb was taped. Observe the position and action of your thumb and other fingers as you perform each activity.

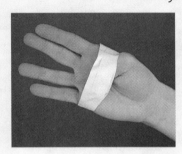

Think It Over
Inferring Humans, chimpanzees, and gorillas all have thumbs that can touch the other four fingers. What advantage does that kind of thumb give to the animal?

How is a koala similar to a panda? Both are furry, cuddly-looking mammals that eat leaves. How is a koala different from a panda? Surprisingly, koalas and pandas belong to very different groups of mammals—koalas are marsupials, and pandas are placental mammals. **Members of the three groups of mammals—monotremes, marsupials, and placental mammals—are classified on the basis of how their young develop.**

GUIDE FOR READING

◆ What characteristic is used to classify mammals into three groups?

Reading Tip As you read this section, write a definition in your own words for each new science term.

Giant panda (left) and koala (right)

Figure 12 The spiny anteater, left, and the duck-billed platypus, right, could share the "Weirdest Mammal" award. Both are monotremes, the only mammals whose young hatch from eggs.

Monotremes

If you held a "Weirdest Mammal in the World" contest, two main contenders would be spiny anteaters and duck-billed platypuses. There are two species of spiny anteaters and only one species of duck-billed platypus, all living in Australia and New Guinea. These are the only species of monotremes that are alive today. **Monotremes** are mammals that lay eggs.

Spiny Anteaters These monotremes look like pincushions with long noses. They have sharp spines scattered throughout their brown hair. As their name implies, spiny anteaters eat ants, which they dig up with their powerful claws.

A female spiny anteater lays one to three leathery-shelled eggs directly into the pouch on her belly. After the young hatch, still in the pouch, they drink milk that seeps out of pores on the mother's skin. They stay in the pouch until they are six to eight weeks old, when their spines start to irritate the mother anteater, and she scratches them out of her pouch.

Duck-billed Platypuses The duck-billed platypus has webbed feet and a bill, but it also has fur and feeds its young with milk. Platypuses, which live in the water, construct a maze of tunnels in muddy banks. The female lays her eggs in an underground nest. The eggs hatch about two weeks later. After they hatch, the tiny offspring feed by lapping at the milk that oozes onto the fur of their mother's belly.

Marsupials

Koalas, kangaroos, bandicoots, wallabies, and opossums are some of the better known marsupials. **Marsupials** are mammals whose young are born alive, but at an early stage of development, and they usually continue to develop in a pouch on their mother's body. Marsupials were once widespread, but today they are found mostly in South America, Australia, and New Guinea. Opossums are the only marsupials found in North America.

Marsupials have a very short **gestation period,** the length of time between fertilization and birth. Opossums, for example, have a gestation period of only about 13 days. Newborn marsupials are tiny—the newborns of one opossum species are only about 10 millimeters long! When they are born, marsupials are blind, hairless, and pink. They crawl along the wet fur of their mother's belly until they reach her pouch. Once inside, they find one of her nipples and attach to it. They remain in the pouch at least until they have grown enough to peer out of the pouch opening.

Figure 13 Gray kangaroos, above, and opossums, below, are marsupials, mammals whose young live for a time in the mother's pouch. *Classifying How do marsupials differ from monotremes?*

Kangaroos The largest marsupials are kangaroos, which are found in Australia and nearby islands. Some male kangaroos are over 2 meters tall—taller than most humans. Kangaroos have powerful hind legs for jumping and long tails that help them keep their balance. A female kangaroo gives birth to only one baby, called a joey, at a time. Kangaroos are herbivores, so they eat foods such as leaves and grasses.

Opossums The common opossum is an omnivore that comes out of its nest at dusk to search for fruits, plants, insects, or other small animals to eat. Opossums are good climbers. They can grasp branches with their long tails. If a predator attacks it, an opossum will often "play dead"—its body becomes limp, its mouth gapes open, and its tongue lolls out of its mouth. Female opossums may give birth to 21 young at a time, but most female opossums have only 13 nipples. The first 13 young opossums that get into the pouch and attach to nipples are the only ones that survive.

☑ *Checkpoint* **What do the young of marsupials do immediately after they are born?**

Placental Mammals

Unlike a monotreme or a marsupial, a **placental mammal** develops inside its mother's body until its body systems can function independently. In *Exploring Placental Mammals* on the next page, you can see some members of this group.

EXPLORING *Placental Mammals*

From tiny moles to huge elephants, placental mammals exhibit a great variety of size and body form. Note how each group is adapted for obtaining food or for living in a particular environment.

▲ Insect-eaters
Star-nosed moles and their relatives have sharp cutting surfaces on all of their teeth. Star-nosed moles spend much of their time in water searching for prey with their sensitive, tentacled snouts.

Flying Mammals ▲
Bats fly, but they are mammals, not birds. The wings of bats are made of a thin skin that stretches from their wrists to the tips of their long finger bones.

▲ Rabbits and Hares
Leaping mammals like this black-tailed jack rabbit have long hind legs specialized for spectacular jumps. Rabbits and hares have long, curved incisors for gnawing.

Rodents ▲
Rodents are gnawing mammals such as rats, beavers, squirrels, mice, and the North American porcupine shown here. Their teeth are adapted to grind down their food. The four incisors of most rodents keep growing throughout their lives but are constantly worn down by gnawing.

▲ Primates
This group of mammals with large brains includes humans, monkeys, and apes such as this chimpanzee. Many primates have opposable thumbs—thumbs that can touch the other four fingers. An opposable thumb makes the hand capable of complex movements, such as grasping and throwing.

▲ Hoofed Mammals

Mammals with hooves are divided into two groups—those with an even number of toes and those with an odd number of toes. Cows, deer, and pigs all have an even number of toes, while horses and zebras belong to the odd-numbered group.

▲ Toothless Mammals

Sloths, such as the one shown here, are toothless mammals, as are armadillos. Although a few members of this group have small teeth, most have none.

Carnivores ▶

This river otter belongs to the group known as carnivores, or meat eaters. Other mammals in this group include dogs, cats, raccoons, bears, weasels, and seals. Large canine teeth and toes with claws help carnivores catch and eat their prey.

Marine Mammals

Whales, manatees, and these Atlantic spotted dolphins are ocean-dwelling mammals that evolved from cowlike, land-dwelling ancestors. The bodies of marine mammals show no external trace of hind limbs, although hind limbs have been found in their fossilized ancestors. ▼

Mammals With Trunks ▲

Elephants' noses are long trunks that they use for collecting food and water.

Figure 14 Young mammals usually require much parental care. On a rocky slope in Alaska, this Dall's sheep, a placental mammal, keeps a close watch on her lamb.

The name of this group comes from the **placenta,** an organ in pregnant female mammals that passes materials between the mother and the developing embryo. Food and oxygen pass from the mother to her young through the placenta. Wastes pass from the young through the placenta to the mother, where they are eliminated by her body. The umbilical cord connects the young to the placenta. Most mammals, including humans, are placental mammals.

Placental mammals are classified into groups on the basis of characteristics such as how they eat and how their bodies are adapted for moving. For example, whales, dolphins, and porpoises all form one group of mammals that have adaptations for swimming. The mammals in the carnivore group, which includes cats, dogs, otters, and seals, are all predators that have enlarged canine teeth. Primates, which include monkeys, apes, and humans, all have large brains and eyes that face forward. In addition, the forelimbs of many primates have adaptations for grasping. For example, the human thumb can touch all four other fingers. As you learned if you did the Discover activity, it is difficult to grasp objects if you cannot use your thumb.

Placental mammals vary in the length of their gestation periods. Generally, the larger the placental mammal, the longer its gestation period. For example, African elephants are the largest land-dwelling placental mammals. The gestation period for an elephant averages about 21 months. A house mouse, on the other hand, gives birth after a gestation period of only about 20 days.

Section 4 Review

1. Explain the difference in the development of the young of monotremes, marsupials, and placental mammals.
2. What is the function of the placenta?
3. Describe the feeding adaptations of three groups of placental mammals.
4. **Thinking Critically** Inferring Many hoofed mammals feed in large groups, or herds. What advantage could this behavior have?

Check Your Progress

CHAPTER PROJECT
4

Continue to observe bird behavior at your bird feeder and record your observations in your notebook. Now is the time to plan your presentation. You may want to include the following information in your presentation: drawings of the different birds you observed, detailed descriptions of bird behaviors, and other interesting observations you made. (Hint: Prepare bar graphs to present numerical data, such as the number of times that different species visited the feeder.)

SECTION 1 Birds

Key Ideas

◆ Birds are endothermic vertebrates that have feathers and a four-chambered heart and lay eggs. Most birds can fly.

◆ Contour feathers give shape to a bird's body and aid in flight. Down feathers provide insulation.

◆ Birds care for their young by keeping the eggs warm until hatching and by protecting the young at least until they can fly.

◆ Birds have adaptations, such as the shapes of their toes and bills, for living and obtaining food in different environments.

Key Terms
bird
contour feather
down feather
insulator
crop
gizzard

SECTION 2 The Physics of Bird Flight

INTEGRATING PHYSICS

Key Ideas

◆ Air flowing over the curved upper surface of a moving wing exerts less downward pressure than the upward pressure from the air flowing beneath the wing. The difference in pressure produces lift that causes the wing to rise.

◆ Birds fly in three basic ways—flapping flight, soaring, and gliding. Flapping flight requires more energy than soaring or gliding.

Key Term
lift

SECTION 3 What Is a Mammal?

Key Ideas

◆ Mammals are vertebrates that are endothermic, have skin covered with hair or fur, feed their young with milk from the mother's mammary glands, and have teeth of different shapes adapted to their diets.

◆ A mammal's fur or hair provides insulation that helps reduce the loss of body heat.

◆ Mammals use a large muscle called the diaphragm to breathe in and out. Mammals have a four-chambered heart and a two-loop circulation.

Key Terms
mammal   incisors   canines
premolars   molars   diaphragm
mammary gland

SECTION 4 Diversity of Mammals

Key Ideas

◆ Mammals are classified into three groups on the basis of how their young develop. Monotremes lay eggs. Marsupials give birth to live young who continue to develop in the mother's pouch. The young of placental mammals develop more fully before birth than do the young of marsupials.

◆ Placental mammals are divided into groups on the basis of adaptations, such as those for feeding and moving.

Key Terms
monotreme
marsupial
gestation period
placental mammal
placenta

USING THE INTERNET

ACTIVITY

www.science-explorer.phschool.com

Reviewing Content

 For more review of key concepts, see the Interactive Student Tutorial CD-ROM.

Multiple Choice
Choose the letter of the best answer.

1. Which of these characteristics is found only in birds?
   a. scales
   b. wings
   c. feathers
   d. four-chambered heart
2. A four-chambered heart is an advantage because
   a. it keeps oxygen-rich and oxygen-poor blood separate.
   b. it allows oxygen-rich and oxygen-poor blood to mix.
   c. blood can move through it quickly.
   d. it slows the flow of blood.
3. What causes the lift that allows a bird's wing to rise?
   a. reduced air pressure beneath the wing
   b. reduced air pressure above the wing
   c. air that is not moving
   d. jet propulsion
4. Which muscle helps mammals move air into and out of their lungs?
   a. air muscle   b. diaphragm
   c. placenta   d. gestation
5. Kangaroos, koalas, and opossums are all
   a. monotremes.
   b. primates.
   c. marsupials.
   d. placental mammals.

True or False
If the statement is true, write true. If it is false, change the underlined word or words to make the statement true.

6. *Archaeopteryx* shows the link between birds and reptiles.
7. A bird's <u>gizzard</u> grinds food.
8. The <u>slower</u> air moves, the less pressure it exerts.
9. Fur and <u>down</u> feathers have a similar function.
10. <u>Marsupials</u> are mammals that lay eggs.

Checking Concepts

11. Explain how the skeleton of a bird is adapted for flight.
12. How is a bird's ability to fly related to the shape of its wings?
13. Explain how soaring birds like vultures use rising air currents in their flight.
14. Contrast the structure and function of incisors and molars.
15. Identify and explain two ways in which mammals are adapted to live in cold climates.
16. How is a mammal's ability to move a function of its nervous system?
17. What is one way in which the bodies of dolphins are different from those of land mammals?
18. **Writing to Learn** You are a documentary filmmaker preparing to make a short film about spiny anteaters. First, think of a title for the film. Then plan two scenes that you would include in the film and write the narrator's script. Your scenes should show what the animals look like and what they do.

Thinking Visually

19. **Compare/Contrast Table** The table below compares three groups of mammals. Copy the table onto a separate sheet of paper. Then complete it and add a title. (For more on compare/contrast tables, see the Skills Handbook.)

Characteristic	Monotremes	Marsupials	Placental Mammals
How Young Begin Life	a. ?	b. ?	c. ?
How Young Are Fed	milk from pores or slits on mother's skin	d. ?	e. ?
Example	f. ?	g. ?	h. ?

Applying Skills

The data table below shows the approximate gestation period of several mammals and the approximate length of time that those mammals care for their young after birth. Use the information in the table to answer Questions 20–22.

Mammal	Gestation Period	Time Spent Caring for Young After Birth
Deer mouse	0.75 month	1 month
Chimpanzee	8 months	24 months
Harp seal	11 months	0.75 month
Elephant	21 months	24 months
Bobcat	2 months	8 months

20. Graphing Decide which kind of graph would be best for showing the data in the table. Then construct two graphs—one for gestation period and the other for time spent caring for young.

21. Interpreting Data Which mammals in the table care for their young for the longest time? The shortest time?

22. Drawing Conclusions What seems to be the general relationship between the size of the mammal and the length of time for which it cares for its young? Which animal is the exception to this pattern?

Thinking Critically

23. Predicting If a rodent were fed a diet consisting only of soft food that it did not need to gnaw, what might its front teeth look like after several months?

24. Making Generalizations What is the general relationship between whether an animal is an endotherm and whether it has a four-chambered heart? Relate this to the animal's need for energy.

25. Comparing and Contrasting Why might monotremes be considered a link between reptiles and mammals?

Performance Assessment

CHAPTER PROJECT 4 — Wrap Up

Presenting Your Project When you present your project to your classmates, display the graphs, charts, and pictures you constructed. Be sure to include a description of the ways in which birds eat and interesting examples of bird behavior that you observed.

Reflect and Record In your journal, analyze how successful the project was. Was the bird feeder located in a good place for attracting birds and observing them? Did many birds come to the feeder—if not, why might this have happened? What are the advantages and limitations of using field guides for identifying birds? What did you learn from completing the project?

Getting Involved

In Your Community Many communities have animal shelters that try to find homes for stray animals. Find a shelter in or near your community. Find out how the shelter finds homes for animals and how the animals at the shelter are cared for. What requirements must a family fulfill before adopting an animal? Make up an information sheet about the shelter. With your teacher's permission, post it or distribute it in your school.

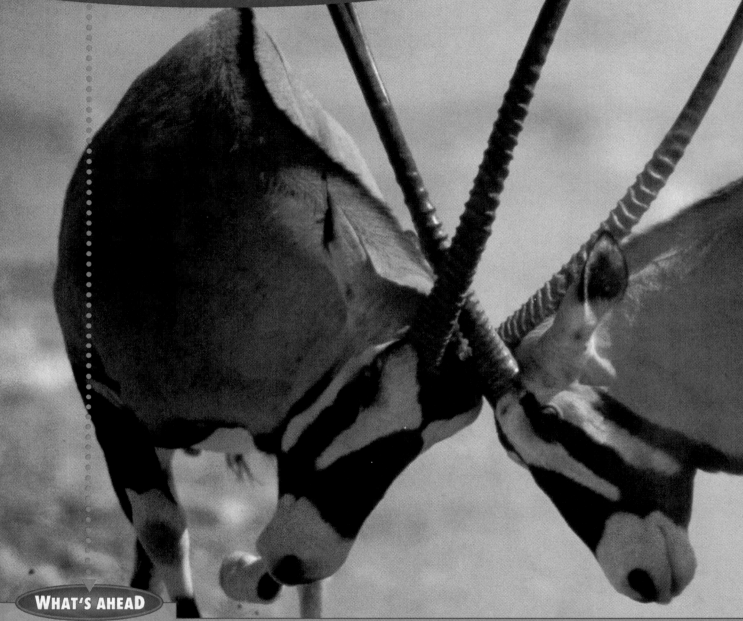

WHAT'S AHEAD

Horn-butting is a common way for male antelopes, like these gemsboks in Africa, to compete for food, water, and mates.

Learning New Tricks

These male gemsboks are butting horns in a contest to see which one is stronger. The victorious gemsbok will become the leader of a herd consisting of himself and several females. Have you ever watched dogs or other animals interacting like the gemsboks on this page? If so, did you wonder whether the animals were playing or fighting? Were they born knowing how to act this way, or did they have to learn this behavior? These and other kinds of questions are part of the study of animal behavior.

As you learn in this chapter about animal behavior, you will have a chance to study an animal on your own. Your challenge will be to teach the animal a new behavior.

Your Goal To monitor an animal's learning process as you teach it a new skill.

To complete the project successfully, you must
- observe an animal to learn about its general behavior patterns
- choose one new skill for the animal to learn, and develop a plan to teach it the new skill
- monitor the animal's learning over a specific period of time
- follow the safety guidelines in Appendix A

Get Started Select an animal to train from those to which you have access. The animal could be a family pet, a neighbor's pet, or another animal approved by your teacher. Begin by observing the animal carefully to learn about its natural behaviors. Then think about an appropriate new skill to teach to the animal.

Check Your Progress You'll be working on this project as you study this chapter. To keep your project on track, look for Check Your Progress boxes at the following points.

Section 1 Review, page 158: Develop a day-by-day plan.
Section 3 Review, page 172: Make and record observations.

Wrap Up At the end of the chapter (page 175), your animal will be a star! As your animal demonstrates its new accomplishment, you will describe your training technique.

SECTION

1 Why Do Animals Behave as They Do?

DISCOVER **••** **ACTIVITY**

What Can You Observe About a Vertebrate's Behavior?

1. For a few minutes, carefully observe the behavior of a small vertebrate, such as a gerbil or a goldfish. Write down your observations.

2. Place some food near the animal and watch what the animal does.

3. If there are other animals in the cage or aquarium, observe how the animals interact—for example, do they fight, groom each other, or ignore each other?

4. Tap gently on the cage or aquarium and see how the animal reacts. Note any other events that seem to make the animal change its behavior (from resting to moving, for example).

Think It Over
Predicting What are some circumstances under which you might expect an animal's behavior to change suddenly?

GUIDE FOR READING

◆ What are the functions of most of an animal's behaviors?

◆ How does instinctive behavior compare with learned behavior?

Reading Tip Before you read, rewrite the headings in the section as *how, why,* or *what* questions. As you read, write answers to those questions.

A male anole—a kind of lizard—stands in a patch of sun. As another male approaches, the first anole begins to lower and raise its head and chest in a series of quick push-ups. From beneath its neck a dewlap, a bright red flap of skin, flares out and then collapses, over and over. The anoles stare at one another, looking like miniature dinosaurs about to do battle. The first anole seems to be saying, "This area belongs to me. You'll have to leave or fight!"

The push-ups, piercing stares, and dewlap displays are all behaviors that warn another male to go away.

Figure 1 These two anoles are displaying their dewlaps in a dispute over space.

An animal's **behavior** consists of all the actions it performs—for example, the things that it does to obtain food, avoid predators, and find a mate. To understand animals, it is important to know not only what their body structures are like, but also how and why they behave as they do. Like their body structures, the behaviors of animals are adaptations that have evolved over long periods of time.

Most behavior is a complicated process in which different parts of an animal's body work together. The first anole saw the second anole with his eyes and interpreted the sight with his brain. His brain and nervous system then directed his muscles to perform the push-up movement and to display his bright red dewlap.

Why Behavior Is Important

When an animal looks for food or hides to avoid a predator, it is obviously doing something that helps it stay alive. When animals search for mates and build nests for young, they are behaving in ways that help them reproduce. **Most behaviors help an animal survive or reproduce.**

As an example of a survival behavior, consider what happens when a water current carries a small crustacean to a hydra's tentacles. After stinging cells on the tentacles paralyze the prey, the tentacles bend, pulling the captured crustacean toward the hydra's mouth. At the same time, the hydra's mouth opens to receive the food. If the tentacles didn't pull the food toward the hydra's mouth, or if the mouth didn't open, then the hydra couldn't take the food into its body. If the hydra couldn't feed, it would die.

The small crustacean acted as a stimulus to the hydra. A **stimulus** (plural *stimuli*) is a signal that causes an organism to react in some way. The organism's reaction to the stimulus is called a **response**. The hydra responded to the crustacean by stinging it and then eating it. All animal behavior is caused by stimuli. Some stimuli come from an animal's external environment, while other stimuli, such as hunger, come from inside the animal's body. An animal's response may include external actions, internal changes (such as a faster heartbeat), or both.

☑ *Checkpoint* *Give an example of a stimulus to which a hydra would respond.*

Figure 2 When a hungry sea star finds a clam, the clam acts as a stimulus. The sea star's response is to approach the clam, grab the clam's shell with its tube feet, and open it. The sea star can then force its stomach inside the shell and consume the clam. *Applying Concepts How is this behavior important to the sea star's survival?*

Sharpen your Skills

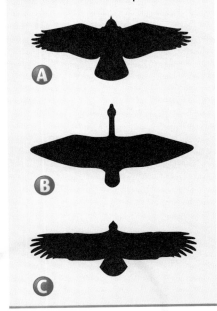
Instinctive Behavior

Some animal behaviors must be learned, while others are inborn—the animal knows how to do them by **instinct**, without being taught. An instinct is a behavior pattern that is inborn and that an animal performs correctly the first time. For example, a newborn kangaroo instinctively crawls into its mother's pouch and attaches itself to a nipple. A dragonfly nymph will instinctively shoot out its lower jaw and catch any bite-sized animal that comes within range. The dragonfly nymph has not been taught how to capture food. Rather, it knows instinctively how to use its mouthparts to do that. Most behaviors of invertebrates, such as insects, echinoderms, and worms, are instinctive.

Like learned behaviors, instinctive behaviors are responses to stimuli. Earthworms, for example, instinctively crawl away from a bright light. The light is the stimulus, and the earthworms respond by moving away from it.

The behavior of earthworms in response to strong light is fairly simple. However, some instinctive behaviors are complex. Spiders instinctively spin complicated webs without making mistakes in the pattern. Most birds build their nests without ever being taught how.

☑ *Checkpoint* *What is instinctive behavior?*

Learning

Think back to the first time you rode a bicycle. It probably took a few tries before you could do it well—you had to learn how. **Learning** is the process that leads to changes in behavior based on practice or experience. In general, the larger an animal's brain is, the more the animal can learn.

Unlike instincts, learned behaviors result from an animal's experience and are not usually done perfectly the first time. Lion cubs must practice many times before they can successfully kill prey. Gradually, by participating in hunting and imitating their mother's behavior, cubs learn to creep up on a prey animal, pounce on it, and kill it.

All learned behaviors depend in part on inherited traits that have passed from parents to offspring. Even though lion cubs must learn specific methods of hunting, they are born with claws that help them capture prey. In addition, lion cubs will instinctively pounce on any object that attracts their attention. The cubs have inherited some physical features and skills that are necessary for hunting, in much the same way that a talented basketball player has inherited above-average height and good eye-hand coordination. But both lions and athletes must practice in order to develop their abilities.

Animals learn new behaviors in different ways. These include conditioning, trial-and-error learning, and insight learning.

Conditioning   When a dog sees its owner approaching with a leash, the dog may get excited, eager to go for a walk. The dog has learned to associate the sight of the leash with a walk. Learning to connect some kind of stimulus with a good or bad event is called **conditioning**. In the case of the dog and the leash, the stimulus of the leash is associated with a pleasant event—a brisk walk. Animals can also be conditioned to avoid bad outcomes. Think of what happens when a predator tries to attack a skunk. The skunk sprays the predator with a substance that stings and smells awful. In the future, the predator is likely to avoid skunks, because the predator associates the sight of a skunk with its terrible spray.

During the early 1900s, the Russian scientist Ivan Pavlov performed a series of experiments involving conditioning. In Figure 3, see how Pavlov conditioned a dog to respond to the stimulus of a bell.

Figure 3 Steps 1, 2, and 3 show the procedure that Pavlov used when he conditioned a dog to salivate at the sound of a bell. *Predicting* Predict what the dog would do if it heard a bell ringing in another part of the house.

1. When a hungry dog sees or smells food, it produces saliva. Food is the stimulus, and the dog's response is salivation. Dogs do not usually salivate in response to other stimuli, such as the sound of a ringing bell.

2. For many days, when Pavlov gave food to a dog, he also rang a bell at the same time. The sight and smell of food were associated with the ringing of a bell. Pavlov did this every time he fed the dog. The dog salivated each time the two stimuli were introduced.

3. Finally, Pavlov rang a bell but did not give the dog food. The dog still produced saliva. The stimulus of the bell by itself produced the same response— salivation—that only food would normally produce.

Figure 4 Rescue dogs, like this English springer spaniel, are specially trained to find and rescue people trapped by accidents or natural disasters. Trainers use conditioning to teach rescue dogs these skills.

Conditioning is often used to train animals. Suppose, for example, that you want to train a dog to come to you when you call it. Every time the dog comes when you call, you reward it with a dog biscuit and a friendly pat. Your dog soon will learn to associate the pleasant experience of food and a pat with the behavior of coming when called. So the dog is likely to repeat that behavior.

Trial-and-Error Learning When a young chicken first hatches and begins to look for food, it will peck at almost any spot on the ground. Gradually the chick learns that only some of these spots are seeds or insects that are good to eat. The chicken has learned through trial and error which objects are food. **Trial-and-error learning** occurs when an animal, through repeated practice, learns to perform a behavior more and more skillfully. When you learned to ride a bicycle, you did it by trial and error. You may have wobbled or even fallen at first, especially when turning corners, but after a while you learned to ride smoothly. You got better because you learned that some movements were more likely to keep you upright than others.

Insight Learning The first time you try out a new video game, you may not need someone to explain how to play it. Instead, you may use what you already know about other video games to figure out how the new one works. When you solve a problem or learn how to do something new by applying what you already know, without a period of trial and error, you are using **insight learning**.

Insight learning is most common in primates, such as gorillas, chimpanzees, and humans. Figure 5 shows the results of an experiment done with chimpanzees. The animals used insight to come up with a way to reach a bunch of bananas—they stacked boxes on top of one another. In contrast, if a dog accidentally wraps its leash around a pole, the dog cannot figure out how to unwrap the leash.

INTEGRATING TECHNOLOGY People once thought that machines were incapable of learning. However, some computers can now learn and solve problems. **Artificial intelligence** is the capacity of a computer to perform complex tasks such as learning from experience and solving problems. Computers with artificial intelligence can play chess and beat human opponents. The computer, like a human chess player, can figure out

Figure 5 In this experiment, a hungry chimpanzee faced a problem—it couldn't reach the bananas. The chimpanzee figured out how to reach the bananas by stacking the boxes and climbing to the top of the stack. *Applying Concepts* *Explain how the chimpanzee's behavior shows insight learning.*

strategies and moves in advance. As scientists working in the field of artificial intelligence try to program computers to learn, they have a growing appreciation for the amazing abilities of the human brain.

✓ *Checkpoint* *In which animals is insight learning most common?*

Imprinting

A female Canada goose swims across a stream. One by one, her goslings paddle after her. The goslings follow their mother wherever she goes because they have undergone a process called imprinting. In **imprinting**, certain newly hatched birds and newborn mammals learn to recognize and follow the first moving object they see, which is usually their mother. Imprinting occurs very shortly after a young animal hatches or is born.

Imprinting involves a combination of instinctive behavior and learning. The young animal has an instinct to follow a moving object, but the youngster is not born knowing what its mother looks like. The young animal must learn from experience what object to follow.

Imprinting is valuable for two reasons. First, it keeps young animals close to their mothers, who know where to find food and how to avoid predators. Second, imprinting allows young

Line Them Up

Try to solve the following problem.

There are five girls: Maureen, Lupita, Jill, PoYee, and Tanya. They are standing in a row. Neither Maureen nor Lupita is next to PoYee. Neither Lupita nor Maureen is next to Tanya. Neither PoYee nor Lupita is next to Jill. Tanya is just to the right of Jill. Name the girls from left to right.

Inferring What kind or kinds of learning did you use to solve the problem? Explain.

Figure 6 These ducks imprinted on scientist Konrad Lorenz when they were ducklings. Even as adults, they followed him when he went for a swim.

animals to learn what other animals of their own species look like. This ability protects the animals while they are young. In addition, it is important later in life when the animals are searching for mates.

Once imprinting takes place, it cannot be changed—even if the animal has imprinted on something other than its mother, such as a moving toy, or even a human. Konrad Lorenz, an Austrian scientist who first described imprinting in 1935, conducted experiments in which he, rather than the mother, was the first moving object that newly hatched birds saw. Figure 6 shows the result of one such experiment. Since the newly hatched birds imprinted on Lorenz, even as adults they followed him around.

Lorenz's experiments sometimes caused surprising results. One bird that had imprinted on Lorenz, a male jackdaw, apparently thought that Lorenz was a possible mate. Because jackdaws feed one another as part of their mating behavior, this bird often tried to feed worms to Lorenz—who politely refused to eat them!

Section 1 Review

1. Explain what roles behavior plays for animals.
2. Contrast instinctive behavior with learned behavior.
3. How is trial-and-error learning different from insight learning?
4. **Thinking Critically Predicting** Right after hatching, before seeing anything else, a duckling sees a child riding a tricycle. What will probably happen the next time the child rides the tricycle in front of the duckling? Explain, and identify the type of behavior that this shows.

Check Your Progress

CHAPTER PROJECT 5

By now, you should have written out a day-by-day plan for teaching your animal a new behavior. You may find ideas in books on training pets. Make sure that your plan will not harm the animal. Obtain your teacher's approval for your plan and begin training your animal. *(Hint: Decide how you will monitor learning in your animal. What responses will show that the animal has mastered the skill?)*

BECOME A LEARNING DETECTIVE

In this lab, you will design an experiment to investigate how people learn.

Problem

What are some factors that make it easier for people to learn new things?

Suggested Materials

paper and pencil

Design a Plan

1. Look over the two lists of words in the table. Researchers use groups of words like these to investigate how people learn. Notice the way the two groups differ. The words in List A have no meanings in ordinary English. List B contains familiar, but unrelated, words.
2. What do you think will happen if people try to learn the words in each list? Write a hypothesis about which list will be easier to learn. How much easier will it be to learn that list?
3. With a partner, design an experiment to test your hypothesis. Brainstorm a list of the variables you will need to control in order to make your results reliable. Then write out your plan and present it to your teacher.
4. If necessary, revise your plan according to your teacher's instructions. Then perform your experiment using people your teacher has approved as test subjects. Keep careful records of your results.

Analyze and Conclude

1. Find the average (mean) number of words people learned from each list. How did these results compare with your hypothesis?

List A	List B
zop	bug
rud	rag
tig	den
wab	hot
hev	fur
paf	wax
mel	beg
kib	cut
col	sip
nug	job

2. What factors may have made one list easier to learn than the other?
3. Share your results with the rest of the class. How do the results of the different experiments in your class compare? What might explain the similarities or differences?
4. **Think About It** Look back at your experimental plan. Think about how well you were able to carry it out in the actual experiment. What difficulties did you encounter? What improvements could you make, either in your plan or in the way you carried it out?

More to Explore

Plan an experiment to investigate how long people remember what they learn. Write a hypothesis, and design an experiment to test your hypothesis. Obtain your teacher's permission before carrying out your experiment.

2 Patterns of Behavior

• ACTIVITY

What Can You Express Without Words?

1. Think of a feeling or situation that you can communicate without words, such as surprise or how to play a sport. Use facial expressions and body movements, but no words, to communicate it to your partner.

2. By observing your behavior, your partner should infer what you are communicating. Your partner should also note the behavior clues that led to this inference.

3. Now your partner should try to communicate a feeling or situation to you without words. Infer what your partner is trying to communicate, and note the behavior clues that led to your inference.

Think It Over
Forming Operational Definitions
Write your own definition of *communication.* How did this activity change your idea of communication?

GUIDE FOR READING

◆ **What is the function of courtship behavior?**

◆ **How do animals benefit from living in groups?**

◆ **How is migration important for an animal's survival?**

Reading Tip As you read, write an outline of this section. Use the headings as the main topics.

At this very moment, somewhere in Earth's oceans, blue whales are calling to one another. Whales communicate with a variety of sounds that scientists call songs. These songs consist of brassy trumpetings, long wails, clicks, and deep grunts. Whales locate one another using these sounds.

Icebergs dot the cold polar waters where these giant mammals spend their summers. After fattening up on small, shrimp-like animals called krill, blue whales migrate to warmer waters near the equator. It is in these tropical seas that the females give birth, usually to one calf.

Blue whales communicate with one another and migrate to breeding and resting places—behavior characteristics that they share with many other animals. In this section you will learn about some common behavior patterns of animals.

Blue whale ▼

Figure 7 These Arctic hares are resolving their conflict by boxing. *Inferring* *What event might have led to this behavior?*

Competition and Aggression

Animals compete with one another for limited resources, such as food, water, space, shelter, and mates. Competition occurs among different species of animals, as when a pride of lions tries to steal a prey animal from a troop of hyenas that has just killed it. However, competition also occurs between members of the same species, as when a female aphid, a type of insect, kicks and shoves another female aphid while competing for the best leaf on which to lay eggs.

When they compete, animals may display **aggression**, which is a threatening behavior that one animal uses to gain control over another. Before a pride of lions settles down to eat its prey, individual lions show aggression by snapping, clawing, and snarling. First the most aggressive members of the pride eat their fill. Then the less aggressive and younger members of the pride get a chance to feed.

Aggression between members of the same species hardly ever results in the injury or death of any of the competitors. Usually the loser communicates "I give up" with its behavior. For example, to protect themselves from the aggressive attacks of older dogs, puppies roll over on their backs, showing their bellies. This signal calms the older dog, and the puppy can then creep away.

Establishing a Territory

On an early spring day, a male oriole fills the warm air with a flutelike song. You may think he is singing just because it is a beautiful day. But in fact, he is alerting other orioles that he is the "owner" of a particular territory. A **territory** is an area that is occupied and defended by an animal or group of animals.

If another animal of the same species enters the territory, the owner will attack the newcomer and try to drive it away. While birds use songs and aggressive behaviors to maintain their territories, other animals use calls, scratches, droppings, and scents. Cougars rake trees and earth with their claws and leave scent markings that advertise the boundaries of their territories.

By establishing a territory, an animal gains unlimited access to its resources, such as food and possible mates. A territory also provides a safe area in which animals can raise their young without competition from other members of their species. In most songbird species, and in many other animal species, a male cannot attract a mate unless he holds a territory.

☑ *Checkpoint* *How does a territory help an animal survive?*

Mating and Raising Young

A male and female salamander swim gracefully in the water, twining elegantly around one another. They are engaging in **courtship behavior**, which is behavior in which males and females of the same species prepare for mating. Males of some spider species court females by presenting them with prey before mating. Fireflies use light signals to indicate readiness for mating. **Courtship behavior ensures that the males and females of the same species recognize one another, so that mating and reproduction can take place.**

Birds have some of the most dramatic courtship behaviors. Figure 8 shows the elaborate bower that male bowerbirds prepare during courtship. Peregrine falcons have an acrobatic flight display as part of their courtship. As they soar through the air at

Figure 8 In the rain forest of Australia, a male satin bowerbird, left, creates a colorful welcome mat. He is decorating the entrance to the archlike bower he has built to attract a mate. By entering the bower, right, the green female bird lets the male know that she agrees to be his mate.

top speed, the male and female falcons dive and do figure eights and rolls.

Animal species differ in the amount of care they provide for their young. Most fishes, amphibians, and reptiles provide little or no parental care for their young. In contrast, most parent birds and mammals care for their young after hatching or birth. Not only do they feed and protect their young, but they also teach them survival skills, such as hunting.

Living in Groups

Although many animals are solitary and only rarely meet one of their own kind, other animals live in groups. Some fishes form schools, some insects live in large groups, and hoofed mammals, such as bison, often form herds. **Living in a group usually helps animals survive—group members protect each other and work together to find food.** Group members may help one another. If an elephant gets stuck in a mud hole, for example, other members of its herd will dig it out. When animals such as lions hunt in a group, they usually can kill larger prey than a single hunter can.

Safety in Groups Group living often protects animals against predators. Fishes that swim in schools are often safer than fishes that swim alone, because it is harder for predators to see and select an individual fish. In a herd, some animals may watch for danger while others feed. Furthermore, animals in a group sometimes cooperate in fighting off a predator. For example, North American musk oxen make a defensive circle against a predator, such as a wolf. Their young calves are sheltered in the middle of the circle while the adult musk oxen stand with their horns lowered, ready to charge. The predator often gives up rather than face a whole herd of angry musk oxen.

Worker Bees

In this activity, you will determine whether it is more productive to work alone or in a group, as honeybees do.

1. Make a paper chain by cutting paper strips for loops and gluing or taping the loops together. After 5 minutes, count the loops in the chain.

2. Now work in a small group to make a paper chain. Decide how to divide up the work before beginning. After 5 minutes, count the loops in the chain.

Calculating Find the difference between the number of loops in your individual and group chains. For Step 2, calculate the number of loops made per person by dividing the total number of loops by the number of people in your group. Was it more productive to work individually or as a group?

Figure 9 When a predator threatens, musk oxen form a horn-rimmed circle with their young sheltered in the center. *Predicting* Would a potential predator be more or less likely to attack a group arranged in this way?

Animal Societies Some animals, including ants, termites, honeybees, naked mole rats, and pistol shrimp, live in groups called societies. A **society** is a group of closely related animals of the same species that work together for the benefit of the whole group. You can see an example in *Exploring a Honeybee Society.* Different members perform specific tasks, such as gathering food or caring for young. The behavior of the animals is instinctive and rigid—an animal in a society is "preprogrammed" to perform a specific job.

Communication

If you've ever seen one cat hissing at another, you've watched two animals communicating. Although animals don't use spoken or written language, they do communicate. Animals use sounds, body positions, movements, and scent to convey information to one another. Hissing cats, for example, are usually communicating aggression.

Animals communicate various kinds of information. Much animal communication is involved in courtship. Female crickets, for example, are attracted to the sound of a male's chirping. Other animal communication relates to defense and aggression. While attacking other animals or defending themselves, animals may growl, snarl, hiss, or assume positions that make them look larger—and thus more frightening—than they really are. Animals may also communicate warnings. When it sees a coyote or other predator approaching, a prairie dog makes a yipping sound that warns other prairie dogs to take cover in their burrows. This yipping sound is something like a dog barking—that's how prairie dogs got their name.

Animals also communicate information about food sources. One of the most complex systems of animal communication is used by honeybees to inform one another about the location of food—flower nectar and pollen. A worker bee that has found a new source of food will return to the hive and begin an excited "dance." The pattern of her movement communicates both the quality of the food and its distance and direction from the hive.

✓ Checkpoint *What are four ways that animals communicate with one another?*

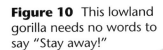

Figure 10 This lowland gorilla needs no words to say "Stay away!"

EXPLORING *a Honeybee Society*

A honeybee hive usually consists of one queen bee, thousands of female worker bees, and a few hundred male drones.

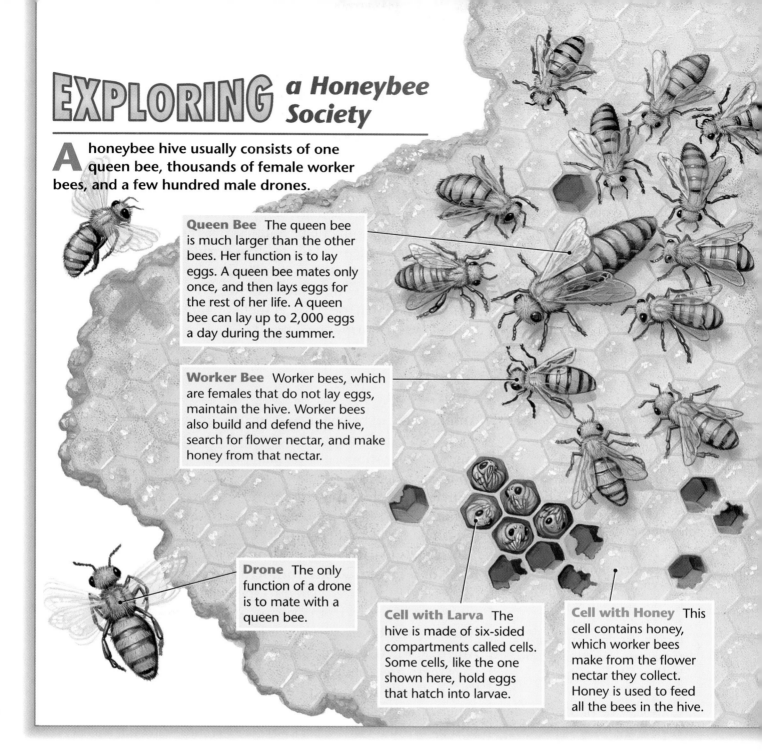

Queen Bee The queen bee is much larger than the other bees. Her function is to lay eggs. A queen bee mates only once, and then lays eggs for the rest of her life. A queen bee can lay up to 2,000 eggs a day during the summer.

Worker Bee Worker bees, which are females that do not lay eggs, maintain the hive. Worker bees also build and defend the hive, search for flower nectar, and make honey from that nectar.

Drone The only function of a drone is to mate with a queen bee.

Cell with Larva The hive is made of six-sided compartments called cells. Some cells, like the one shown here, hold eggs that hatch into larvae.

Cell with Honey This cell contains honey, which worker bees make from the flower nectar they collect. Honey is used to feed all the bees in the hive.

Behavior Cycles

Some animal behavior occurs in regular, predictable patterns. While blowflies, for example, search for food during the day, they are inactive at night. In contrast, field mice are active during the night and quiet by day. These daily behavior cycles of blowflies and mice are examples of **circadian rhythms** (sur KAY dee uhn rhythms), which are behavior cycles that occur over a period of approximately one day.

Other behavior cycles are related to seasons. Some animals, such as woodchucks and chipmunks, are active during warm seasons, but hibernate during the winter. **Hibernation** is a state of greatly reduced body activity that occurs during the winter. During hibernation, all of an animal's body processes, such as breathing and heartbeat, slow down. Hibernating animals do not eat. Their bodies use stored fat to meet their reduced nutrition needs.

Behavior cycles usually help animals survive in some way. Hibernation not only helps animals live through severe cold, it also eliminates the need for feeding during a season when food is scarce. Animals that are active during the day can take advantage of sunlight, which makes food easy to see. On the other hand, animals that are active at night do not encounter predators that are active during the day.

✓ *Checkpoint* **What happens to an animal during hibernation?**

Migration

Another kind of behavior cycle involves movement from place to place. While many animals spend their lives in a single area, others migrate. **Migration** is the regular, periodic journey of an animal from one place to another and then back again. Some migrating animals travel thousands of kilometers. Arctic terns, for example, fly more than 17,000 kilometers between their summer homes in the Arctic Circle to their winter residence near the South Pole.

Animals usually migrate to an area that provides abundant food, or a favorable environment for reproduction, or both. Most migrations are related to the changing seasons and take place twice a year, in the spring and fall. American redstarts, insect-eating birds, spend the long days of summer in North America, where they mate and raise young. In the fall, however, days there grow shorter and cooler, and insects become scarce. The redstarts then migrate south to Central America, South America, and islands in the Caribbean Sea, where they can again find plentiful food.

Many other animals, such as salmon, migrate to the areas in which they reproduce. Adult salmon live in oceans. However, to mate and lay eggs, an adult salmon must migrate from the ocean to the same stream where it once hatched from an egg—sometimes more than 3,000 kilometers away. In her "home" stream, the female lays her eggs and the male fertilizes them. The young salmon that hatch from those eggs will eventually migrate back to the ocean, and the cycle will begin again.

While there is much yet to learn about how migrating animals find their way, scientists have discovered

that animals use sight, taste, and other senses, including some that humans do not have. Some birds and sea turtles, for example, have a magnetic sense that acts something like a compass needle. Migrating birds also seem to navigate by using the positions of the sun, moon, and stars, as human sailors have always done. Salmon use scent and taste to locate the streams where they were born.

 INTEGRATING ENVIRONMENTAL SCIENCE Human activities sometimes interfere with animal migration. For example, when fuel and water pipelines are built above ground, migrating animals cannot easily cross over them. Dams across streams and rivers can block the path of fish migration. Bright city lights can confuse birds that migrate at night. Each year, millions of birds strike skyscraper windows and die during migration. But humans are learning how to help migrating animals. During the spring migration of 1998, the lights in more than 80 skyscrapers in Toronto, Ontario, were turned off at night to make a safer path for the birds. The lights of the Empire State Building in New York City also darken at night during migration.

Figure 11 This caribou herd is migrating across Alaska on the same path its ancestors used for thousands of years. Recently, human construction and oil drilling have begun to threaten this migration path. Both native people, who rely on the caribou for food, and corporations are working to find a way to save the path.

Section 2 Review

1. Define courtship behavior and describe an example.
2. Identify two ways in which animals benefit from living in groups.
3. What are the two major advantages that animals gain by migrating?
4. **Thinking Critically** **Applying Concepts** A mockingbird sings from a tree on the left side of the schoolyard. Soon it flies to the pine tree on the right side of the schoolyard and sings again. When another mockingbird flies into the schoolyard, the first mockingbird flies at it and tries to peck it. Explain what is probably happening.

Science at Home

With a family member, spend some time making detailed observations of the behavior of an animal—a pet, an insect, a bird, or another animal. Watch the animal for signs of aggressive behavior or other communication. Try to figure out why the animal is behaving aggressively or what it is trying to communicate.

ONE FOR ALL

H ave you ever stopped to watch a group of busy ants? In this lab, you will find out what goes on in an ant colony.

Problem

How does an ant society show organization and cooperative behavior?

Skills Focus

observing, inferring, posing questions

Materials

large glass jar	sandy soil	shallow pan
water	wire screen	sponge
20–30 ants	hand lens	bread crumbs
sugar	black paper	tape
glass-marking pencil		forceps
large, thick rubber band		

Procedure

1. Read over the entire lab to preview the kinds of observations you will be making. Copy the data table into your notebook. You may also want to leave space for sketches.

2. Mark the outside of a large jar with four evenly spaced vertical lines, as shown in the photograph on the next page. Label the sections with the letters A, B, C, and D. You can use these labels to identify the sections of soil on and below the surface.

3. Fill the jar about three-fourths full with soil. Place the jar in a shallow pan of water to prevent any ants from escaping. Place a wet sponge on the surface of the soil as a water source for the ants.

4. Observe the condition of the soil, both on the surface and along the sides of the jar. Record your observations.

5. Add the ants to the jar. Immediately cover the jar with the wire screen, using the rubber band to hold the screen firmly in place.

6. Observe the ants for at least 10 minutes. Look for differences in the appearance of adult ants, and look for eggs, larvae, and pupae. Examine both individual behavior and interactions between the ants.

7. Remove the screen cover, and add small amounts of bread crumbs and sugar to the soil surface. Close the cover. Observe the ants for at least 10 more minutes.

8. Create dark conditions for the ants by covering the jar with black paper above the water line. Remove the paper only when you are making your observations.

9. Observe the ant colony every day for two weeks. Remove the dark paper, and make and record your observations. Look at the soil as well as the ants, and always examine the food. If any food has started to mold, use forceps to remove it. Place the moldy food in a plastic bag, seal the bag, and throw it away. Add more food as necessary, and keep the sponge moist. When you finish your observations, replace the dark paper.

10. At the end of the lab, follow your teacher's directions for returning the ants.

DATA TABLE

Date	Section A	Section B	Section C	Section D

Analyze and Conclude

1. Describe the various types of ants you observed. What differences, if any, did you observe in their behavior? What evidence did you observe that different kinds of ants perform different tasks?
2. How do the different behaviors you observed contribute to the survival of the colony?
3. How did the soil change over the period of your observations? What caused those changes? How do you know?
4. **Apply** What kinds of environmental conditions do you think ant colonies need to thrive outdoors? Use the evidence obtained in this lab to support your answer.

Design an Experiment

Design an experiment to investigate how an ant colony responds when there is a change in the ants' environment, such as the introduction of a new type of food. Obtain your teacher's approval before carrying out your experiment.

SECTION 3 The Chemistry of Communication

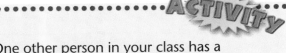

DISCOVER ······················ACTIVITY···

Can You Match the Scents?

1. From your teacher, obtain a container covered with aluminum foil with holes punched in it.

2. Carefully sniff the contents of the container. **CAUTION:** *Never sniff an unknown substance directly. When testing an odor, use a waving motion with your hand to direct the vapor toward your nose.*

3. One other person in your class has a container with the same substance. Use your sense of smell to find the container whose scent matches the one in your container.

Think It Over

Observing How easy was it for you and your classmates to match scents? What advantage might identifying or detecting scents have to an animal?

GUIDE FOR READING

◆ **How do animals use pheromones to communicate?**

Reading Tip As you read, make a list of main ideas and supporting details about pheromones and bioluminescence.

Figure 12 These ants are finding their way to the sugar by following a pheromone trail. The first ant to find the sugar began the trail, and each ant adds to its strength.

Oh no—ants have gotten into the sugar! As you watch in dismay, a stream of ants moves along the kitchen counter, heading right for the sugar bowl. Using their sense of smell, the ants follow a chemical trail that was first laid down by the ant that discovered the sugar. Each ant contributes to the trail by depositing a tiny droplet of scent onto the counter. If you watch carefully, you may see the ants doing this. The droplet quickly evaporates, making an invisible cloud of scent that hangs in the air above the path of the ants.

All the ants running to and from the sugar bowl are enveloped in an ant-sized tunnel of scent. It's like an invisible ant highway. The ants hold their antennae forward and use them to sniff their way to the sugar bowl. Then they turn around and follow the same chemical signal back to their nest.

Pheromones

The scent tunnel that leads ants to the sugar bowl is made of pheromones. A **pheromone** (FER uh mohn) is a chemical released by one animal that affects the behavior of another

animal of the same species. **Animals communicate with pheromones to establish territories, locate food, attract mates, and distinguish members of their own group from members of other groups.** Animals release these very powerful chemicals only in tiny quantities.

Why Pheromones Are Specific

Most pheromones are chemical compounds that are made up of long chains of atoms. Each pheromone has a unique combination of atoms in it. Because the atoms join together in specific ways, each pheromone has a different chemical shape. The different shapes of pheromones make them highly specific—when an animal releases a pheromone, it usually only causes a response in other animals of the same species. Just as the key to your front door will not work in the lock of your neighbor's door, the pheromones released by a luna moth will not trigger a response in a gypsy moth.

Pheromones and Behavior Pheromones enable many animals to recognize group members and establish territories. Every ant colony, for example, has its own pheromones that identify colony members. If an ant wanders into a colony other than its own, the intruder ant's pheromones will be recognized as foreign. The intruder will be attacked and killed. Many mammals mark their territories with pheromones in urine or sprays. Male house cats often spray the trees in their yards with a musky scent containing pheromones. The pheromones advertise the presence of that male cat to other cats in the neighborhood.

Pheromones play an important role in mating and reproduction. A female silkworm moth, for example, releases a pheromone when she is ready to mate. When the sense organs on a male's antennae pick up the scent of the pheromone, the male flies toward the scent to mate with the female.

✓ *Checkpoint* *How do pheromones enable ants to identify members of another ant colony?*

Figure 13 The antennae of this male Atlas silkworm moth allow him to find females that are ready to mate. Sense organs on the antennae pick up the female pheromone scent. The male moth then follows the scent to the female. *Predicting* *How might injured antennae affect a male moth's ability to find a mate?*

Pheromones and Pest Control Some pheromones can be

***INTEGRATING
ENVIRONMENTAL SCIENCE***

made in laboratories and then used to attract and eliminate pest insects. Manufactured pheromones lure insects into traps. In some cases, the insects are killed in the traps. In some other cases, male insects that collect in these traps can be exposed to X-rays that kill their sperm cells. Even though these altered males will mate with females after they are released, no offspring will result. The population of the insects will eventually decrease. A common pheromone trap lures Japanese beetles, which damage rosebushes. They are lured into a bag from which they can't escape. Then they can be killed or relocated.

Figure 14 This flashlight fish uses a bioluminescent organ beneath its eye to see. The organ is also used to attract prey, to confuse predators, and to communicate with other flashlight fish.

Communicating with Light

Pheromones are only one form of chemical communication used by animals. Some animals, such as fireflies and some species of fish, use light to communicate. **Bioluminescence** (by oh loo muh NEHS uhns) is the production of light by a living organism. That light is generated by chemical reactions that take place in the organism's cells.

On a warm summer night, when you see a meadow lit up with fireflies, you are actually watching fireflies using bioluminescence in courtship. A male firefly sends a blinking signal to female fireflies in the grass below. Each species of firefly has a distinctive signal. When an interested female sees the signal of a male of her species, she flashes a reply. If the male sees her signal, he will land near her and they may mate.

Section 3 Review

1. List three things that animals communicate with pheromones. Using a specific animal, give an example of each type of communication.
2. How are pheromones used to control insect pests?
3. What do fireflies communicate with their bioluminescence?
4. **Thinking Critically** **Predicting** While a stream of ants is traveling to and from the sugar bowl, you take a sponge and wash away a six-inch section of their path. Predict how the ants will respond.

Check Your Progress
At this point, you should be continuing with your training plan and monitoring your animal's progress. Be sure to keep good records of your animal's daily progress. Make modifications to your plan now if they are needed. Also begin to think about how you will present your results to the class. (*Hint:* You may want to make drawings or take photos of your animal in action to use in your presentation.)

CHAPTER PROJECT
5

STUDY GUIDE

SECTION 1 — Why Do Animals Behave as They Do?

Key Ideas

◆ Most behaviors help an animal survive and reproduce. Examples include behaviors involved in obtaining food, avoiding predators, and finding a mate.

◆ An instinct is an inborn behavior pattern that the animal performs correctly the first time. Most behaviors of invertebrates are instinctive.

◆ Learning changes an animal's behavior as a result of experience. Some ways in which animals learn include conditioning, trial-and-error learning, and insight learning.

◆ Imprinting, in which very young animals learn to follow the first moving object they see, involves both instinct and learning.

Key Terms

behavior
response
learning
trial-and-error learning
artificial intelligence
stimulus
instinct
conditioning
insight learning
imprinting

SECTION 2 — Patterns of Behavior

Key Ideas

◆ Animals use aggression to compete for limited resources, such as food or shelter.

◆ Many animals establish territories from which they exclude other members of their species.

◆ Courtship behavior ensures that males and females of the same species recognize one another so that they can reproduce.

◆ There is usually some survival advantage to living in a group, such as cooperation in getting food and protection from danger.

◆ Animals use sounds, scents, body positions, and movements to communicate.

◆ Some animal behaviors occur in regular patterns. Circadian rhythms are one-day behavior cycles. Hibernation is a period of inactivity during winter.

◆ Some animals migrate to places where they can more easily find food, reproduce, or both.

Key Terms

aggression
courtship behavior
circadian rhythm
migration
territory
society
hibernation

SECTION 3 — The Chemistry of Communication

INTEGRATING CHEMISTRY

Key Ideas

◆ Pheromones are chemicals that animals use to establish a territory, locate food, attract a mate, and identify group members.

◆ Male fireflies use bioluminescence, or the production of light by a living organism, to attract mates.

Key Terms

pheromone
bioluminescence

USING THE INTERNET
www.science-explorer.phschool.com

CHAPTER 5 REVIEW

Chapter 5 **B ◆ 173**

Reviewing Content

For more review of key concepts, see the Interactive Student Tutorial CD-ROM.

Multiple Choice

Choose the letter of the best answer.

1. The scent of a female moth causes a male to fly toward her. The scent is an example of
   a. a response.　　b. a stimulus.
   c. aggression.　　d. insight learning.

2. If you could play the saxophone by instinct, you would
   a. play well the first time you tried.
   b. need someone to teach you.
   c. have to practice frequently.
   d. know how to play other instruments.

3. When a male and female falcon perform an acrobatic flight display with each other, they are exhibiting
   a. learning.　　b. imprinting.
   c. migration.　　d. courtship behavior.

4. When an American redstart travels from its winter home in South America to its nesting area in New York, this is called
   a. learning.　　b. conditioning.
   c. migration.　　d. bioluminescence.

5. A trap contains strong-smelling chemicals. Insects fly into the trap because of
   a. conditioning.　b. insight learning.
   c. pheromones.　d. bioluminescence.

True or False

If the statement is true, write true. If it is false, change the underlined word or words to make the statement true.

6. A spider building a web exhibits <u>learned</u> behavior.

7. Every day after school, you take your dog for a walk. Lately, he greets your arrival with his leash in his mouth. Your dog's behavior is an example of <u>instinct</u>.

8. A <u>territory</u> is an area that an animal will fight to defend.

9. When salmon return to freshwater streams to reproduce, their behavior is an example of <u>circadian rhythm</u>.

10. The production of light by an organism is called <u>bioluminescence</u>.

Checking Concepts

11. Explain how both instinct and learning are involved in imprinting.

12. Your German shepherd puppy has just shredded your favorite pair of sneakers. When you loudly scold him, he rolls over on his back. What kind of behavior are you exhibiting to the dog? What is the meaning of his response?

13. Explain how courtship and territorial behavior are related.

14. Because a highway has been constructed through a forest, many of the animals that once lived there have had to move to a different wooded area. Is their move an example of migration? Explain.

15. How does a pheromone's structure account for the fact that it usually affects the behavior of only one species?

16. **Writing to Learn**　After landing on a distant planet, you discover creatures who look something like humans but whose society is organized like that of honeybees. Write an interview with one creature, who explains the structure of the society and the roles of different members.

Thinking Visually

17. **Concept Map**　Copy the concept map below onto a separate sheet of paper. Then complete the map. (For more on concept maps, see the Skills Handbook.)

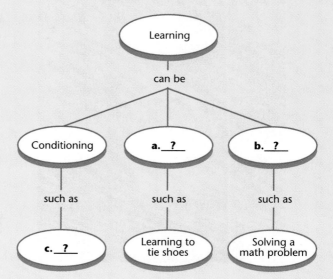

Applying Skills

The toad in the pictures below caught a bee and then spit it out. Use the pictures to answer Questions 18–20.

18. **Inferring** Explain why the toad probably behaved as it did in picture B.
19. **Predicting** If another bee flies by, how will the toad probably behave? Give a reason to support your prediction.
20. **Classifying** What type of learning will probably result from the toad's experience? Explain.

Thinking Critically

21. **Applying Concepts** Give an example of something you have learned by insight learning. Explain how you used past knowledge and experience in learning it.
22. **Predicting** Suppose a disease blinded a population of fireflies. How might the reproduction rate be affected? Explain.
23. **Applying Concepts** Explain how a racehorse's ability to win races is a combination of inherited and learned characteristics.
24. **Problem Solving** A dog keeps jumping onto a sofa. Describe a procedure that the owner might use to train the dog not to do this. The procedure must not involve any pain or harm to the dog.

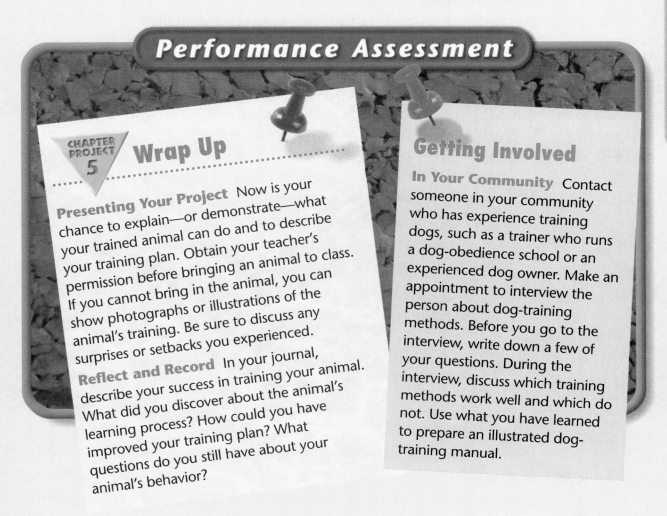

Performance Assessment

CHAPTER PROJECT 5 Wrap Up

Presenting Your Project Now is your chance to explain—or demonstrate—what your trained animal can do and to describe your training plan. Obtain your teacher's permission before bringing an animal to class. If you cannot bring in the animal, you can show photographs or illustrations of the animal's training. Be sure to discuss any surprises or setbacks you experienced.

Reflect and Record In your journal, describe your success in training your animal. What did you discover about the animal's learning process? How could you have improved your training plan? What questions do you still have about your animal's behavior?

Getting Involved

In Your Community Contact someone in your community who has experience training dogs, such as a trainer who runs a dog-obedience school or an experienced dog owner. Make an appointment to interview the person about dog-training methods. Before you go to the interview, write down a few of your questions. During the interview, discuss which training methods work well and which do not. Use what you have learned to prepare an illustrated dog-training manual.

The Secret of Silk

What animal—

was a secret for thousands of years?

was smuggled across mountains in a hollow cane?

is good to eat, especially stir-fried with garlic and ginger?

is not really what its name says it is?

If you guessed that this amazing animal is the silkworm, you are right. The silk thread that this caterpillar spins is woven into silk cloth. For at least 4,000 years people have treasured silk.

Chinese legends say that in 2640 B.C., a Chinese empress accidentally dropped a silkworm cocoon in warm water and watched the thread unravel. She had discovered silk. But for thousands of years, the Chinese people kept the work of silkworms a secret. Death was the penalty for telling the secret.

Then, it is said, in A.D. 552, two travelers from Persia visited China and returned to the West carrying silkworm eggs hidden in their hollow canes. Ever since then, the world has enjoyed the beauty of silk—its warmth, strength, softness, and shimmer.

Metamorphosis of the Silkworm

The silkworm is not really a worm; it's the larva of an insect—a moth named *Bombyx mori*. In its entire feeding period, this larva consumes about 20 times its own weight in mulberry leaves. The silkworm undergoes complete metamorphosis during its life.

1 The adult female moth lays 300 to 500 eggs, each the size of a pinhead. After about ten days at 27°C, the larvae—which people call silkworms—hatch from the eggs and begin to eat. Mulberry leaves are the insects' source of food.

2 For the next 40 to 45 days, the larvae consume great quantities of mulberry leaves. The silkworms molt each time their exoskeletons become too tight. After the last molting and feeding stage, the silkworms begin to build their cocoons.

3 To spin its cocoon, each silkworm produces two single strands from its two silk glands. Another pair of glands produces a sticky substance that binds the two strands together. The silkworm pushes this single strand out through a small tube in its head. Once in the air, the strand hardens and the silkworm winds the strand around itself in many layers to make a thick cocoon. The single silk strand may be as long as 900 meters— more than two laps around an Olympic track.

Science Activity

Examine a silkworm cocoon. After softening the cocoon in water, find the end of the strand of silk. Pull this strand, wind it onto an index card, and measure its length.

With a partner, design an experiment to compare the strength of the silk thread you just collected to that of cotton and/or nylon thread of the same weight or thickness.

◆ Develop a hypothesis about the strength of the threads.

◆ Decide on the setup you will use to test the threads.

◆ Check your safety plan with your teacher.

4 After 14 to 18 days, the adult moths emerge from the cocoons. The new moth does not eat or fly. It mates, the female lays eggs, and 2 to 3 days later both the male and female die.

The Silk Road

Long before the rest of the world learned how silk was made, the Chinese were trading this treasured fabric with people west of China. Merchants who bought and sold silk traveled along a system of hazardous routes that came to be known as the Silk Road. The Silk Road stretched 6,400 kilometers from Ch'ang-an in China to the Mediterranean Sea. Silk, furs, and spices traveled west toward Rome along the road. Gold, wool, glass, grapes, garlic, and walnuts moved east toward China.

Travel along the Silk Road was treacherous and difficult. For safety, traders traveled in caravans of many people and animals. Some kinds of pack animals were better equipped to handle certain parts of the journey than others. Camels, for instance, were well suited to the desert; they could store large amounts of water and withstand most sandstorms. Yaks were often used in the high mountains.

The entire journey along the Silk Road could take years. Many people and animals died along the way. Very few individuals or caravans traveled the length of the Silk Road.

Silk fabric became highly prized in Rome. In fact, it was said that the first silk products to reach Rome after 50 B.C. were worth their weight in gold. The Chinese, of course, kept the secret of the silkworm and controlled silk production. They were pleased that the Romans thought that silk grew on trees. It was not until about A.D. 550 that the Roman Empire learned the secret of silk.

In time, silk production spread around the world. The Silk Road, though, opened forever the exchange of goods and ideas between China and the West.

EUROPE

Rome

Black Sea

ASIA MINOR

7 Antioch

The Silk Road
200 B.C. to
A.D. 200

1 Ch'ang-an
From Ch'ang-an in northern China, the Silk Road headed west along a corridor between the Nan Shan Mountains and the Gobi Desert.

2 Dunhuang
At Dunhuang, in an oasis, or fertile green area, of the Gobi Desert, caravans took on rested pack animals. Beyond Dunhuang, the silk route split.

3 Takla Makan Desert
The desert is well named—Takla Makan means "Go in and you won't come out!" Most travelers avoided the scorching heat of the desert and journeyed along the edges of this great wasteland of sand.

Social Studies Activity

Suppose you are a merchant traveling from Dunhuang to Kashgar. You will be carrying silk, furs, and cinnamon to Kashgar where you'll trade for gold, garlic, and glass, which you will carry back to Dunhuang. Plan your route and hire a guide.

- Look at the map to find the distances and the physical features you will see on your journey.
- Explain why you chose the route you did.
- List the animals and supplies that you will take.
- Write a help-wanted ad for a guide to lead your caravan.

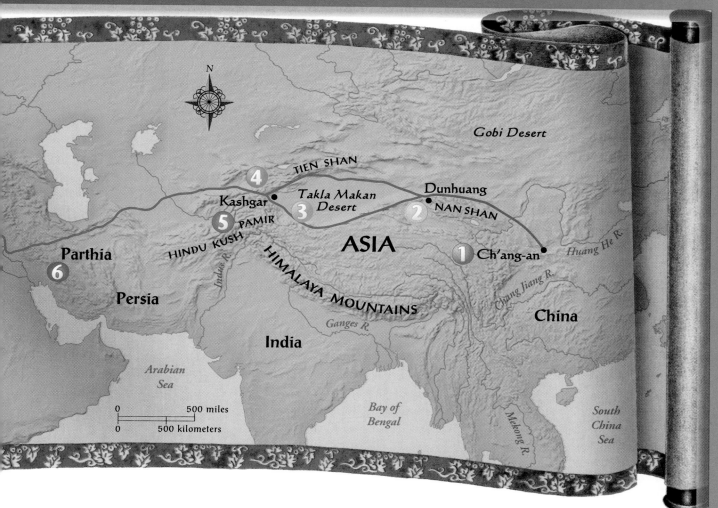

TIEN SHAN

Gobi Desert

④ Kashgar

Takla Makan Desert

③

② NAN SHAN

Dunhuang

⑤ PAMIR

Kashgar

HINDU KUSH

Indus R.

HIMALAYA MOUNTAINS

ASIA

① Ch'ang-an

Huang He R.

Chang Jiang R.

⑥

Parthia

Persia

Ganges R.

India

China

Arabian Sea

Bay of Bengal

Mekong R.

South China Sea

N

| 0 | 500 miles |
| 0 | 500 kilometers |

④ Kashgar

The silk routes along the northern and southern edges of the Takla Makan Desert came together at Kashgar. The perilous part of the Silk Road was still ahead.

⑤ Pamir Mountains

Traveling west from Kashgar, caravans faced some of the highest mountains in the world. The towering Pamir Mountains are more than 6,000 meters high. Once traders crossed the mountains, though, travel on the Silk Road was less difficult. Traders journeyed west through Persia to cities on the Mediterranean Sea.

⑥ Parthia

For a while, Parthian traders controlled part of the Silk Road. In 53 B.C., Rome was a mighty power around the Mediterranean Sea. That year when the Roman and Parthian armies were at battle, the Parthians suddenly turned to face their enemy and attacked with deadly arrows. Then, in the bright light of noon, the Parthians unrolled huge banners of gold-embroidered silk. The Romans were so dazzled by the brilliance that they surrendered.

⑦ Antioch

Trade flourished in Antioch, where silk was traded for gold. Ships carried silk and spices on the Mediterranean Sea from Antioch to Rome, Egypt, and Greece.

Language Arts

The Gift of Silk

A myth is a story handed down from past cultures—often to explain an event or natural phenomenon. Myths may be about gods and goddesses or about heroes.

The Yellow Emperor, Huang Di, who is mentioned in this Chinese myth, was a real person. Some stories say that he was the founder of the Chinese nation. He was thought to be a god who came to rule on Earth. Here the silkworm goddess appears to him at a victory celebration.

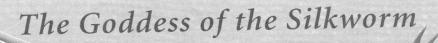

The Goddess of the Silkworm

A GODDESS descended from the heavens with a gift for the Yellow Emperor. Her body was covered with a horse's hide, and she presented two shining rolls of silk to the god. She was the "goddess of the silkworm", sometimes called the "lady with a horse's head". Long, long ago she had been a beautiful girl, but now a horse's skin grew over her body. If she pulled the two sides of the skin close to her body she became a silkworm with a horse's head, spinning a long, glittering thread of silk from her mouth. It is said she lived in a mulberry tree, producing silk day and night in the wild northern plain. This is her story.

Once in ancient times there lived a man, his daughter and their horse. Often the man had to travel, leaving his daughter alone at home to take care of the beast. And often the girl was lonely. One day, because she missed her father she teased the horse: "Dear long-nosed one, if you could bring my father home right how, I'd marry you and be your wife." At that the horse broke out of his harness. He galloped away and came quickly to the place where the master was doing business. The master, surprised to see his beast, grasped his mane and jumped up on his back. The horse stood mournfully staring in the direction he had come from, so the man decided there must be something amiss at home and hurried back.

When they arrived home, the daughter explained that she had only remarked that she missed her father and the horse had dashed off wildly. The man said nothing but was secretly pleased to own such a remarkable animal and fed him special sweet hay. But the horse would not touch it and whinnied and reared each time he saw the girl.

The man began to worry about the horse's strange behavior, and one day he said to the girl,

Luxurious hand-embroidered silk fabric has been made in China for thousands of years.

"Why is it that our horse behaves so strangely whenever you are about?"

So the young girl confessed the teasing remark she had made.

When he heard this the father was enraged, "For shame to say such a thing to an animal! No one must know of this! You will stay locked in the house!"

Now the man had always liked this horse, but he would not hear of its becoming his son-in-law. That night, to prevent any more trouble, he crept quietly into the stable with his bow and arrow and shot the horse through the heart. Then he skinned it and hung up the hide in the courtyard.

Next day, when the father was away, the girl ran out of the house to join some other children playing in the courtyard near the horse hide. When she saw it she kicked it angrily and said, "Dirty horse hide! What made you think such an ugly long-snouted creature as you could become my . . . ."

But before she could finish, the hide suddenly flew up and wrapped itself around her, swift as the wind, and carried her away out of sight. The other children watched dumbfounded; there was nothing they could do but wait to tell the old man when he arrived home.

Her father set out immediately in search of his daughter, but in vain. Some days later a neighbouring family found the girl wrapped up in the hide in the branches of a mulberry tree. She had turned into a wormlike creature spinning a long thread of shining silk from her horse-shaped head, spinning it round and round her in a soft cocoon.

Such is the story of the goddess of the silkworm. The Yellow Emperor was delighted to receive her exquisite gift of silk . . . . He ordered his official tailor, Bo Yu, to create new ceremonial robes and hats. And Lei Zu, the revered queen mother of gods and people, wife of the Emperor, began then to collect silkworms and grow them. And so it was that the Chinese people learned of silk.

—Yuan Ke, *Dragons and Dynasties*, translated by Kim Echlin and Nie Zhixiong

Language Arts Activity

What two details in the myth tell you that silkworms were important to the Chinese people?

The girl in the myth gets into trouble because she breaks her promise. Write a story of your own using the idea of a broken promise.

◆ Decide on the place, time, and main characters.
◆ Think about the events that will happen and how your story will conclude.

Mathematics

Counting on Caterpillars

Lai opened the door to the silkworm room. She was greeted by the loud sound of thousands of silkworms crunching on fresh leaves from mulberry trees. Lai enjoyed raising silkworms, but it was hard work. Over its lifetime, each silkworm eats about twenty times its own weight.

Lai had a chance to care for more silkworms. But first she had to figure out how many more she could raise. She now had 6,000 silkworms that ate the leaves from 125 mulberry trees. Should she have her parents buy another piece of land with another 100 mulberry trees? If she had 100 more trees, how many more silkworms could she feed?

Analyze. 125 trees can feed 6,000 silkworms. You want to know the number of silkworms 100 trees will feed. Write a proportion, using n to represent the number of silkworms.

Write the proportion.

$$\frac{\text{trees}}{\text{silkworms}} \overset{\rightarrow}{\underset{\rightarrow}{}} \frac{125}{6{,}000} = \frac{100}{n} \overset{\leftarrow}{\underset{\leftarrow}{}} \frac{\text{trees}}{\text{silkworms}}$$

Cross multiply. $125 \times n = 6{,}000 \times 100$

Simplify. $125n = 600{,}000$

Solve. $n = \dfrac{600{,}000}{125}$ $n = 4{,}800$

Think about it. "Yes," she decided. She could raise 4,800 more silkworms!

▲ Silkworms are fed fresh mulberry leaves every four hours, around the clock.

Math Activity

Solve the following problems.

1. Lai's friend Cheng also raises silkworms. He buys mulberry leaves. If 20 sacks of leaves feed 12,000 silkworms a day, how many sacks of leaves will 9,600 silkworms eat per day?

2. When Lai's silkworms are ready to spin, she places them in trays. If 3 trays can hold 150 silkworms, how many trays does Lai use for her 6,000 silkworms?

3. A silkworm spins silk at a rate of about 30.4 centimeters per minute. (a) How many centimeters can it spin in an hour? (b) It takes a silkworm 60 hours to spin the entire cocoon. How many centimeters is that?

4. Lai's silk thread contributes to the creation of beautiful silk clothes. It takes the thread of 630 cocoons to make a blouse and the thread of 110 cocoons to make a tie. (a) If each of Lai's 6,000 silkworms produces a cocoon, how many blouses can be made from the thread? (b) How many ties can be made?

Tie It Together

Plan a Silk Festival

People use silk in many ways other than just to make fine clothing. Did you know that silk was used for parachutes during World War II? Or that some bicycle racers choose tires containing silk because they provide good traction? Today, silk is used for a variety of purposes, including:

◆ recreation: fishing lines and nets, bicycle tires;

◆ business: electrical insulations, typewriter and computer ribbons, surgical sutures;

◆ decoration: some silkscreen printing, artificial flowers

Work in small groups to learn about one of the ways that people have used silk in the past or are using it today. Devise an interesting way to share your project with the class, such as

◆ a booth to display or advertise a silk product;

◆ a skit in which you wear silk;

◆ a historical presentation on the uses of silk in other countries;

◆ a presentation about a process, such as silkscreen painting or silk flowers.

Ask volunteers to bring pictures or silk products to class. After rehearsing or reviewing your presentation, work with other groups to decide how to organize your Silk Festival.

▼ **Racers at the Tour de France often use tires containing silk on their bicycles.**

Think Like a Scientist

Although you may not know it, you think like a scientist every day. Whenever you ask a question and explore possible answers, you use many of the same skills that scientists do. Some of these skills are described on this page.

Observing

When you use one or more of your five senses to gather information about the world, you are **observing.** Hearing a dog bark, counting twelve green seeds, and smelling smoke are all observations. To increase the power of their senses, scientists sometimes use microscopes, telescopes, or other instruments that help them make more detailed observations.

An observation must be factual and accurate—an exact report of what your senses detect. It is important to keep careful records of your observations in science class by writing or drawing in a notebook. The information collected through observations is called evidence, or data.

Inferring

When you explain or interpret an observation, you are **inferring,** or making an inference. For example, if you hear your dog barking, you may infer that someone is at your front door. To make this inference, you combine the evidence—the barking dog—and your experience or knowledge—you know that your dog barks when strangers approach—to reach a logical conclusion.

Notice that an inference is not a fact; it is only one of many possible explanations for an observation. For example, your dog may be barking because it wants to go for a walk. An inference may turn out to be incorrect even if it is based on accurate observations and logical reasoning. The only way to find out if an inference is correct is to investigate further.

Predicting

When you listen to the weather forecast, you hear many predictions about the next day's weather—what the temperature will be, whether it will rain, and how windy it will be. Weather forecasters use observations and knowledge of weather patterns to predict the weather. The skill of **predicting** involves making an inference about a future event based on current evidence or past experience.

Because a prediction is an inference, it may prove to be false. In science class, you can test some of your predictions by doing experiments. For example, suppose you predict that larger paper airplanes can fly farther than smaller airplanes. How could you test your prediction?

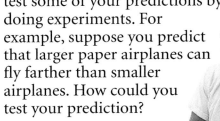

ACTIVITY Use the photograph to answer the questions below.

Observing Look closely at the photograph. List at least three observations.

Inferring Use your observations to make an inference about what has happened. What experience or knowledge did you use to make the inference?

Predicting Predict what will happen next. On what evidence or experience do you base your prediction?

Classifying

Could you imagine searching for a book in the library if the books were shelved in no particular order? Your trip to the library would be an all-day event! Luckily, librarians group together books on similar topics or by the same author. Grouping together items that are alike in some way is called **classifying.** You can classify items in many ways: by size, by shape, by use, and by other important characteristics.

Like librarians, scientists use the skill of classifying to organize information and objects. When things are sorted into groups, the relationships among them become easier to understand.

Classify the objects in the photograph into two groups based on any characteristic you choose. Then use another characteristic to classify the objects into three groups.

Making Models

Have you ever drawn a picture to help someone understand what you were saying? Such a drawing is one type of model. A model is a picture, diagram, computer image, or other representation of a complex object or process. **Making models** helps people understand things that they cannot observe directly.

Scientists often use models to represent things that are either very large or very small, such as the planets in the solar system, or the parts of a cell. Such models are physical models—drawings or three-dimensional structures that look like the real thing. Other models are mental models—mathematical equations or words that describe how something works.

This student is using a model to demonstrate what causes day and night on Earth. What do the flashlight and the tennis ball in the model represent?

Communicating

Whenever you talk on the phone, write a letter, or listen to your teacher at school, you are communicating. **Communicating** is the process of sharing ideas and information with other people. Communicating effectively requires many skills, including writing, reading, speaking, listening, and making models.

Scientists communicate to share results, information, and opinions. Scientists often communicate about their work in journals, over the telephone, in letters, and on the Internet. They also attend scientific meetings where they share their ideas with one another in person.

On a sheet of paper, write out clear, detailed directions for tying your shoe. Then exchange directions with a partner. Follow your partner's directions exactly. How successful were you at tying your shoe? How could your partner have communicated more clearly?

Making Measurements

When scientists make observations, it is not sufficient to say that something is "big" or "heavy." Instead, scientists use instruments to measure just how big or heavy an object is. By measuring, scientists can express their observations more precisely and communicate more information about what they observe.

Measuring in SI

The standard system of measurement used by scientists around the world is known as the International System of Units, which is abbreviated as SI (in French, *Système International d'Unités*). SI units are easy to use because they are based on multiples of 10. Each unit is ten times larger than the next smallest unit and one tenth the size of the next largest unit. The table lists the prefixes used to name the most common SI units.

Common SI Prefixes		
Prefix	**Symbol**	**Meaning**
kilo-	k	1,000
hecto-	h	100
deka-	da	10
deci-	d	0.1 (one tenth)
centi-	c	0.01 (one hundredth)
milli-	m	0.001 (one thousandth)

Length To measure length, or the distance between two points, the unit of measure is the **meter (m).** One meter is the approximate distance from the floor to a doorknob. Long distances, such as the distance between two cities, are measured in kilometers (km). Small lengths are measured in centimeters (cm) or millimeters (mm). Scientists use metric rulers and meter sticks to measure length.

Common Conversions
1 km = 1,000 m
1 m = 100 cm
1 m = 1,000 mm
1 cm = 10 mm

The larger lines on the metric ruler in the picture show centimeter divisions, while the smaller, unnumbered lines show millimeter divisions. How many centimeters long is the shell? How many millimeters long is it? **ACTIVITY**

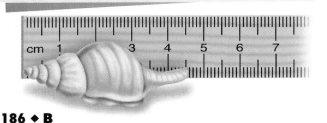

Liquid Volume To measure the volume of a liquid, or the amount of space it takes up, you will use a unit of measure known as the **liter (L).** One liter is the approximate volume of a medium-sized carton of milk. Smaller volumes are measured in milliliters (mL). Scientists use graduated cylinders to measure liquid volume.

Common Conversion
1 L = 1,000 mL

The graduated cylinder in the picture is marked in milliliter divisions. Notice that the water in the cylinder has a curved surface. This curved surface is called the *meniscus.* To measure the volume, you must read the level at the lowest point of the meniscus. What is the volume of water in this graduated cylinder? **ACTIVITY**

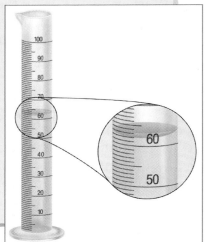

Mass To measure mass, or the amount of matter in an object, you will use a unit of measure known as the **gram (g)**. One gram is approximately the mass of a paper clip. Larger masses are measured in kilograms (kg). Scientists use a balance to find the mass of an object.

Common Conversion

1 kg = 1,000 g

The electronic balance displays the mass of an apple in kilograms. What is the mass of the apple? Suppose a recipe for applesauce called for one kilogram of apples. About how many apples would you need?

ACTIVITY

Temperature
To measure the temperature of a substance, you will use the **Celsius scale**. Temperature is measured in degrees Celsius (°C) using a Celsius thermometer. Water freezes at 0°C and boils at 100°C.

ACTIVITY

What is the temperature of the liquid in degrees Celsius?

Converting SI Units

To use the SI system, you must know how to convert between units. Converting from one unit to another involves the skill of **calculating**, or using mathematical operations. Converting between SI units is similar to converting between dollars and dimes because both systems are based on multiples of ten.

Suppose you want to convert a length of 80 centimeters to meters. Follow these steps to convert between units.
1. Begin by writing down the measurement you want to convert—in this example, 80 centimeters.
2. Write a conversion factor that represents the relationship between the two units you are converting. In this example, the relationship is *1 meter = 100 centimeters*. Write this conversion factor as a fraction, making sure to place the units you are converting from (centimeters, in this example) in the denominator.

3. Multiply the measurement you want to convert by the fraction. When you do this, the units in the first measurement will cancel out with the units in the denominator. Your answer will be in the units you are converting to (meters, in this example).

Example

80 centimeters = ___?___ meters

$$80 \text{ centimeters} \times \frac{1 \text{ meter}}{100 \text{ centimeters}} = \frac{80 \text{ meters}}{100}$$

$$= 0.8 \text{ meters}$$

Convert between the following units.

ACTIVITY

1. 600 millimeters = _?_ meters
2. 0.35 liters = _?_ milliliters
3. 1,050 grams = _?_ kilograms

Conducting a Scientific Investigation

In some ways, scientists are like detectives, piecing together clues to learn about a process or event. One way that scientists gather clues is by carrying out experiments. An experiment tests an idea in a careful, orderly manner. Although all experiments do not follow the same steps in the same order, many follow a pattern similar to the one described here.

Posing Questions

Experiments begin by asking a scientific question. A scientific question is one that can be answered by gathering evidence. For example, the question "Which freezes faster— fresh water or salt water?" is a scientific question because you can carry out an investigation and gather information to answer the question.

Developing a Hypothesis

The next step is to form a hypothesis. A **hypothesis** is a prediction about the outcome of the experiment. Like all predictions, hypotheses are based on your observations and previous knowledge or experience. But, unlike many predictions, a hypothesis must be something that can be tested. A properly worded hypothesis should take the form of an *If . . . then . . .* statement. For example, a hypothesis might be *"If I add salt to fresh water, then the water will take longer to freeze."* A hypothesis worded this way serves as a rough outline of the experiment you should perform.

Designing an Experiment

Next you need to plan a way to test your hypothesis. Your plan should be written out as a step-by-step procedure and should describe the observations or measurements you will make.

Two important steps involved in designing an experiment are controlling variables and forming operational definitions.

Controlling Variables In a well-designed experiment, you need to keep all variables the same except for one. A **variable** is any factor that can change in an experiment. The factor that you change is called the **manipulated variable.** In this experiment, the manipulated variable is the amount of salt added to the water. Other factors, such as the amount of water or the starting temperature, are kept constant.

The factor that changes as a result of the manipulated variable is called the responding variable. The **responding variable** is what you measure or observe to obtain your results. In this experiment, the responding variable is how long the water takes to freeze.

An experiment in which all factors except one are kept constant is a **controlled experiment.** Most controlled experiments include a test called the control. In this experiment, Container 3 is the control. Because no salt is added to Container 3, you can compare the results from the other containers to it. Any difference in results must be due to the addition of salt alone.

Forming Operational Definitions
Another important aspect of a well-designed experiment is having clear operational definitions. An **operational definition** is a statement that describes how a particular variable is to be measured or how a term is to be defined. For example, in this experiment, how will you determine if the water has frozen? You might decide to insert a stick in each container at the start of the experiment. Your operational definition of "frozen" would be the time at which the stick can no longer move.

EXPERIMENTAL PROCEDURE

1. Fill 3 containers with 300 milliliters of cold tap water.

2. Add 10 grams of salt to Container 1; stir. Add 20 grams of salt to Container 2; stir. Add no salt to Container 3.

3. Place the 3 containers in a freezer.

4. Check the containers every 15 minutes. Record your observations.

Interpreting Data

The observations and measurements you make in an experiment are called data. At the end of an experiment, you need to analyze the data to look for any patterns or trends. Patterns often become clear if you organize your data in a data table or graph. Then think through what the data reveal. Do they support your hypothesis? Do they point out a flaw in your experiment? Do you need to collect more data?

Drawing Conclusions

A conclusion is a statement that sums up what you have learned from an experiment. When you draw a conclusion, you need to decide whether the data you collected support your hypothesis or not. You may need to repeat an experiment several times before you can draw any conclusions from it. Conclusions often lead you to pose new questions and plan new experiments to answer them.

Is a ball's bounce affected by the height from which it is dropped? Using the steps just described, plan a controlled experiment to investigate this problem. **ACTIVITY**

Thinking Critically

Has a friend ever asked for your advice about a problem? If so, you may have helped your friend think through the problem in a logical way. Without knowing it, you used critical-thinking skills to help your friend. Critical thinking involves the use of reasoning and logic to solve problems or make decisions. Some critical-thinking skills are described below.

Comparing and Contrasting

When you examine two objects for similarities and differences, you are using the skill of **comparing and contrasting.** Comparing involves identifying similarities, or common characteristics. Contrasting involves identifying differences. Analyzing objects in this way can help you discover details that you might otherwise overlook.

ACTIVITY Compare and contrast the two animals in the photo. First list all the similarities that you see. Then list all the differences.

Applying Concepts

When you use your knowledge about one situation to make sense of a similar situation, you are using the skill of **applying concepts.** Being able to transfer your knowledge from one situation to another shows that you truly understand a concept. You may use this skill in answering test questions that present different problems from the ones you've reviewed in class.

ACTIVITY You have just learned that water takes longer to freeze when other substances are mixed into it. Use this knowledge to explain why people need a substance called antifreeze in their car's radiator in the winter.

Interpreting Illustrations

Diagrams, photographs, and maps are included in textbooks to help clarify what you read. These illustrations show processes, places, and ideas in a visual manner. The skill called **interpreting illustrations** can help you learn from these visual elements. To understand an illustration, take the time to study the illustration along with all the written information that accompanies it. Captions identify the key concepts shown in the illustration. Labels point out the important parts of a diagram or map, while keys identify the symbols used in a map.

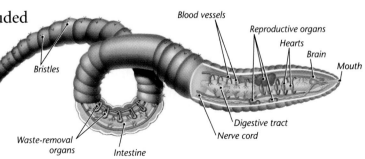

Blood vessels
Reproductive organs
Hearts
Brain
Mouth
Bristles
Digestive tract
Nerve cord
Waste-removal organs
Intestine

▲ Internal anatomy of an earthworm

ACTIVITY Study the diagram above. Then write a short paragraph explaining what you have learned.

Relating Cause and Effect

If one event causes another event to occur, the two events are said to have a cause-and-effect relationship. When you determine that such a relationship exists between two events, you use a skill called **relating cause and effect.** For example, if you notice an itchy, red bump on your skin, you might infer that a mosquito bit you. The mosquito bite is the cause, and the bump is the effect.

It is important to note that two events do not necessarily have a cause-and-effect relationship just because they occur together. Scientists carry out experiments or use past experience to determine whether a cause-and-effect relationship exists.

ACTIVITY

You are on a camping trip and your flashlight has stopped working. List some possible causes for the flashlight malfunction. How could you determine which cause-and-effect relationship has left you in the dark?

Making Generalizations

When you draw a conclusion about an entire group based on information about only some of the group's members, you are using a skill called **making generalizations.** For a generalization to be valid, the sample you choose must be large enough and representative of the entire group. You might, for example, put this skill to work at a farm stand if you see a sign that says, "Sample some grapes before you buy." If you sample a few sweet grapes, you may conclude that all the grapes are sweet—and purchase a large bunch.

ACTIVITY

A team of scientists needs to determine whether the water in a large reservoir is safe to drink. How could they use the skill of making generalizations to help them? What should they do?

Making Judgments

When you evaluate something to decide whether it is good or bad, or right or wrong, you are using a skill called **making judgments.** For example, you make judgments when you decide to eat healthful foods or to pick up litter in a park. Before you make a judgment, you need to think through the pros and cons of a situation, and identify the values or standards that you hold.

ACTIVITY

Should children and teens be required to wear helmets when bicycling? Explain why you feel the way you do.

Problem Solving

When you use critical-thinking skills to resolve an issue or decide on a course of action, you are using a skill called **problem solving.** Some problems, such as how to convert a fraction into a decimal, are straightforward. Other problems, such as figuring out why your computer has stopped working, are complex. Some complex problems can be solved using the trial and error method—try out one solution first, and if that doesn't work, try another. Other useful problem-solving strategies include making models and brainstorming possible solutions with a partner.

Organizing Information

As you read this textbook, how can you make sense of all the information it contains? Some useful tools to help you organize information are shown on this page. These tools are called *graphic organizers* because they give you a visual picture of a topic, showing at a glance how key concepts are related.

Concept Maps

Concept maps are useful tools for organizing information on broad topics. A concept map begins with a general concept and shows how it can be broken down into more specific concepts. In that way, relationships between concepts become easier to understand.

A concept map is constructed by placing concept words (usually nouns) in ovals and connecting them with linking words. Often, the most general concept word is placed at the top, and the words become more specific as you move downward. Often the linking words, which are written on a line extending between two ovals, describe the relationship between the two concepts they connect. If you follow any string of concepts and linking words down the map, it should read like a sentence.

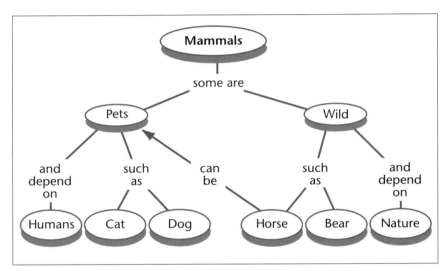

Some concept maps include linking words that connect a concept on one branch of the map to a concept on another branch. These linking words, called cross-linkages, show more complex interrelationships among concepts.

Compare/Contrast Tables

Compare/contrast tables are useful tools for sorting out the similarities and differences between two or more items. A table provides an organized framework in which to compare items based on specific characteristics that you identify.

To create a compare/contrast table, list the items to be compared across the top of a table. Then list the characteristics that will form the basis of your comparison in the left-hand column. Complete the table by filling in information about each characteristic, first for one item and then for the other.

Characteristic	Baseball	Basketball
Number of Players	9	5
Playing Field	Baseball diamond	Basketball court
Equipment	Bat, baseball, mitts	Basket, basketball

Venn Diagrams

Another way to show similarities and differences between items is with a Venn diagram. A Venn diagram consists of two or more circles that partially overlap. Each circle represents a particular concept or idea. Common characteristics, or similarities, are written within the area of overlap between the two circles. Unique characteristics, or differences, are written in the parts of the circles outside the area of overlap.

To create a Venn diagram, draw two overlapping circles. Label the circles with the names of the items being compared. Write the unique characteristics in each circle outside the area of overlap. Then write the shared characteristics within the area of overlap.

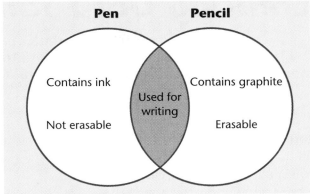

Flowcharts

A flowchart can help you understand the order in which certain events have occurred or should occur. Flowcharts are useful for outlining the stages in a process or the steps in a procedure.

To make a flowchart, write a brief description of each event in a box. Place the first event at the top of the page, followed by the second event, the third event, and so on. Then draw an arrow to connect each event to the one that occurs next.

Preparing Pasta

Boil water → Cook pasta → Drain water → Add sauce

Cycle Diagrams

A cycle diagram can be used to show a sequence of events that is continuous, or cyclical. A continuous sequence does not have an end because, when the final event is over, the first event begins again. Like a flowchart, a cycle diagram can help you understand the order of events.

To create a cycle diagram, write a brief description of each event in a box. Place one event at the top of the page in the center. Then, moving in a clockwise direction around an imaginary circle, write each event in its proper sequence. Draw arrows that connect each event to the one that occurs next, forming a continuous circle.

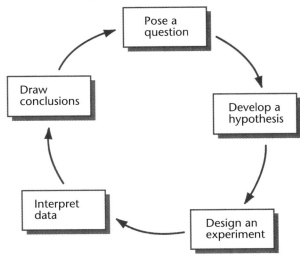

Steps in a Science Experiment

Creating Data Tables and Graphs

How can you make sense of the data in a science experiment? The first step is to organize the data to help you understand them. Data tables and graphs are helpful tools for organizing data.

Data Tables

You have gathered your materials and set up your experiment. But before you start, you need to plan a way to record what happens during the experiment. By creating a data table, you can record your observations and measurements in an orderly way.

Suppose, for example, that a scientist conducted an experiment to find out how many Calories people of different body masses burn while doing various activities. The data table shows the results.

Notice in this data table that the manipulated variable (body mass) is the heading of one column. The responding

variable (for Experiment 1, the number of Calories burned while bicycling) is the heading of the next column. Additional columns were added for related experiments.

CALORIES BURNED IN 30 MINUTES OF ACTIVITY			
Body Mass	Experiment 1 Bicycling	Experiment 2 Playing Basketball	Experiment 3 Watching Television
30 kg	60 Calories	120 Calories	21 Calories
40 kg	77 Calories	164 Calories	27 Calories
50 kg	95 Calories	206 Calories	33 Calories
60 kg	114 Calories	248 Calories	38 Calories

Bar Graphs

To compare how many Calories a person burns doing various activities, you could create a bar graph. A bar graph is used to display data in a number of separate, or distinct, categories. In this example, bicycling, playing basketball, and watching television are three separate categories.

To create a bar graph, follow these steps.

1. On graph paper, draw a horizontal, or *x-*, axis and a vertical, or *y-*, axis.
2. Write the names of the categories to be graphed along the horizontal axis. Include an overall label for the axis as well.
3. Label the vertical axis with the name of the responding variable. Include units of measurement. Then create a scale along the axis by marking off equally spaced numbers that cover the range of the data collected.
4. For each category, draw a solid bar using the scale on the vertical axis to determine the

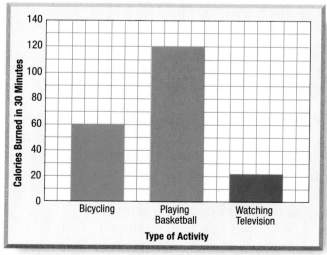

Calories Burned by a 30-kilogram Person in Various Activities

appropriate height. For example, for bicycling, draw the bar as high as the 60 mark on the vertical axis. Make all the bars the same width and leave equal spaces between them.
5. Add a title that describes the graph.

Line Graphs

To see whether a relationship exists between body mass and the number of Calories burned while bicycling, you could create a line graph. A line graph is used to display data that show how one variable (the responding variable) changes in response to another variable (the manipulated variable). You can use a line graph when your manipulated variable is *continuous*, that is, when there are other points between the ones that you tested. In this example, body mass is a continuous variable because there are other body masses between 30 and 40 kilograms (for example, 31 kilograms). Time is another example of a continuous variable.

Line graphs are powerful tools because they allow you to estimate values for conditions that you did not test in the experiment. For example, you can use the line graph to estimate that a 35-kilogram person would burn 68 Calories while bicycling.

To create a line graph, follow these steps.

1. On graph paper, draw a horizontal, or *x*-, axis and a vertical, or *y*-, axis.
2. Label the horizontal axis with the name of the manipulated variable. Label the vertical axis with the name of the responding variable. Include units of measurement.
3. Create a scale on each axis by marking off equally spaced numbers that cover the range of the data collected.
4. Plot a point on the graph for each piece of data. In the line graph above, the dotted lines show how to plot the first data point (30 kilograms and 60 Calories). Draw an imaginary vertical line extending up from the horizontal axis at the 30-kilogram mark. Then draw an imaginary horizontal line extending across from the vertical axis at the 60-Calorie mark. Plot the point where the two lines intersect.

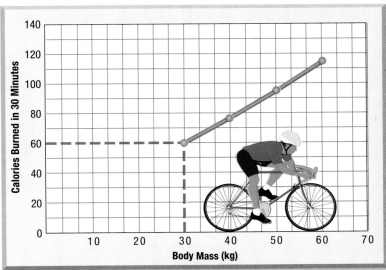

Effect of Body Mass on Calories Burned While Bicycling

5. Connect the plotted points with a solid line. (In some cases, it may be more appropriate to draw a line that shows the general trend of the plotted points. In those cases, some of the points may fall above or below the line.)
6. Add a title that identifies the variables or relationship in the graph.

> **ACTIVITY**
> Create line graphs to display the data from Experiment 2 and Experiment 3 in the data table.

> **ACTIVITY**
> You read in the newspaper that a total of 4 centimeters of rain fell in your area in June, 2.5 centimeters fell in July, and 1.5 centimeters fell in August. What type of graph would you use to display these data? Use graph paper to create the graph.

Circle Graphs

Like bar graphs, circle graphs can be used to display data in a number of separate categories. Unlike bar graphs, however, circle graphs can only be used when you have data for *all* the categories that make up a given topic. A circle graph is sometimes called a pie chart because it resembles a pie cut into slices. The pie represents the entire topic, while the slices represent the individual categories. The size of a slice indicates what percentage of the whole a particular category makes up.

The data table below shows the results of a survey in which 24 teenagers were asked to identify their favorite sport. The data were then used to create the circle graph at the right.

Sports That Teens Prefer

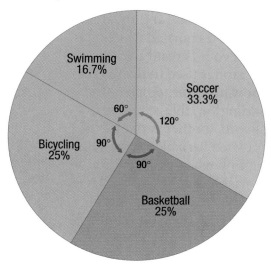

FAVORITE SPORTS	
Sport	Number of Students
Soccer	8
Basketball	6
Bicycling	6
Swimming	4

To create a circle graph, follow these steps.

1. Use a compass to draw a circle. Mark the center of the circle with a point. Then draw a line from the center point to the top of the circle.
2. Determine the size of each "slice" by setting up a proportion where x equals the number of degrees in a slice. (NOTE: A circle contains 360 degrees.) For example, to find the number of degrees in the "soccer" slice, set up the following proportion:

$$\frac{\text{students who prefer soccer}}{\text{total number of students}} = \frac{x}{\text{total number of degrees in a circle}}$$

$$\frac{8}{24} = \frac{x}{360}$$

Cross-multiply and solve for x.

$$24x = 8 \times 360$$
$$x = 120$$

The "soccer" slice should contain 120 degrees.

3. Use a protractor to measure the angle of the first slice, using the line you drew to the top of the circle as the 0° line. Draw a line from the center of the circle to the edge for the angle you measured.
4. Continue around the circle by measuring the size of each slice with the protractor. Start measuring from the edge of the previous slice so the wedges do not overlap. When you are done, the entire circle should be filled in.
5. Determine the percentage of the whole circle that each slice represents. To do this, divide the number of degrees in a slice by the total number of degrees in a circle (360), and multiply by 100%. For the "soccer" slice, you can find the percentage as follows:

$$\frac{120}{360} \times 100\% = 33.3\%$$

6. Use a different color to shade in each slice. Label each slice with the name of the category and with the percentage of the whole it represents.
7. Add a title to the circle graph.

> **ACTIVITY**
> In a class of 28 students, 12 students take the bus to school, 10 students walk, and 6 students ride their bicycles. Create a circle graph to display these data.

Laboratory Safety

Safety Symbols

These symbols alert you to possible dangers in the laboratory and remind you to work carefully.

Safety Goggles Always wear safety goggles to protect your eyes in any activity involving chemicals, flames or heating, or the possibility of broken glassware.

Lab Apron Wear a laboratory apron to protect your skin and clothing from damage.

Breakage You are working with materials that may be breakable, such as glass containers, glass tubing, thermometers, or funnels. Handle breakable materials with care. Do not touch broken glassware.

Heat-resistant Gloves Use an oven mitt or other hand protection when handling hot materials. Hot plates, hot glassware, or hot water can cause burns. Do not touch hot objects with your bare hands.

Heating Use a clamp or tongs to pick up hot glassware. Do not touch hot objects with your bare hands.

Sharp Object Pointed-tip scissors, scalpels, knives, needles, pins, or tacks are sharp. They can cut or puncture your skin. Always direct a sharp edge or point away from yourself and others. Use sharp instruments only as instructed.

Electric Shock Avoid the possibility of electric shock. Never use electrical equipment around water, or when the equipment is wet or your hands are wet. Be sure cords are untangled and cannot trip anyone. Disconnect the equipment when it is not in use.

Corrosive Chemical You are working with an acid or another corrosive chemical. Avoid getting it on your skin or clothing, or in your eyes. Do not inhale the vapors. Wash your hands when you are finished with the activity.

Poison Do not let any poisonous chemical come in contact with your skin, and do not inhale its vapors. Wash your hands when you are finished with the activity.

Physical Safety When an experiment involves physical activity, take precautions to avoid injuring yourself or others. Follow instructions from your teacher. Alert your teacher if there is any reason you should not participate in the activity.

Animal Safety Treat live animals with care to avoid harming the animals or yourself. Working with animal parts or preserved animals also may require caution. Wash your hands when you are finished with the activity.

Plant Safety Handle plants in the laboratory or during field work only as directed by your teacher. If you are allergic to certain plants, tell your teacher before doing an activity in which those plants are used. Avoid touching harmful plants such as poison ivy, poison oak, or poison sumac, or plants with thorns. Wash your hands when you are finished with the activity.

Flames You may be working with flames from a lab burner, candle, or matches. Tie back loose hair and clothing. Follow instructions from your teacher about lighting and extinguishing flames.

No Flames Flammable materials may be present. Make sure there are no flames, sparks, or other exposed heat sources present.

Fumes When poisonous or unpleasant vapors may be involved, work in a ventilated area. Avoid inhaling vapors directly. Only test an odor when directed to do so by your teacher, and use a wafting motion to direct the vapor toward your nose.

Disposal Chemicals and other laboratory materials used in the activity must be disposed of safely. Follow the instructions from your teacher.

Hand Washing Wash your hands thoroughly when finished with the activity. Use antibacterial soap and warm water. Lather both sides of your hands and between your fingers. Rinse well.

General Safety Awareness You may see this symbol when none of the symbols described earlier appears. In this case, follow the specific instructions provided. You may also see this symbol when you are asked to develop your own procedure in a lab. Have your teacher approve your plan before you go further.

Science Safety Rules

To prepare yourself to work safely in the laboratory, read over the following safety rules. Then read them a second time. Make sure you understand and follow each rule. Ask your teacher to explain any rules you do not understand.

Dress Code

1. To protect yourself from injuring your eyes, wear safety goggles whenever you work with chemicals, burners, glassware, or any substance that might get into your eyes. If you wear contact lenses, notify your teacher.
2. Wear a lab apron or coat whenever you work with corrosive chemicals or substances that can stain.
3. Tie back long hair to keep it away from any chemicals, flames, or equipment.
4. Remove or tie back any article of clothing or jewelry that can hang down and touch chemicals, flames, or equipment. Roll up or secure long sleeves.
5. Never wear open shoes or sandals.

General Precautions

6. Read all directions for an experiment several times before beginning the activity. Carefully follow all written and oral instructions. If you are in doubt about any part of the experiment, ask your teacher for assistance.
7. Never perform activities that are not assigned or authorized by your teacher. Obtain permission before "experimenting" on your own. Never handle any equipment unless you have specific permission.
8. Never perform lab activities without direct supervision.
9. Never eat or drink in the laboratory.
10. Keep work areas clean and tidy at all times. Bring only notebooks and lab manuals or written lab procedures to the work area. All other items, such as purses and backpacks, should be left in a designated area.
11. Do not engage in horseplay.

First Aid

12. Always report all accidents or injuries to your teacher, no matter how minor. Notify your teacher immediately about any fires.
13. Learn what to do in case of specific accidents, such as getting acid in your eyes or on your skin. (Rinse acids from your body with lots of water.)
14. Be aware of the location of the first-aid kit, but do not use it unless instructed by your teacher. In case of injury, your teacher should administer first aid. Your teacher may also send you to the school nurse or call a physician.
15. Know the location of emergency equipment, such as the fire extinguisher and fire blanket, and know how to use it.
16. Know the location of the nearest telephone and whom to contact in an emergency.

Heating and Fire Safety

17. Never use a heat source, such as a candle, burner, or hot plate, without wearing safety goggles.
18. Never heat anything unless instructed to do so. A chemical that is harmless when cool may be dangerous when heated.
19. Keep all combustible materials away from flames. Never use a flame or spark near a combustible chemical.
20. Never reach across a flame.
21. Before using a laboratory burner, make sure you know proper procedures for lighting and adjusting the burner, as demonstrated by your teacher. Do not touch the burner. It may be hot. And never leave a lighted burner unattended!
22. Chemicals can splash or boil out of a heated test tube. When heating a substance in a test tube, make sure that the mouth of the tube is not pointed at you or anyone else.
23. Never heat a liquid in a closed container. The expanding gases produced may blow the container apart.
24. Before picking up a container that has been heated, hold the back of your hand near it. If you can feel heat on the back of your hand, the container is too hot to handle. Use an oven mitt to pick up a container that has been heated.

Using Chemicals Safely

25. Never mix chemicals "for the fun of it." You might produce a dangerous, possibly explosive substance.

26. Never put your face near the mouth of a container that holds chemicals. Never touch, taste, or smell a chemical unless you are instructed by your teacher to do so. Many chemicals are poisonous.

27. Use only those chemicals needed in the activity. Read and double-check labels on supply bottles before removing any chemicals. Take only as much as you need. Keep all containers closed when chemicals are not being used.

28. Dispose of all chemicals as instructed by your teacher. To avoid contamination, never return chemicals to their original containers. Never simply pour chemicals or other substances into the sink or trash containers.

29. Be extra careful when working with acids or bases. Pour all chemicals over the sink or a container, not over your work surface.

30. If you are instructed to test for odors, use a wafting motion to direct the odors to your nose. Do not inhale the fumes directly from the container.

31. When mixing an acid and water, always pour the water into the container first and then add the acid to the water. Never pour water into an acid.

32. Take extreme care not to spill any material in the laboratory. Wash chemical spills and splashes immediately with plenty of water. Immediately begin rinsing with water any acids that get on your skin or clothing, and notify your teacher of any acid spill at the same time.

Using Glassware Safely

33. Never force glass tubing or thermometers into a rubber stopper or rubber tubing. Have your teacher insert the glass tubing or thermometer if required for an activity.

34. If you are using a laboratory burner, use a wire screen to protect glassware from any flame. Never heat glassware that is not thoroughly dry on the outside.

35. Keep in mind that hot glassware looks cool. Never pick up glassware without first checking to see if it is hot. Use an oven mitt. See rule 24.

36. Never use broken or chipped glassware. If glassware breaks, notify your teacher and dispose of the glassware in the proper broken-glassware container. Never handle broken glass with your bare hands.

37. Never eat or drink from lab glassware.

38. Thoroughly clean glassware before putting it away.

Using Sharp Instruments

39. Handle scalpels or other sharp instruments with extreme care. Never cut material toward you; cut away from you.

40. Immediately notify your teacher if you cut your skin when working in the laboratory.

Animal and Plant Safety

41. Never perform experiments that cause pain, discomfort, or harm to mammals, birds, reptiles, fishes, or amphibians. This rule applies at home as well as in the classroom.

42. Animals should be handled only if absolutely necessary. Your teacher will instruct you as to how to handle each animal species brought into the classroom.

43. If you know that you are allergic to certain plants, molds, or animals, tell your teacher before doing an activity in which these are used.

44. During field work, protect your skin by wearing long pants, long sleeves, socks, and closed shoes. Know how to recognize the poisonous plants and fungi in your area, as well as plants with thorns, and avoid contact with them.

45. Never eat any part of an unidentified plant or fungus.

46. Wash your hands thoroughly after handling animals or the cage containing animals. Wash your hands when you are finished with any activity involving animal parts, plants, or soil.

End-of-Experiment Rules

47. After an experiment has been completed, clean up your work area and return all equipment to its proper place.

48. Dispose of waste materials as instructed by your teacher.

49. Wash your hands after every experiment.

50. Always turn off all burners or hot plates when they are not in use. Unplug hot plates and other electrical equipment. If you used a burner, check that the gas-line valve to the burner is off as well.

Glossary

abdomen The hind section of an arachnid's body that contains its reproductive organs and part of its digestive tract; the hind section of an insect's body. (p. 58)

adaptation A characteristic that helps an organism survive in its environment or reproduce. (p. 19)

aggression A threatening behavior that one animal uses to gain control over another. (p. 161)

amphibian An ectothermic vertebrate that spends its early life in water and its adulthood on land, returning to water to reproduce. (p. 96)

antenna An appendage on the head of an animal that contains sense organs. (p. 57)

anus The opening at the end of an organism's digestive system through which wastes exit. (p. 39)

arachnid An arthropod with only two body sections. (p. 58)

arthropod An invertebrate that has an external skeleton, a segmented body, and jointed attachments called appendages. (p. 55)

artificial intelligence The capacity of a computer to perform complex tasks such as learning from experience and solving problems. (p. 156)

asexual reproduction The process by which a single organism produces a new organism identical to itself. (p. 18)

atrium An upper chamber of the heart. (p. 96)

autotroph An organism that makes its own food. (p. 17)

behavior All the actions an animal performs. (p. 153)

bilateral symmetry Line symmetry; the quality of being divisible into two halves that are mirror images. (p. 24)

bioluminescence The production of light by a living organism by means of chemical reactions within the organism's cells. (p. 172)

bird An endothermic vertebrate that has feathers and a four-chambered heart, and lays eggs. (p. 121)

bivalve A mollusk that has two shells held together by hinges and strong muscles. (p. 50)

buoyant force The force that water exerts upward on any underwater object. (p. 92)

camouflage Protective coloration; a common animal defense. (p. 66)

canine teeth Sharply pointed teeth that stab food and tear into it. (p. 136)

carnivore An animal that eats only other animals. (p. 19)

cartilage A flexible, strong tissue that is softer than bone. (p. 83)

cephalopod A mollusk with feet adapted to form tentacles around its mouth. (p. 52)

chitin The tough, flexible material from which arthropod exoskeletons are made. (p. 55)

chordate The phylum whose members have a notochord, a nerve cord, and slits in their throat area at some point in their lives. (p. 82)

circadian rhythms Behavior cycles that occur over a period of approximately one day. (p. 165)

cnidarians Animals whose stinging cells are used to capture their prey and defend themselves, and who take their food into a hollow central cavity. (p. 31)

complete metamorphosis A type of metamorphosis characterized by four dramatically different stages: egg, larva, pupa, and adult. (p. 64)

conditioning The process of learning to connect a stimulus with a good or bad event. (p. 155)

contour feather A large feather that helps give shape to a bird's body. (p. 121)

courtship behavior The behavior that animals of the same species engage in to prepare for mating. (p. 162)

crop A bird's internal storage tank that allows it to store food inside its body after swallowing it. (p. 122)

crustacean An arthropod that has two or three body sections, five or more pairs of legs, two pairs of antennae, and usually three pairs of appendages for chewing. (p. 57)

diaphragm A large muscle in a mammal's chest that functions in breathing. (p. 136)

down feathers Short fluffy feathers that trap heat and keep a bird warm. (p. 122)

echinoderm A radially symmetrical invertebrate that lives on the ocean floor and has a spiny internal skeleton . (p. 73)

ectotherm An animal whose body does not produce much internal heat. (p. 84)

endoskeleton An internal skeleton. (p. 73)

endotherm An animal whose body controls and regulates its temperature by controlling the internal heat it produces. (p. 85)

exoskeleton A waxy, waterproof outer shell. (p. 55)

fertilization The joining of egg and sperm. (p. 18)

fish An ectothermic vertebrate that lives in the water and has fins. (p. 87)

fossil The hardened remains or other evidence of a living thing that existed a long time in the past. (p. 112)

gastropod A mollusk with a single shell or no shell. (p. 50)

gestation period The length of time between fertilization and birth of a mammal. (p. 143)

gill An organism's breathing organ that removes oxygen from water. (p. 49)

gizzard A thick-walled, muscular part of a bird's stomach that squeezes and grinds partially digested food. (p. 123)

gradual metamorphosis A type of metamorphosis in which an egg hatches into a nymph that resembles an adult, and which has no distinctly different larval stage. (p. 64)

habitat The specific environment in which an animal lives. (p. 100)

herbivore An animal that eats only plants. (p. 19)

heterotroph An organism that cannot make food for itself, and must obtain food by eating other organisms. (p. 17)

hibernation A state of greatly reduced body activity that occurs during the winter. (p. 166)

host An organism that provides food to a parasite that lives on or inside it. (p. 36)

hypothesis A prediction about the outcome of an experiment. (p. 188)

imprinting A process in which newly hatched birds or newborn mammals learn to follow the first object they see. (p. 157)

incisors Flat-edged teeth used to bite off and cut parts of food. (p. 136)

insect An arthropod with three body sections, six legs, one pair of antennae, and usually one or two pairs of wings. (p. 63)

insight learning The process of learning how to solve a problem or do something new by applying what is already known. (p. 156)

instinct An inborn behavior pattern that an animal performs correctly the first time. (p. 154)

insulator A material that does not conduct heat well and which therefore helps prevent it from escaping. (p. 122)

invertebrate An animal that does not have a backbone. (p. 22)

kidney An organ that removes the wastes produced by an animal's cells. (p. 49)

larva The immature form of an animal that looks very different from the adult. (p. 30)

learning The process that leads to changes in behavior based on practice or experience. (p. 154)

lift The difference in pressure between the upper and lower surfaces of a bird's wing that produces an upward force that causes the wing to rise. (p. 131)

mammal An endothermic vertebrate with a four-chambered heart, skin covered with fur or hair, and which has young fed with milk from the mother's body. (p. 133)

mammary glands The organs that produce the milk with which mammals feed their young. (p. 138)

manipulated variable The one factor that a scientist changes during an experiment. (p. 189)

marsupial A mammal whose young are born alive at an early stage of development, and which usually continue to develop in a pouch on their mother's body. (p. 142)

medusa The cnidarian body plan characterized by a bowl shape and which is adapted for a free-swimming life. (p. 32)

metamorphosis A process in which an animal's body undergoes dramatic changes in form during its life cycle. (p. 58)

migration The regular, periodic journey of an animal from one place to another and back again for the purpose of feeding or reproduction. (p. 166)

molars Teeth that, along with premolars, grind and shred food into tiny bits. (p. 136)

mollusk An invertebrate with a soft, unsegmented body; most are protected by hard outer shells. (p. 48)

molting The process of shedding an outgrown exoskeleton. (p. 56)

monotreme A mammal that lays eggs. (p. 142)

notochord A flexible rod that supports a chordate's back. (p. 82)

nymph A stage of gradual metamorphosis that usually resembles the adult insect. (p. 64)

omnivore An animal that eats both plants and animals. (p. 20)

operational definition A statement that describes how a particular variable is to be measured or how a term is to be defined. (p. 189)

paleontologist A scientist who studies extinct organisms, examines fossil structure, and makes comparisons to present-day organisms. (p. 114)

parasite An organism that lives inside or on another organism and takes food from the organism in or on which it lives. (p. 36)

pheromone A chemical released by one animal that affects the behavior of another animal of the same species. (p. 170)

phylum One of about 35 major groups into which biologists classify members of the animal kingdom. (p. 20)

placenta An organ in pregnant female placental mammals that passes materials between the mother and the developing embryo. (p. 146)

placental mammal A mammal that develops inside its mother's body until its body systems can function independently. (p. 143)

polyp The cnidarian body plan characterized by a vaselike shape and which is usually adapted for life attached to an underwater surface. (p. 31)

predator A carnivore that hunts and kills other animals and has adaptations that help it capture the animals it preys upon. (p. 19)

premolars Teeth that, along with molars, grind and shred food into tiny bits. (p. 136)

prey An animal that a predator feeds upon. (p. 20)

pupa The second stage of complete metamorphosis, in which an insect is enclosed in a protective covering and gradually changes from a larva to an adult. (p. 64)

radial symmetry The quality of having many lines of symmetry that all pass through a central point. (p. 24)

radula A flexible ribbon of tiny teeth in mollusks. (p. 49)

regeneration The ability of an organism to regrow body parts. (p. 36)

reptile An exothermic vertebrate that has lungs and scaly skin. (p. 101)

responding variable The factor that changes as a result of changes to the manipulated variable in an experiment. (p. 189)

response An organism's reaction to a stimulus. (p. 153)

sedimentary rock Rock formed from hardened layers of sediments—particles of clay, sand, mud, or silt. (p. 112)

sexual reproduction The process by which a new organism forms from the joining of two sex cells. (p. 17)

society A group of closely related animals of the same species that work together for the benefit of the whole group. (p. 164)

species A group of organisms that can mate with each other and produce offspring which can also mate and reproduce. (p. 17)

stimulus A signal that causes an organism to react in some way. (p. 153)

swim bladder An internal gas-filled organ that helps a bony fish stabilize its body at different water depths. (p. 92)

territory An area that is occupied and defended by an animal or group of animals. (p. 161)

thorax An insect's mid-section, to which its wings and legs are attached. (p. 63)

trial-and-error learning The learning that occurs when an animal learns to perform a behavior more and more skillfully. (p. 156)

urine The watery fluid in which the wastes produced by an animal's cells are excreted. (p. 103)

variable Any factor that can change in an experiment. (p. 189)

ventricle The lower chamber of the heart, which pumps blood out to the lungs and body. (p. 96)

vertebrae The bones that make up the backbone of an animal. (p. 83)

vertebrate An animal that has a backbone. (p. 22)

water vascular system A system of fluid-filled tubes in an echinoderm's body. (p. 74)

Index

Acknowledgments

Illustration

Sally Bensusen: 51, 65
Warren Budd Associated Ltd.: 125
Patrice Rossi Calkin: 20, 22, 37, 83, 102, 136, 137, 155
Warren Cutler: 97, 123
John Edwards & Associates: 125
Andrea Golden: 27, 42, 58
Biruta Hansen: 104, 170–171, 173
Martucci Design: 71, 117
Fran Milner: 17, 59, 91, 99
Paul Mirocha: 157
Morgan Cain & Associates: 94, 139
Matt Myerchak: 44, 78, 174
Ortelius Design Inc.: 166
Matthew Pippin: 114
Walter Stuart: 29, 53, 75, 110, 165
J/B Woolsey Associates (Mark Desman): 21, 40, 56, 82, 86, 106–107, 175
J/B Woolsey Associates: 23, 24, 96, 126, 131, 154

Photography

Photo Research Sue McDermott
Cover image Davis/W. Bilenduke/TSI

Nature of Science
Page 10t,10b,12, Heinz Kluetmeier/Sports Illustrated; **13l,13r,** Russell A. Mittermeier, Ph.D./Conservation International

Chapter 1
Pages 14–15, Hal Beral/Visuals Unlimited; **16t,** Richard Haynes; **16–17b,** Gary Bell/Masterfile; **18,** Robert Maier/Animals Animals; **19t,** Oliver Strewe/TSI; **19b,** Frans Lanting/Minden Pictures; **20,** David & Tess Young/Tom Stack & Associates; **23,** Corel Corp.; **24,** William C Jorgensen/Visuals Unlimited; **25l,** Daniel W. Gotshall/Visuals Unlimited; **25r,** Tim Davis/TSI; **26,** Ted Kerasote/Photo Researchers; **28t,** Russ Lappa; **31t,** Biophoto Associates/Photo Researchers; **31bl,** Stuart Westmorland/Natural Selection; **31br,** David B. Fleetham/Tom Stack & Associates; **33t,** Nancy Sefton/Photo Researchers; **33b,** Linda Pitkin/Masterfile; **34,** James Watt/Animals Animals; **35t,** Richard Haynes; **35bl,** Ed Robinson/Tom Stack & Associates; **35br,** Mary Beth Angelo/Photo Researchers; **36,** Kiell B. Sandved/Visuals Unlimited; **38t,** David M. Dennis/Tom Stack & Associates; **38b,** Sinclair Stammers/Science Photo Library/Photo Researchers; **39l, 39r,** Kjell B. Sandved/Visuals Unlimited; **43l,** Corel Corp.; **43r,** Linda Pitkin/Masterfile.

Chapter 2
Pages 46–47, Michael Fogden/DRK Photo; **48b,** Richard Nowitz; **48t,** Corel Corp.; **49l,** Douglas Faulkner/Photo Researchers; **49r,** Bruce Watkins/Animals Animals; **50,** Pete Atkinson/Masterfile; **52,** Kevin & Cat Sweeney/TSI; **54t,** Richard Haynes; **52–53,** Gary Retherford/Photo Researchers; **53r,** Richard Haynes; **54b,** Ron Broda/Masterfile; **55l,** John Gerlach/Tom Stack & Associates; **55r,** Donald Specker/Animals Animals; **56,** Robert A. Lubeck/Animals Animals; **57,** Andrew Syred/Science Photo Library/Photo Researchers; **60t,** Robert Calentine/Visuals Unlimited; **60b,** Tom MuHugh/Photo Researchers; **60m,** Tim Flach/TSI; **61l,** Marty Cordano/DRK Photo; **61r,** Simon D. Pollard/Photo Researchers; **62t,** R Calentine/Visuals Unlimited; **62b,** Patti Murray/Animals Animals; **63,** CNRI/Science Photo Library/Photo Researchers; **64,** Belinda Wright/DRK Photo; **66l,** Valorie Hodgson/Visuals Unlimited; **66r,** Art Wolfe/Tony Stone Images; **67,** John Trager/Visuals Unlimited; **68,** Robert A. Lubeck/Animals Animals; **69, 70,** Richard Haynes; **71t,** Paul Silverman/Fundamental Photographs; **71b,** Richard Magna/Fundamental Photographs; **72,** Russ Lappa; **73t,** Richard Haynes; **73b,** Kjell B. Sandred/Visuals Unlimited; **74,** Ed Robinson/Tom Stack & Associates; **76tl,** Brian Parker/Tom Stack & Associates; **76tr,** Tammy Peluso/Tom Stack & Associates; **76b,** Fred Whitehead/Animals Animals; **77t,** Bruce Watkins/Animals Animals; **77b,** Andrew Syred/Science Photo Library/Photo Researchers.

Chapter 3
Pages 80–81, Norbert Wu/DRK Photo; **82,** Russ Lappa; **83,** G.J. Bernard/ Animals Animals; **84,** Michael Fodgen/DRK Photo; **85,** Corel Corp.; **87t,** Gerard Lacz/Animals Animals; **87b,** Flip Micklin/Minden Pictures; **89tl,** Larry Lipsky/DRK Photo; **89tr,** John d. Cummingham/Visuals Unlimited **89b,** Herve Berthoule Jacana/Photo Researchers; **90t,** Frank Burek/Animals Animals; **90b,** Jeff Rotman; **92l,** Norbert Wu; **92r,** Stuart Westmorland/ Photo Researchers; **93r,** Stuart Westmorland/TSI; **93l,** Norbert Wu/TSI; **95t,** Russ Lappa; **95b,** John M. Burnley/Photo Researchers; **96,** Michael Fogden/Photo Researchers; **98,** Richard Haynes; **100,** Justin W. Verforker/Visuals Unlimited; **101t,** Richard Haynes; **101b,** Joe McDonald/Tom Stack & Associates; **102,** Zig Leszczynski/Animals Animals; **103,** Brian Kenney/Natural Selection; **105l,** Joe McDonald/Tom Stack & Associates; **105r,** A.B. Sheldon/Animals Animals; **108t,** Dave B. Fleetham/Visuals Unlimited; **108m,** T.A. Wiewandt/DRK Photo; **108b,** M.C. Chamberlain/DRK Photo; **109,** Gerald & Buff Corsi/ Tom Stack & Associates; **111t,** Richard Haynes; **111b,** Tom Bean/DRK Photo; **112t,** Ernst Mayr Library of the Museum of Comparative Zoology,Harvard University. ©President and Fellows of Harvard; **112b,** By permission of the Houghton Library, Harvard University; **113t,** Louis Psihoyos Matrix; **113b,** James L. Amos/Photo Researchers; **115l,** Stuart Westmorland/TSI; **115r,** Joe McDonald/Tom Stack & Associates.

Chapter 4
Pages 118–119, Robert A. Tyrrell; **120,** Richard Haynes; **121,** Collection of The New York Historical Society; **122t,** Art Wolfe/TSI; **122m,** Jerome Wexler/Photo Researchers; **122b,** Darrell Gulin/DRK Photo; **124,** Richard Haynes; **127,** David Hosking/TSI; **128tl,** Dave Watts/Tom Stack & Associates; **128tm,** Stephen Krasemann/DRK Photo; **128tr,** S. Nielsen/DRK Photo; **128bl,** D. Allen/Animals Animals; **128br,** Joe McDonald/Visuals Unlimited; **129l,** Manfred Danegger/TSI; **129r,** Wayne Lankinen/DRK Photo; **130t,** Richard Haynes; **130b,** Stephen Dalton/Photo Researchers; **132,** David Tipling/TSI; **133t,** Richard Haynes; **133b,** Eric Valli/Minden Pictures; **134,** Daryl Balfour/ TSI; **135,** Art Wolfe/TSI; **136t,** Hilary Pooley/Animals Animals; **136–137b,** Michael Fogden/DRK Photo; **138,** Joe McDonald/Visuals Unlimited; **140,** Colin Milkins/Animals Animals; **141t,** Richard Haynes; **141bl,** Keren Su/TSI; **141br,** Penny Tweedie/TSI; **142l,142r,** Tom McHugh/Photo Researchers; **143t,** Dave Watts/Tom Stack & Associates; **143b,** Jack Dermid; **144tl,** Michael Habicht/Animals Animals; **144tm,** Art Wolfe/TSI; **144tr,** Roger Aitkenhead/Animals Animals; **144ml,** Stephen Krasemann/TSI; **144mr,** Jeanne Drake/TSI; **144bl,** Renee Lynn/TSI; **145tl,** Corel Corp.; **145tr,** M.P. Kahl/DRK Photo; **145ml,** Stephen Krasemann/TSI; **145bl,** Chuck Davis/TSI; **145br,** Johnny Johnson/DRK Photo; **146,** Johnny Johnson; **147l,** Joe McDonald/Visuals Unlimited; **147r,** Penny Tweedie/TSI.

Chapter 5
Pages 150–151, Tim Davis/TSI; **152t,** Jerome Wexler/Photo Researchers; **152b,** Michael Fogden/DRK Photo; **153,** Fred Winner/Jacana/Photo Researchers; **156,** Robert & Eunice Pearcy/Animals Animals; **158,** Nina Leen/Time-Warner, Life Magazine; **160t,** Richard Haynes; **160b,** Mark Jones/Minden Pictures; **161,** Art Wolfe/TSI; **162l,162r,** Michael Fogden/DRK Photo; **163,** Jeff Lepore/Natural Selection; **164,** John Cancalosi/DRK Photo; **166,** M. A. Chappell/Animals Animals; **167,** Michio Hoshino/Minden Pictures; **168,** Doug Wechsler; **169,** Richard Haynes; **171,** Michael Fogden/Animals Animals; **173l,** John Cancalosi/DRK Photo.

Interdisciplinary Exploration
Page 176, Cary Wolinsky/Stock Boston; **177t,** E.R. Degginger/Animals Animals; **177m,177b,** Cary Wolinsky/Stock Boston; **177r,** Harry Rogers/Photo Researchers; **180,** Russ Lappa; **182t,** Xinhua/Gamma-Liaison International; **183t,** Russ Lappa; **183b,** Jean Marc Barey/Angence Vandystadt/Photo Researchers.

Skills Handbook
Page 184, Mike Moreland/Photo Network; **185t,** Foodpix; **185m,** Richard Haynes; **185b,** Russ Lappa; **188,** Richard Haynes; **190,** Ron Kimball; **191,** Renee Lynn/Photo Researchers.